11

Advanced Harmony and Counterpoint

Essential Music Theory

Mark Sarnecki

San Marco Publications

Essential Music Theory © 2025 by San Marco Publications. All rights reserved.

All right reserved. No part of this book may be reproduced in any form or by electronic or mechanical means including Information storage and retrieval systems without permission in writing from the author.

ISNB: 9781896499543

Contents

Chapter 1: **Modal Mixture and Borrowed Chords** — 4

Chapter 2: **The Neopolitan Chord** — 34

Chapter 3: **Augmented 6th Chords** — 48

Chapter 4: **Chromatically Altered Chords** — 77

Chapter 5: **Common-Tone Chords** — 86

Chapter 6: **Chromatic Mediants** — 98

Chapter 7: **Modulation** — 106

Chapter 8: **Composition** — 130

Chapter 9: **The Bach Chorales** — 138

Chapter 10: **Figured Bass Realization** — 155

Chapter 11: **Counterpoint** — 169

1
Modal Mixture and Borrowed Chords

A number of chromatically altered chords are used in tonal music. These chords act as powerful tools in the harmonic language, offering composers a pallet of expressive possibilities. By temporarily using chords from parallel modes, these techniques create rich harmonic color, emotional depth, and unexpected twists in musical progressions. In this lesson, we are going to explore the theory behind modal mixture and borrowed chords, their uses and their practical applications in composition and music theory.

Modal Mixture

The terms *modal mixture* or *model exchange*, refers to the practice of borrowing chords from the parallel mode. In this context, the word "mode" refers to major and minor keys. Parallel modes are major and minor scales that share the same tonic. For example, in C major, chords may be borrowed from C minor and vice versa. The borrowed chords are used to color the passage and expand the harmonic vocabulary of the composition.

Modal mixture is used to add harmonic variety and colour without changing the original key. Modal mixture can also enhance emotional expression. For example, minor chords in a major key can evoke a mood of melancholy or sadness. It can also create tension and release through unexpected harmonic shifts.

The excerpt in Figure 1.1 is in the key of F major, but the chord marked with an asterisk (*) is a borrowed chord. This chord (G - B♭ - D♭ - F) is the supertonic 7th of F minor. In F minor, it is a *diatonic chord* (that is, a chord that is part of the key), but when it appears in a passage in F major, it is analyzed as a borrowed chord.

Figure 1.1

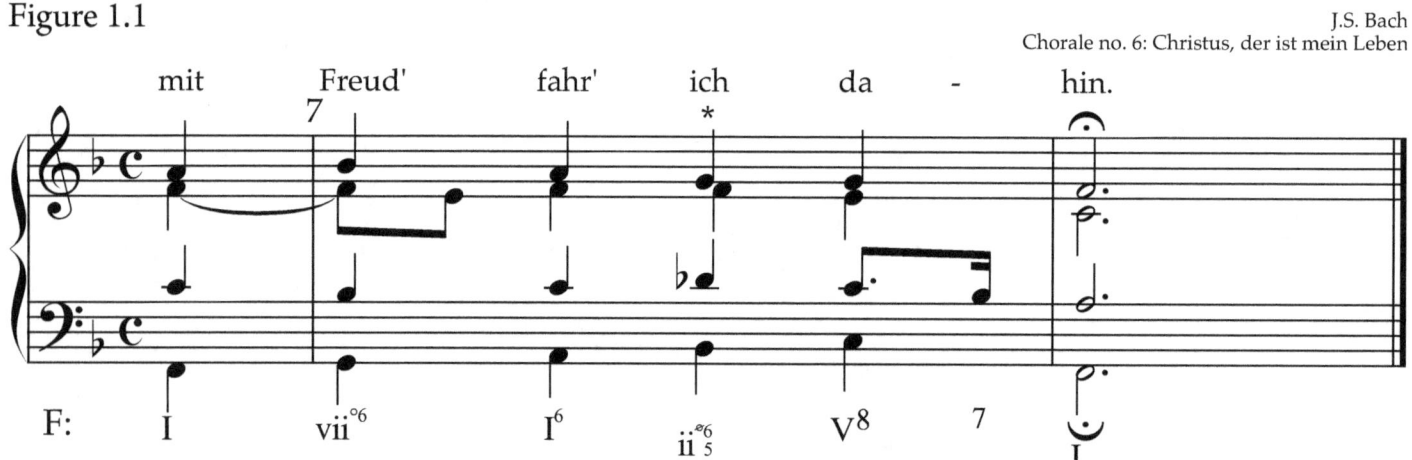

The results of mixing chords from parallel major and minor keys can range from a single borrowed chord, used to supply additional color, to a progression of borrowed chords that changes the mode for several measures. In either case, the key in use is enriched by pitches borrowed from the parallel, major or minor scale. Compare the pitches of the major and minor scales shown in the following chart.

Major scale	$\hat{1}$	$\hat{2}$	$\hat{3}$	$\hat{4}$	$\hat{5}$	$\hat{6}$	$\hat{7}$	$\hat{1}$
Minor scale	$\hat{1}$	$\hat{2}$	$\flat\hat{3}$	$\hat{4}$	$\hat{5}$	$\flat\hat{6}$ $\hat{6}$	$\flat\hat{7}$ $\hat{7}$	$\hat{1}$

In major keys, commonly borrowed chords from the parallel minor include:

- i (minor tonic): e.g., Cm in C major
- ♭III (major flat 3rd): e.g., E♭ in C major
- v (minor dominant): e.g., Gm in C major
- ♭VI (major flat 6th): e.g., A♭ in C major
- ♭VII (major flat 7th): e.g., B♭ in C major
- ii° (diminished supertonic): e.g., Ddim in C major

In minor keys, chords can be borrowed from the parallel major, such as:

- I (major tonic): e.g., C in C minor
- IV (major subdominant): e.g., F in C minor

Borrowed chords are most often taken from the minor mode for use in a major mode. These borrowed chords include the lowered scale degrees ♭3, ♭6, and ♭7 found in the minor mode. Figure 1.2 shows the chords that are most commonly borrowed from a minor mode (in this case, C minor) for use in the major mode (here, C major). All of these chords are diatonic chords in the key of C minor. A composer might use one or more of them to add color, expression, and harmonic variety to a passage in the key C major.

Figure 1.2

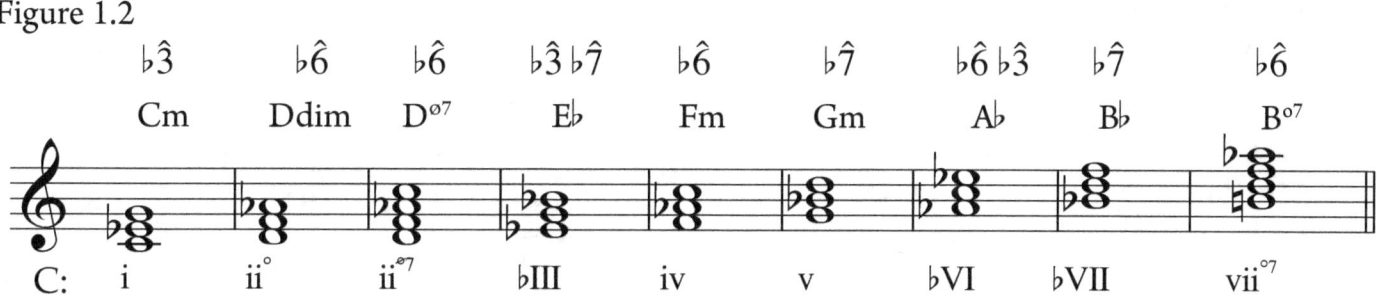

Chapter 1: Modal Mixture and Borrowed Chords

Roman Numerals and Figures for Chromatic Harmonies

Specific figures and symbols are added to the standard Roman numerals to indicate chromatic harmonies using functional chord symbols. Here are some basic guidelines and examples.

1. Uppercase Roman numerals indicate major triads.

2. Lowercase Roman numerals indicate minor triads.

3. An uppercase Roman numeral followed by a + (plus sign) indicates an augmented triad. Some systems use an **x** rather than a plus sign.

4. A lowercase Roman numeral followed by a ° (degree sign) indicates a diminished triad.

Figure 1.3

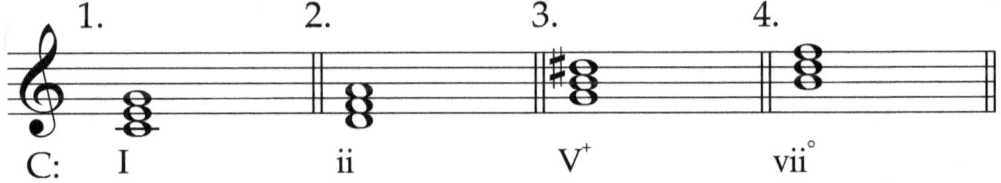

5. A borrowed minor chord in the major key is simply indicated with a lowercase Roman numeral. This indicates that the chord is minor.

6. If the borrowed chord is diminished, a lowercase Roman numeral with the degree sign is placed under the chord to indicate this.

Figure 1.4

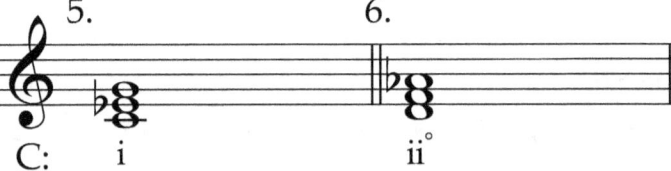

7. A flat placed in front of the Roman numeral indicates that the root of the chord is lowered.

8. A flat is always used to indicate a lowered root, even if the actual accidental needed to lower the root is a natural.

Figure 1.5

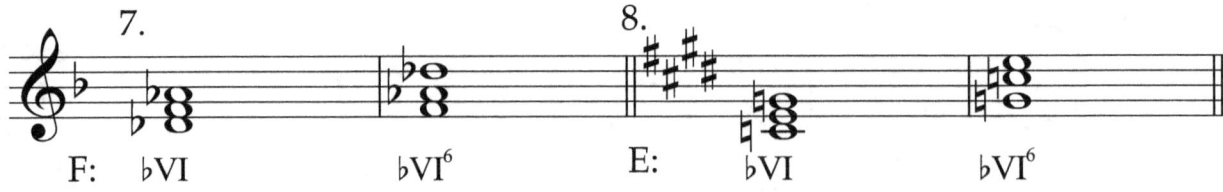

9. A borrowed half diminished 7th chord which consists of a diminished triad and a minor 7th is indicated by ⌀7 after the lowercase Roman numeral.

10. A borrowed diminished 7th chord is indicated by °7 after the lowercase Roman numeral.

Figure 1.6

The functional chord symbol used in the figuration of borrowed chords, reflects the quality and the function of the chord being used in the music.

In general discussion throughout this text, where any key may be assumed, we will use the flat sign (♭) to indicate a lowered note and the sharp sign (♯) to indicate a raised note. In other words, in a general discussion we refer to chords as ♭VI or ♯V but in the context of a particular key, these chords might actually be ♮VI, ♭♭VI, ♮V, or ♯♯V.

It is important to note that different texts use different methods of symbolizing chords. Some texts indicate all of a chords accidentals by writing them in the figuration next to the Roman numeral. Here we are not writing these accidentals after the Roman numeral on the assumption that they are understood because of the upper or lowercase Roman numerals and the symbols used with them. It is important to be aware of the different systems of chord symbols that may be encountered in various textbooks and sources.

Root/Quality Chord Symbols

Roman numerals written under the score are known as functional chord symbols. Functional chord symbols tell us the function of the chord (tonic, predominant, dominant, etc.) Another system of chord symbols placed above the score and covered in previous volumes of this series uses root/quality chord symbols. These chord symbols simply state what the chord is, and not its function. The final two chords in the chart, the dominant 7th with a raised fifth and the dominant 7th with the lower fifth will be covered in detail later in this book.

Review the following chart containing a root/quality chord symbols:

Chord Type	Interval Structure	Symbol	Example
Major triad	Root, maj 3, per 5	letter only	C
Minor triad	Root, min 3, per 5	m	Cm
Diminished triad	Root, min 3, dim 5	dim (or °)	Cdim C°
Augmented triad	Root, maj 3, aug 5	aug	Caug
Dominant 7th chord (major-minor 7th)	Root, maj 3, per 5, min 7	7	C7
Diminished 7th chord	Root, min 3, dim 5, dim 7	dim7 (or °7)	Cdim7 C°7

Chord Type	Interval Structure	Symbol	Example
Half-diminished 7th	Root, min 3, dim 5, min 7	ø7	CØ7
Minor 7th chord	Root, min 3, per 5, min 7	m7	Cm7
Major 7th chord	Root, maj 3, per 5, maj 7	maj7	Cmaj7
Dominant 9th chord	Root, maj 3, (per 5), min 7, maj 9	9	G9
Dominant minor 9th chord	Root, maj 3, (per 5), min 7, min 9	9 (♭9) (or m9)	G7(♭9)
Dominant 13th chord	Root, maj 3, or per 5, min 7, (maj 9), (per 11), maj 13	13	G13
Dominant minor 13th chord	Root, maj 3, (per 5), min 7, (maj 9), (per 11), min 13	7(♭13) (or m13)	G7(♭13)
Dominant 7th 7aug5) raised 5th	Root, maj 3, aug 5, min 7	7#5 (or 7aug5)	G7#5
Dominant 7th 7dim5) lowered 5th	Root, maj 3, dim 5, min 7	7♭5 (or 7dim5)	G7♭5

Chapter 1: Modal Mixture and Borrowed Chords

1. Write the following borrowed chords in the keys indicated.

2. Write the functional and root/quality chord symbols for the following borrowed chords.

Chapter 1: Modal Mixture and Borrowed Chords

3. Write the following chords.

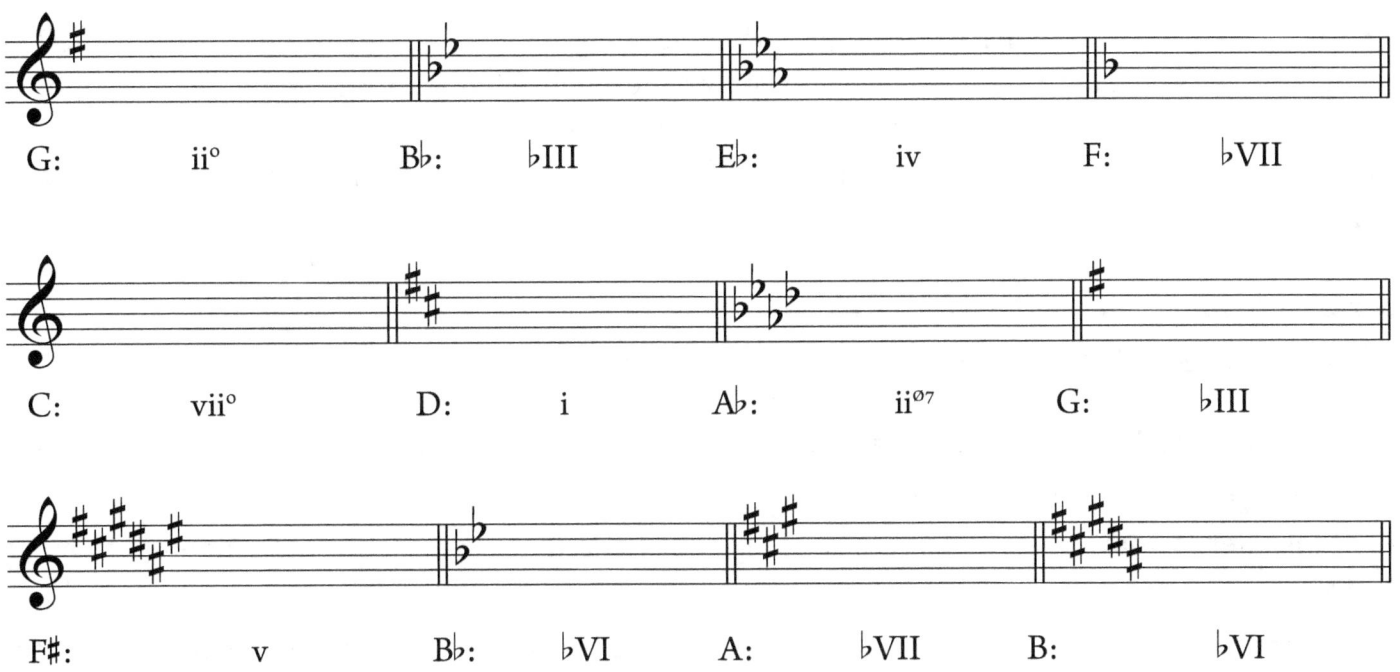

4. Write the chords and their functional chord symbols in the keys indicated according to the following root/quality chord symbols.

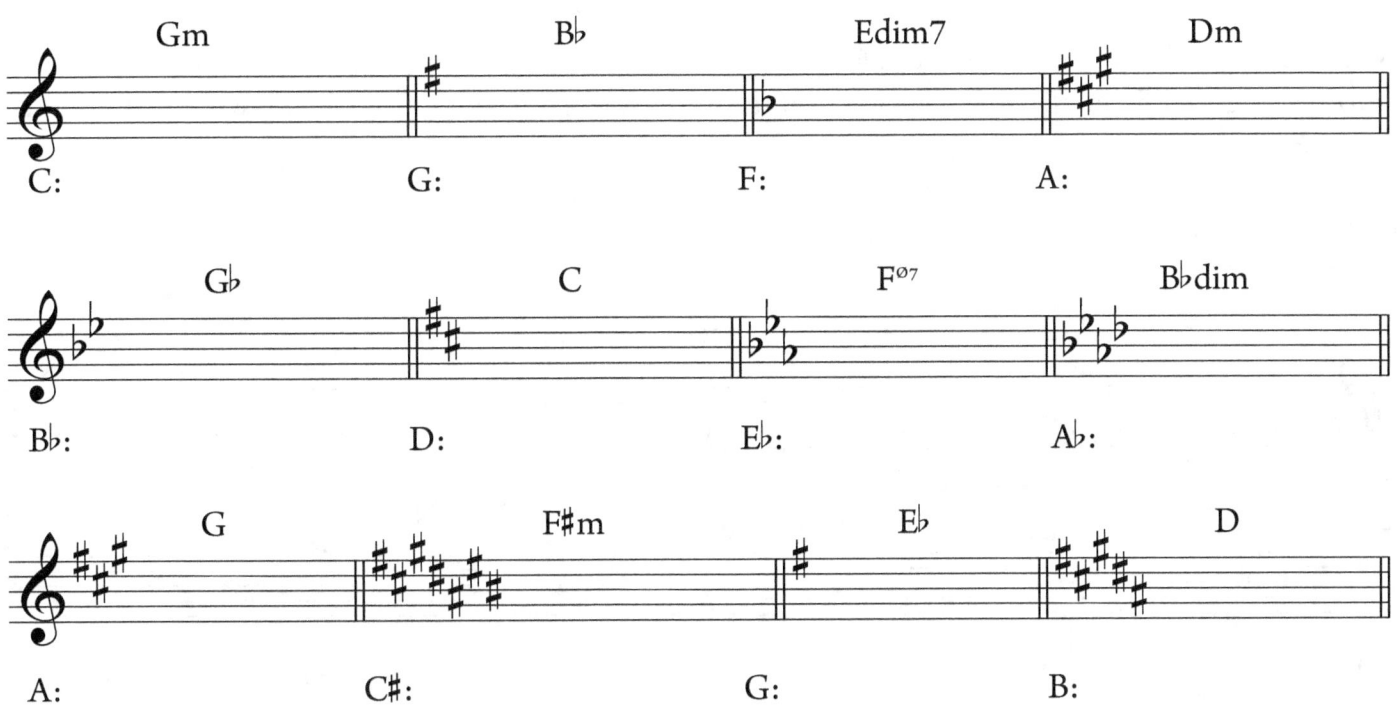

Harmonic Functions of Borrowed Chords

Borrowed chords function in basically the same way as their unaltered, or diatonic, counterparts. The general tendency for a supertonic chord to progress to the dominant chord, applies equally to both diatonic chords and borrowed chords. In other words, the harmonic function of the two types of chords is the same. Borrowed chords are substituted for unaltered chords mainly for their color and tonal variety.

Borrowed chords contain chromatically altered notes that are resolved in various ways.
Here are a few guidelines for resolving these altered notes.

1. If a chromatically lowered note makes a chord more dissonant (as in ii°, ii°7, or even iv), that lowered note usually resolves downward by step.
2. If the altered notes create a major triad (as in ♭III, or ♭VI but not ♭II), the altered note may move freely.
3. Whenever you use an altered chord, take particular care to avoid melodic augmented 2nds or 4ths approaching or leaving the altered note.

Now take a closer look at the excerpt from Bach's setting of the chorale *Christus der is mein Leben* in Figure 1.7. In the borrowed chord, the lowered tone - the tenor D flat - gives the ii°$^6_5$ chord a more dissonant sound. Bach resolves this D flat downward to C.

Note that altered notes are rarely doubled, mainly because of their strong resolution tendency. For example, a doubled D flat in this excerpt would result in parallel octaves when those two notes resolved downward.

Figure 1.7

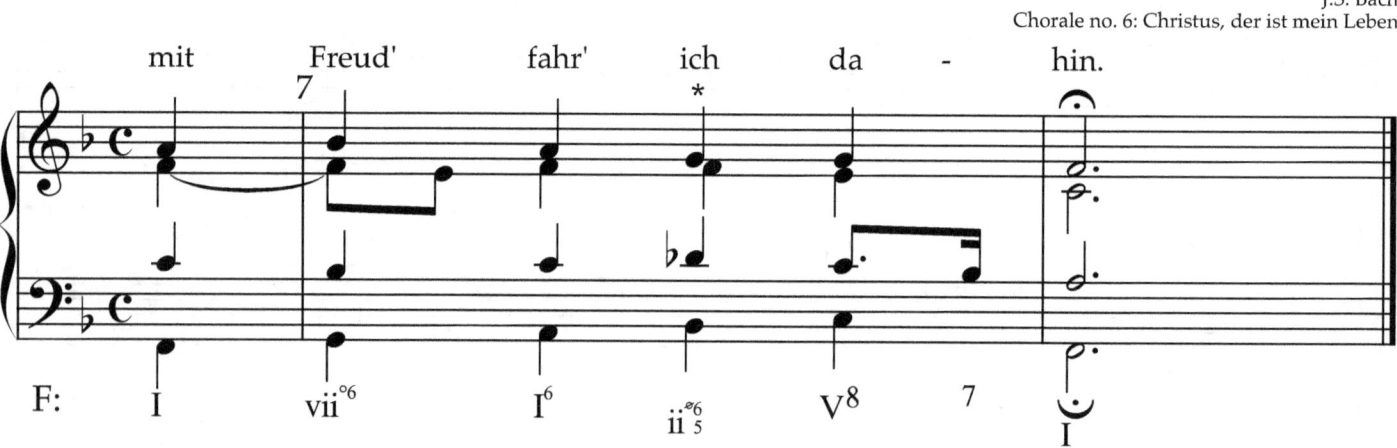

J.S. Bach
Chorale no. 6: Christus, der ist mein Leben

The i Chord

The minor tonic chord can function in several ways. In the excerpt in Figure 1.8, Mozart uses a i to follow a tonic chord, as a momentary chromatic change. Here, the i is borrowed from C Minor, the tonic minor.

Figure 1.8

In Figure 1.8, Mozart uses i as a brief model contrast in the development section. The excerpt in Figure 1.9 is in the key of A flat major. Schubert borrows i from A flat minor, the tonic minor, and uses it as a substitute for the major I chord. He begins his impromptu in A flat minor, and we do not realize that the piece is in A flat major until m. 31.

Figure 1.9

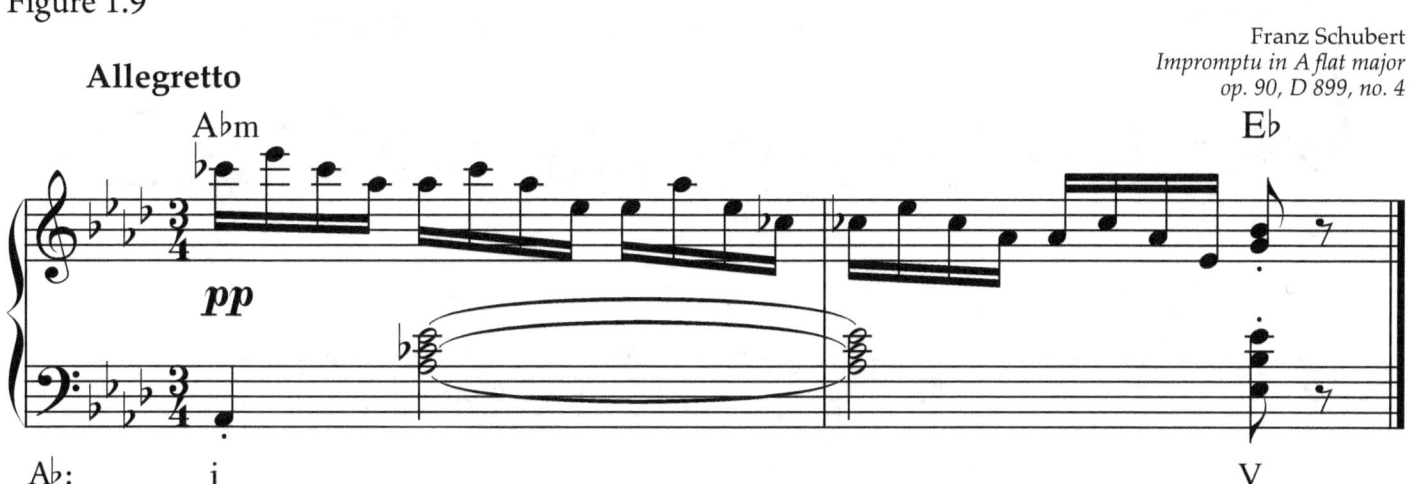

5. Complete the following progressions for four voices.

F: I   i   ii⁶   V⁷   I

key: I   i   ii$^6_5$ V$^6_5$/V   V$^{8\ \ 7}_{4\ \ 3}$ I

The ii° and ii°⁷ Chords

Both ii° and ii°⁷ may function as pre-dominant chords. They may also be used in prolongation of tonic and pre-dominant harmony. In Figure 1.10, ii°$^6_5$ which Mozart borrows from C minor, functions as a pre-dominant chord.

Figure 1.10

W.A. Mozart
Piano Sonata in C major
K 330 (1st mvt.)

14   Chapter 1: Modal Mixture and Borrowed Chords

In Figure 1.11, ii°⁶, ii⁰⁷, and ii⁰⁶₅ act as neighbour chords to I in a prolongation of tonic harmony. The chord ii° is usually used in first inversion because the diminished triad in the root position of this chord has a harsh sound.

In all three progressions, $\flat\hat{6}$ resolves downward to $\hat{5}$. The diminished 5th moving to a perfect 5th (D-A flat to C-G) in examples a and b are correct. In examples b and c, the seventh of ii⁰⁷ (C) is prepared by common tone motion from I and remains a common tone.

Figure 1.11

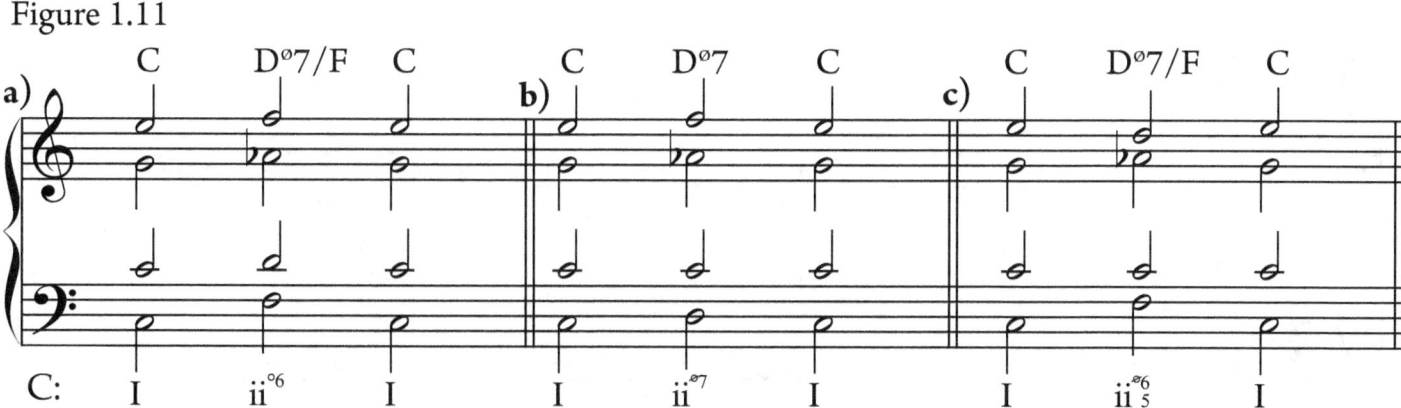

The ii°⁶ chord can function in other prolongations of tonic harmony. In Figure 1.12, ii°⁶ is borrowed from G minor and his followed by V$^4_2$ in a prolongation of I. The $\flat\hat{6}$ resolves downward to $\hat{5}$. When writing this progression, take care to avoid a melodic augmented 2nd (here, between E flat and F sharp). Placing these two notes in different voices will prevent this error.

Figure 1.12

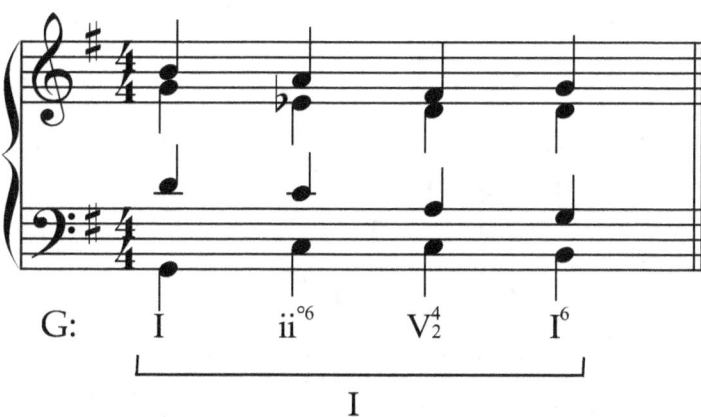

The tonic chord I is a good chord of approach for ii°⁶ and, ii⁰⁷, but ii and IV are also effective options. The use of ii or IV as approach chords will produce a prolongation of pre-dominant harmony. Note that in these progressions (Figure 1.13), the chromatic half-step (A – A flat) remains in the same voice.

Figure 1.13

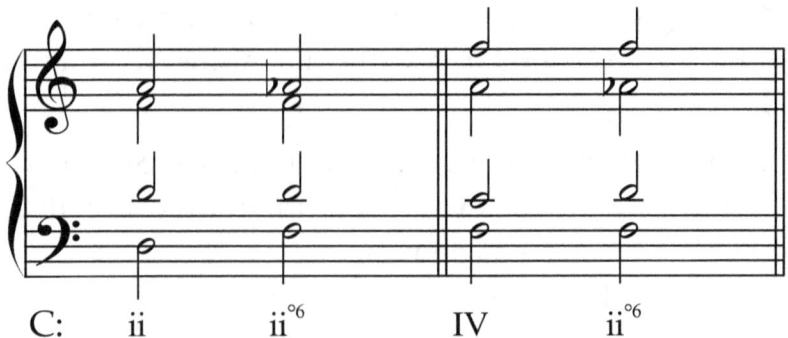

C: ii   ii°⁶   IV   ii°⁶

6. Name the key and complete the following progressions for four voices.

7. Provide a harmonic analysis of the following excerpts. Use both functional and root/quality chord symbols. Circle and identify any non-chord tones.

Gaetono Donizetti
O luce di quest'anima
from Linda de Chamounix (act 1, scene 3)

a)

key:___

16   Chapter 1: Modal Mixture and Borrowed Chords

b)

Robert Schumann
Ich grolle nicht
from Dichterliebe, op. 48

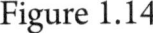
key:___

The ♭III Chord

The ♭III chord is rarely used. It is usually followed by ♭VI and actually acts as the secondary dominant of ♭VI. Note the resolutions of the chromatically altered notes (B flat and E flat) in Figure 1.14.

Figure 1.14

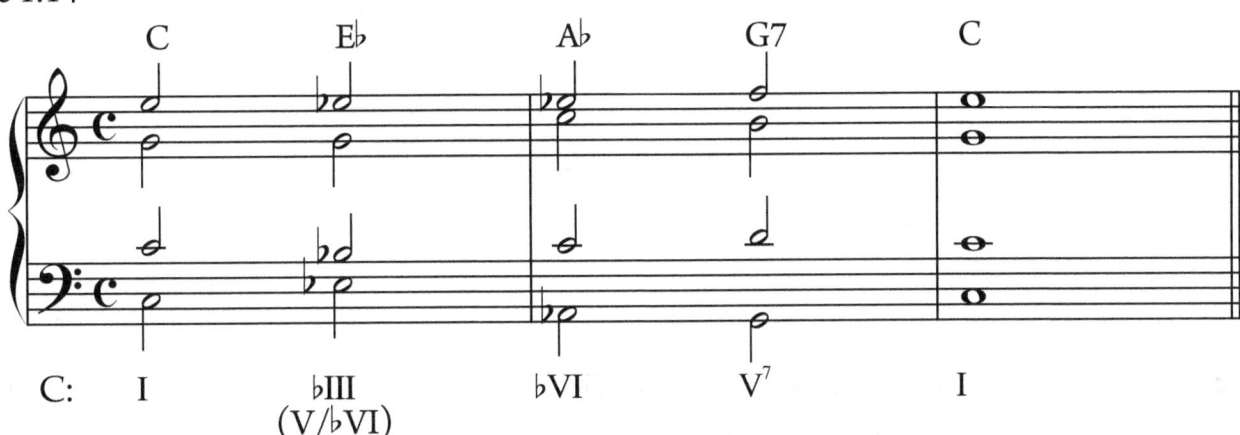

As stated earlier, borrowed chords may serve the same function as their unaltered counterparts. The mediant chord iii is normally used as a link between tonic and pre-dominant chords (usually between I and IV). The ♭III chord may fill this same function. In Figure 1.15 ♭III links the tonic (I) and the pre-dominant (IV).

Figure 1.15

8. Complete the following progressions for four voices.

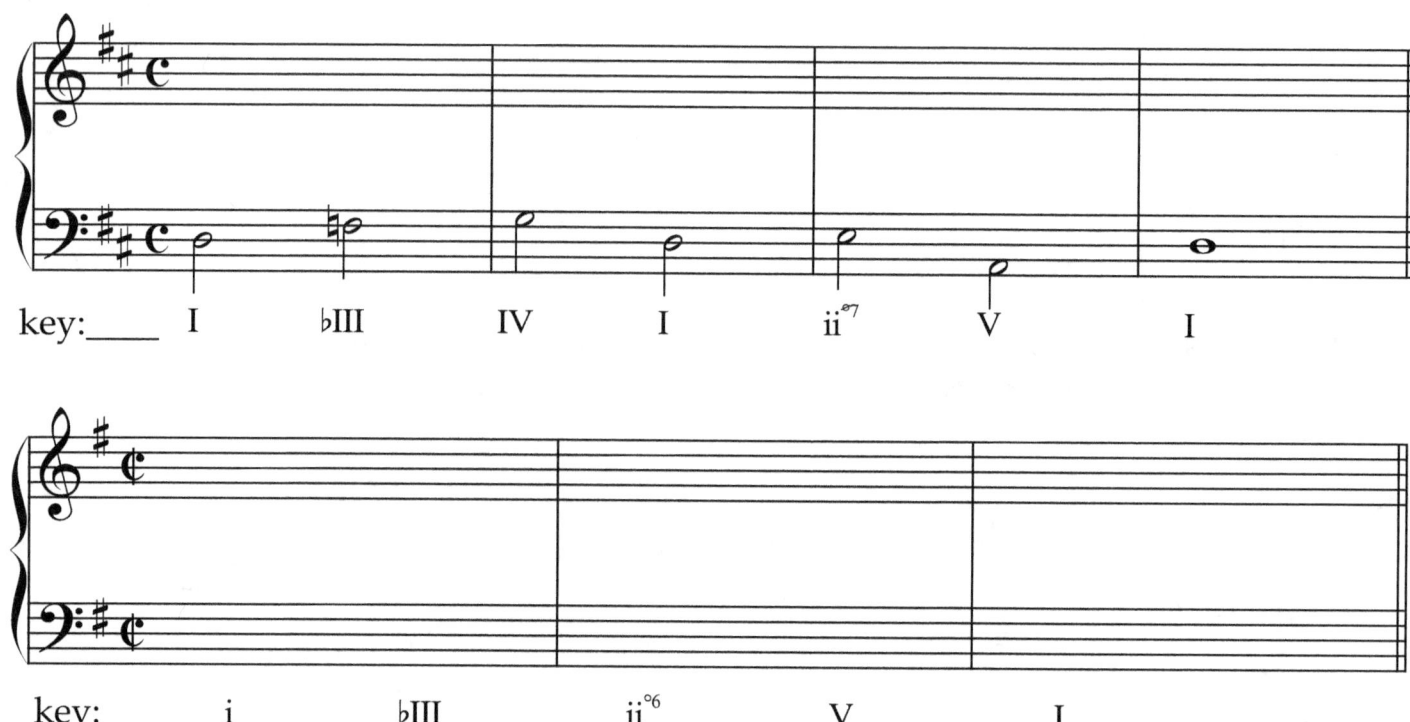

The iv Chord

The iv chord may have several functions. In Figure 1.16, iv functions as a pre-dominant chord leading directly to a dominant function chord in root position.

Figure 1.16

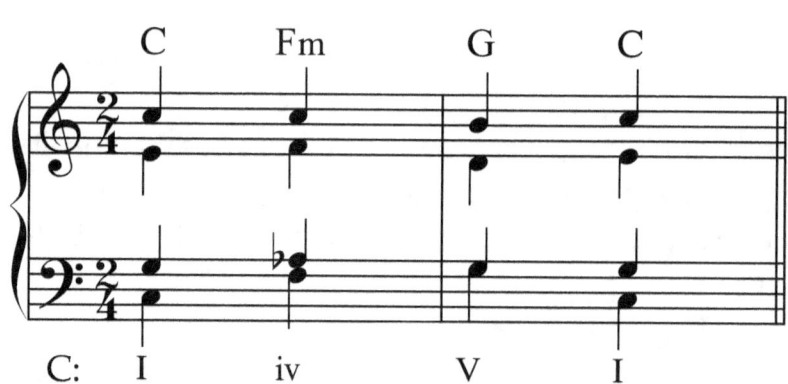

The iv chord may also be used between two statements of I to prolong tonic harmony.

Figure 1.17

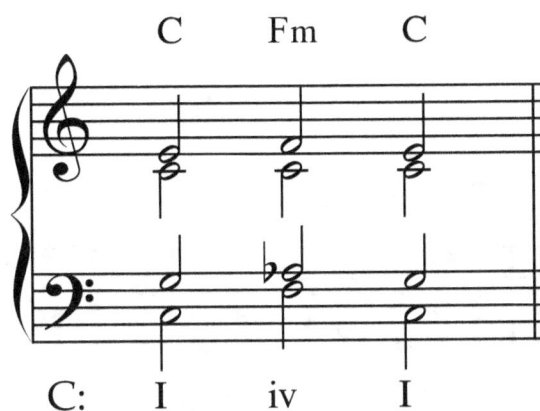

The iv chord may be used before V^6 and inversions of V^7. In Figure 1.18, iv proceeds V^4_2. We can describe this group of chords as a tonic prolongation because the dominant function chord is in inversion. If the dominant function chord was in root position, the group of chords would be considered a harmonic progression.

Figure 1.18

In Figure 1.19, Mendelssohn has used iv between statements of I in a prolongation of tonic harmony. The use of ♭6̂ as a neighbour to 5̂ adds expressiveness, color, and chromatic interest to the passage.

Figure 1.19

Felix Mendelssohn
Song Without Words
op. 102, no. 2

9. Complete the following progressions for four voices.

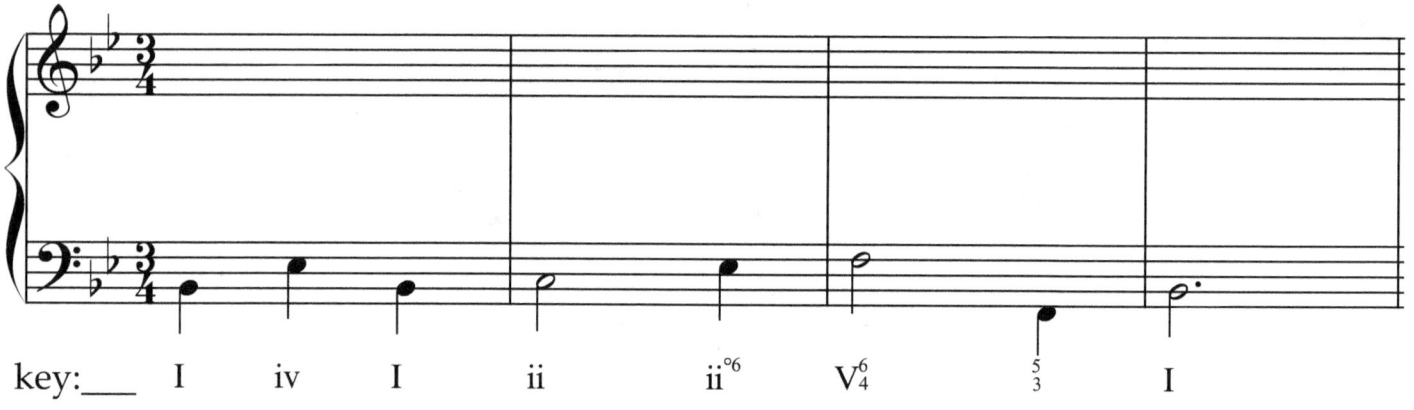

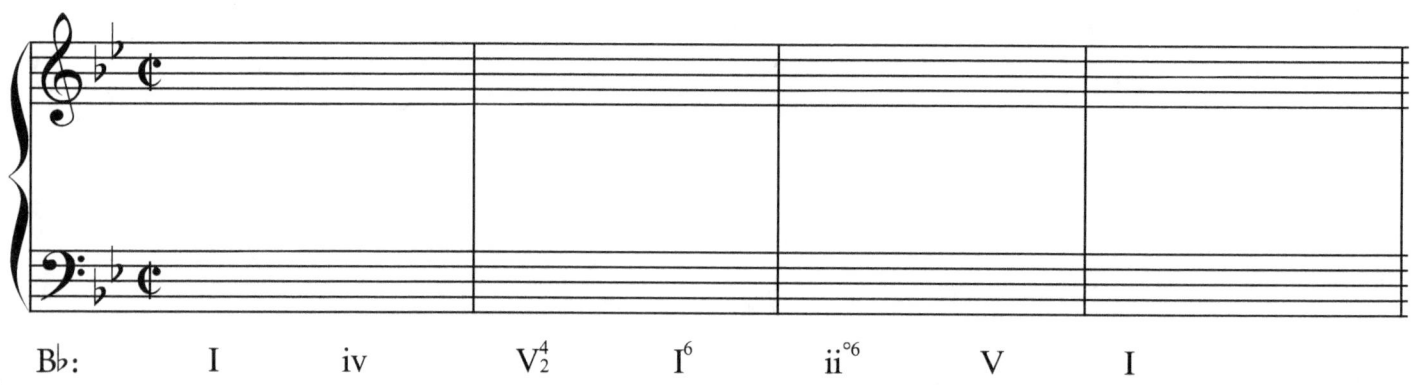

20   Chapter 1: Modal Mixture and Borrowed Chords

10. Provide a harmonic analysis of the following excerpt. Use both functional and root/quality chord symbols. Circle and identify any non-chord tones.

Franz Schubert
Das Wirtshaus
from Winterreise, op. 89, D 911

key:___

The $V^{\flat 9}$ and $V^{\flat 13}$ Chords

The minor versions of V^9 and V^{13} can be seen in major keys. They are borrowed from the tonic minor and are labelled $V^{\flat 9}$ and $V^{\flat 13}$. Take note of the resolutions of these chords. They are written and resolve in the same way as regular V^9 and V^{13} chords. The 9th and the 13th are placed in the soprano. The 9th resolves down by half step and the 13th drops down a 3rd to the root of I (Figure 1.20).

Figure 1.20

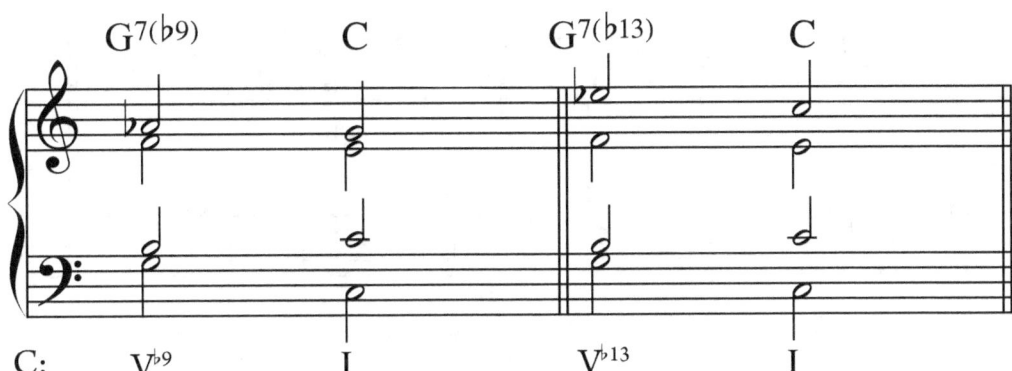

21 Chapter 1: Modal Mixture and Borrowed Chords

The ♭VI Chord

In the ♭VI chord, both the root and the fifth are lowered. This chord is used in the same way as it's unaltered counterpart (vi). It often functions as a substitute for I in a deceptive cadence (V - ♭VI), as shown in Figure 1.21.

Figure 1.21

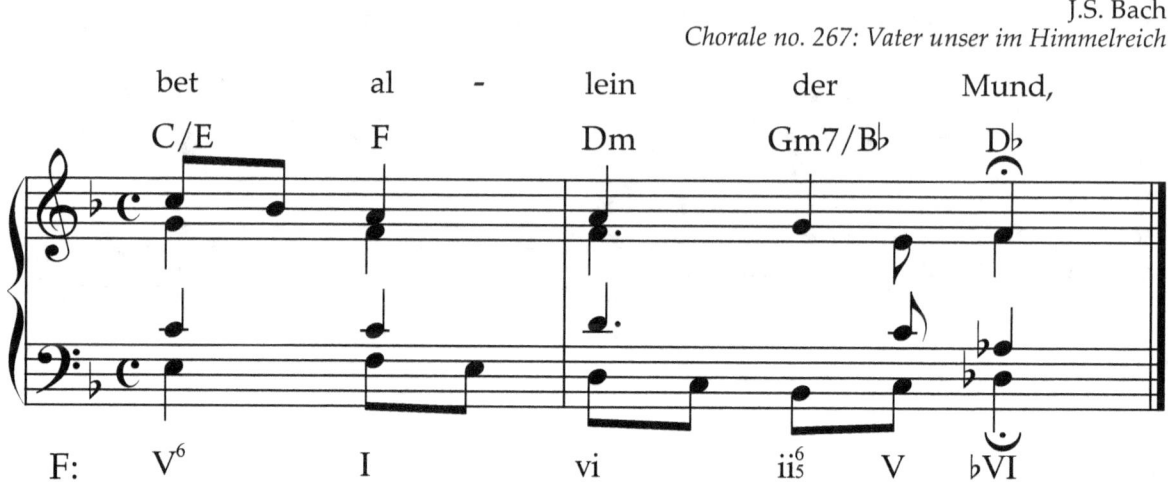

In this progression, the third of ♭VI should be doubled in order to avoid a melodic augmented second, and faulty, parallel, octaves and fifths.

Figure 1.22

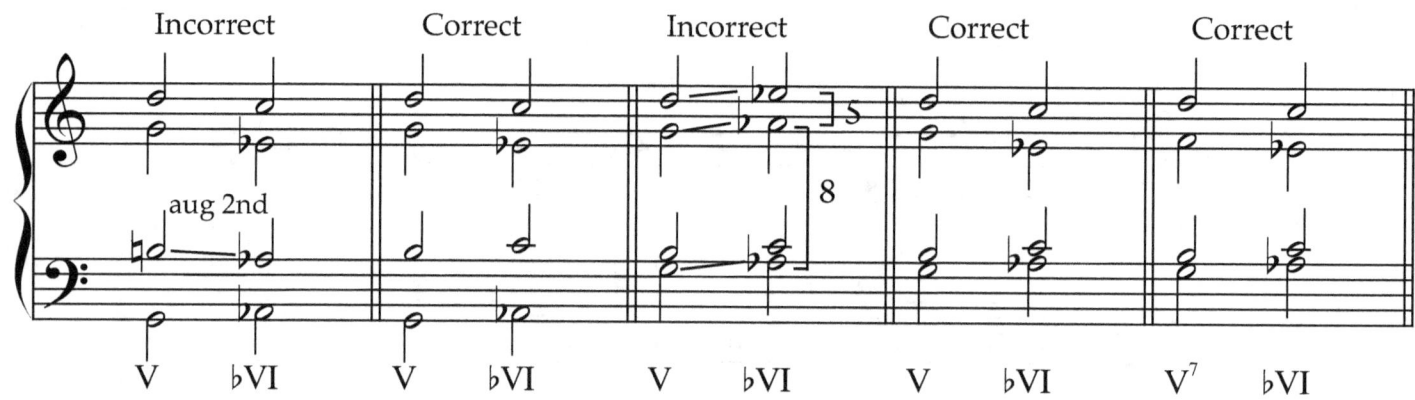

22   Chapter 1: Modal Mixture and Borrowed Chords

A ♭VI chord may function as a link between tonic and predominant chords. It is often found between I and the altered iv in a line of descending 3rds. A ♭VI may also link I and ii or an altered form of ii (ii°6 or ii°7). In Figure 1.23, the chromatic half-step E – E flat occurs in the same voice part. The root of ♭VI can be doubled here since it is not used in conjunction with chord V.

Figure 1.23

C: I   ♭VI   iv   V   I   I   ♭VI   ii°6   V   I

11. Complete the following progressions for four voices.

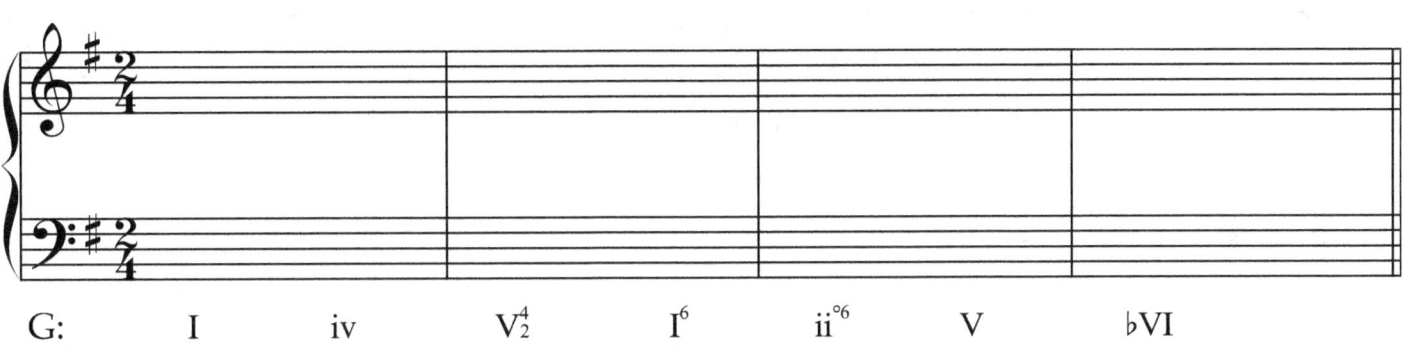

G: I   iv   V$^4_2$ I^6 ii°6   V   ♭VI

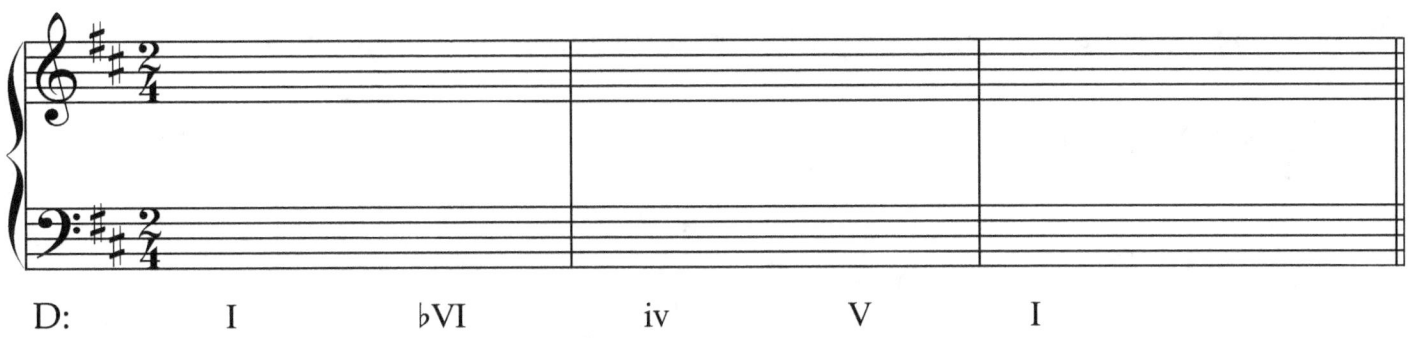

D: I   ♭VI   iv   V   I

12. Provide a harmonic analysis of the following excerpt. Use both functional and root/quality chord symbols. Circle and identify any non-chord tones.

Johannes Brahms
Symphony no. 3 op. 90 (2nd mvt.)

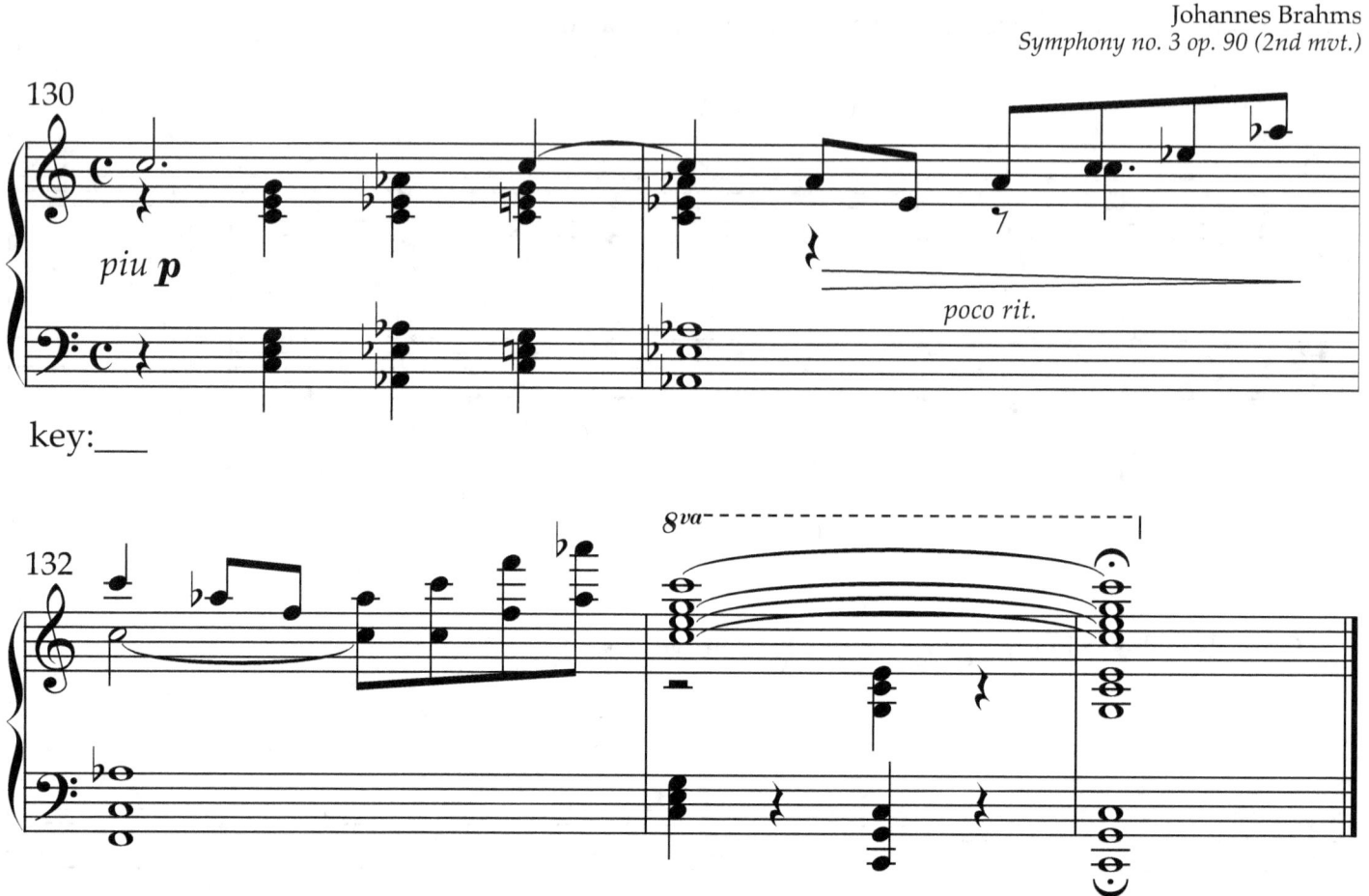

key:___

The vii°7 Chord

The vii°7 chord is described in *Essential Music Theory Level 10*. This chord is one of the most commonly borrowed chords in major keys. It can have the same function as a dominant 7th chord, and it can also be used in a tonic prolongation. It is usually found in root position, first inversion, or second inversion.

The most common resolution of vii°7 to the tonic uses the following voice-leading:

$\flat\hat{6}$ moves to $\hat{5}$
$\hat{4}$ moves to $\hat{3}$
$\hat{2}$ moves to $\hat{3}$
$\hat{7}$ moves to $\hat{1}$

This resolution results in a tonic chord with a doubled third (see Figure 1.24a).

When $\hat{2}$ is above $\flat\hat{6}$, a vii°⁷ chord may resolve to a tonic chord with a doubled root (Figure 1.24b).

$\flat\hat{6}$ moves to $\hat{5}$
$\hat{4}$ moves to $\hat{3}$
$\hat{2}$ moves to $\hat{1}$
$\hat{7}$ moves to $\hat{1}$

This resolution is particularly effective when the soprano voice moves from $\hat{2}$ to $\hat{1}$.

Figure 1.24

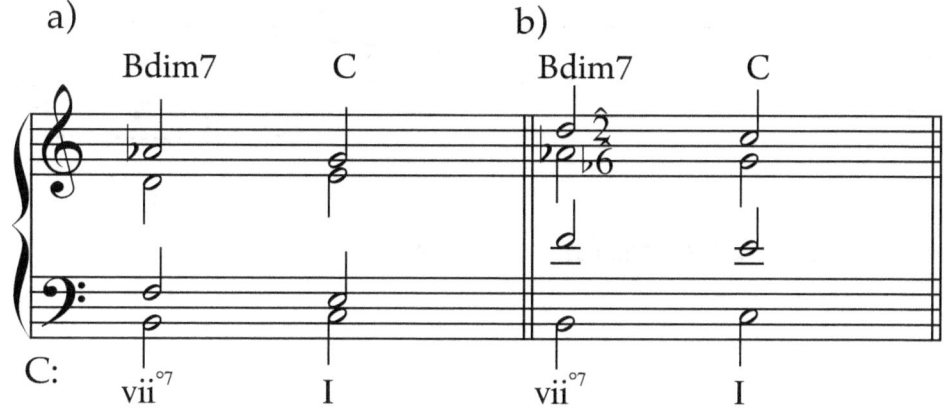

13. The following progressions are in major keys. Name the keys and complete the progressions.

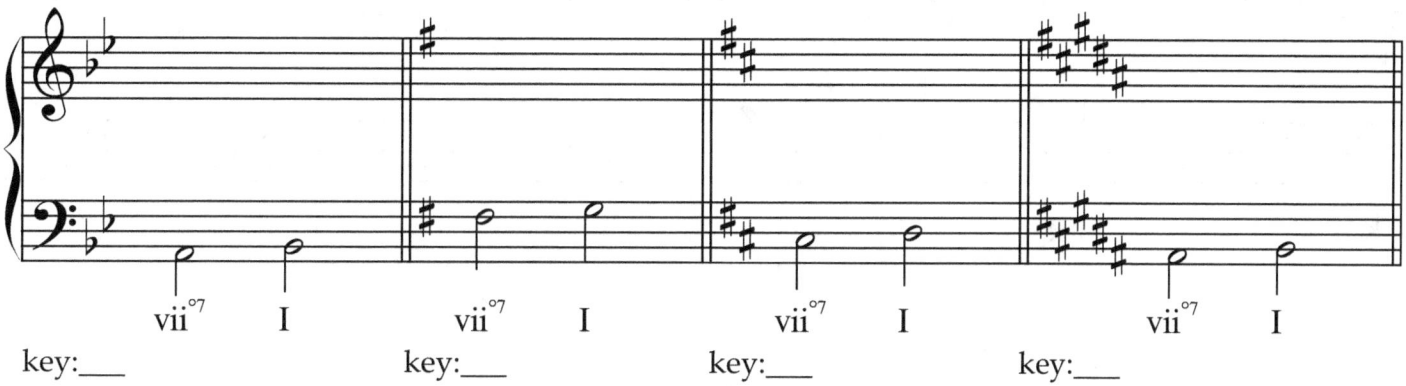

14. Complete the following progression in four parts.

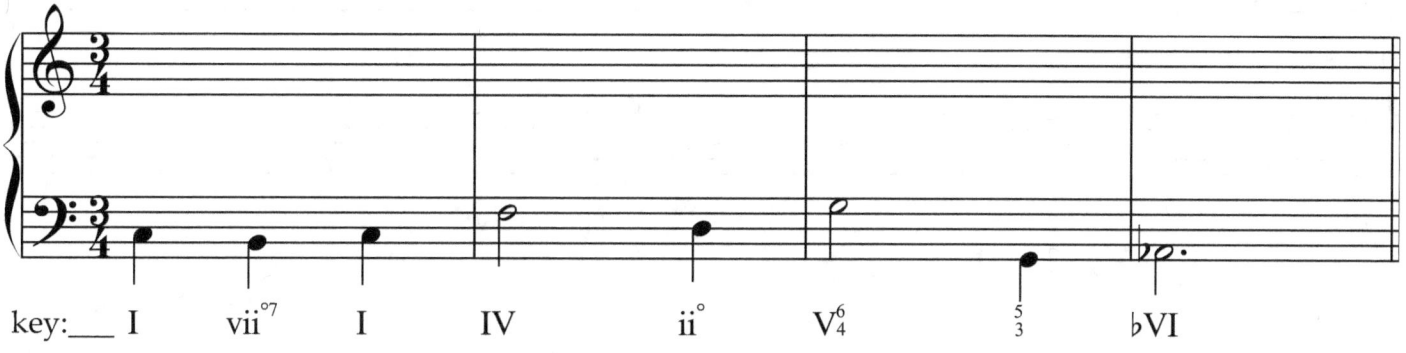

25   Chapter 1: Modal Mixture and Borrowed Chords

15. Provide a harmonic analysis of the following excerpt using functional chord symbols. Circle and identify any non-chord tones.

Johannes Brahms
Ballade op. 10, no. 4

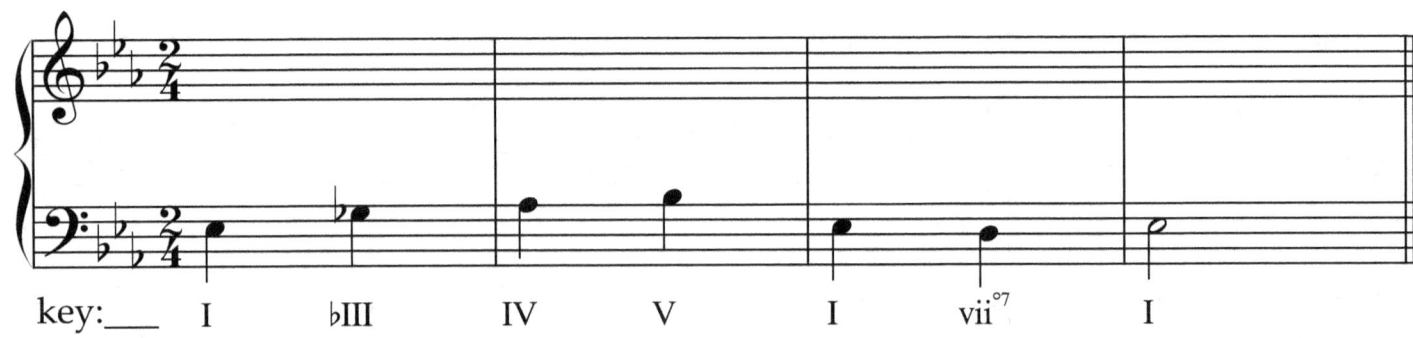

key:___

16. Complete the following progressions for four voices.

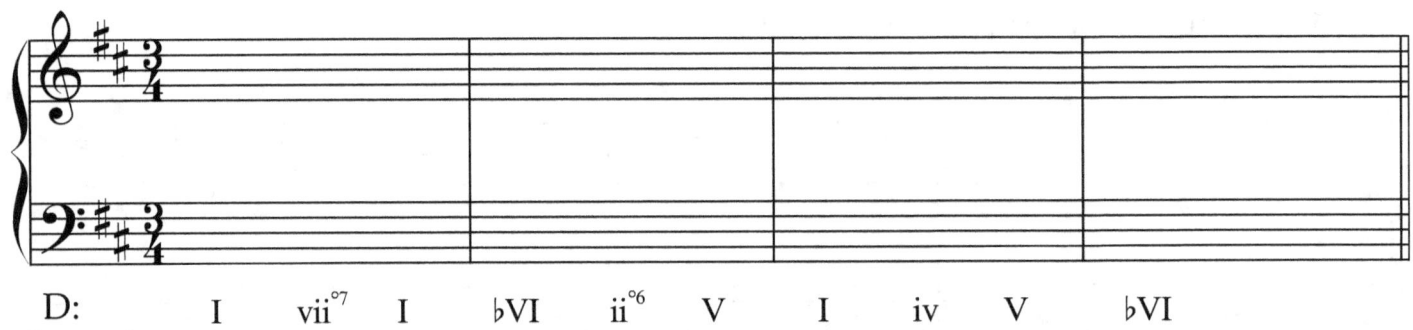

key:___ I   ♭III   IV   V   I   vii°⁷   I

D: I   vii°⁷   I   ♭VI   ii°⁶   V   I   iv   V   ♭VI

The ♭VII Chord

The ♭VII chord is rarely used. It is sometimes found in popular music, where it serves as a model substitute for V. It can also function as the secondary dominant V/♭III.

Figure 1.25

Figure 1.26 in C major is an extended tonic prolongation. Brahms uses ♭VII between two statements of I in a prolongation of tonic harmony. (Since ♭VII does not contain the leading tone, it is referred to as the **subtonic triad**). The iv chord in the last measure is a borrowed chord that functions as a prolongation of I.

Figure 1.26

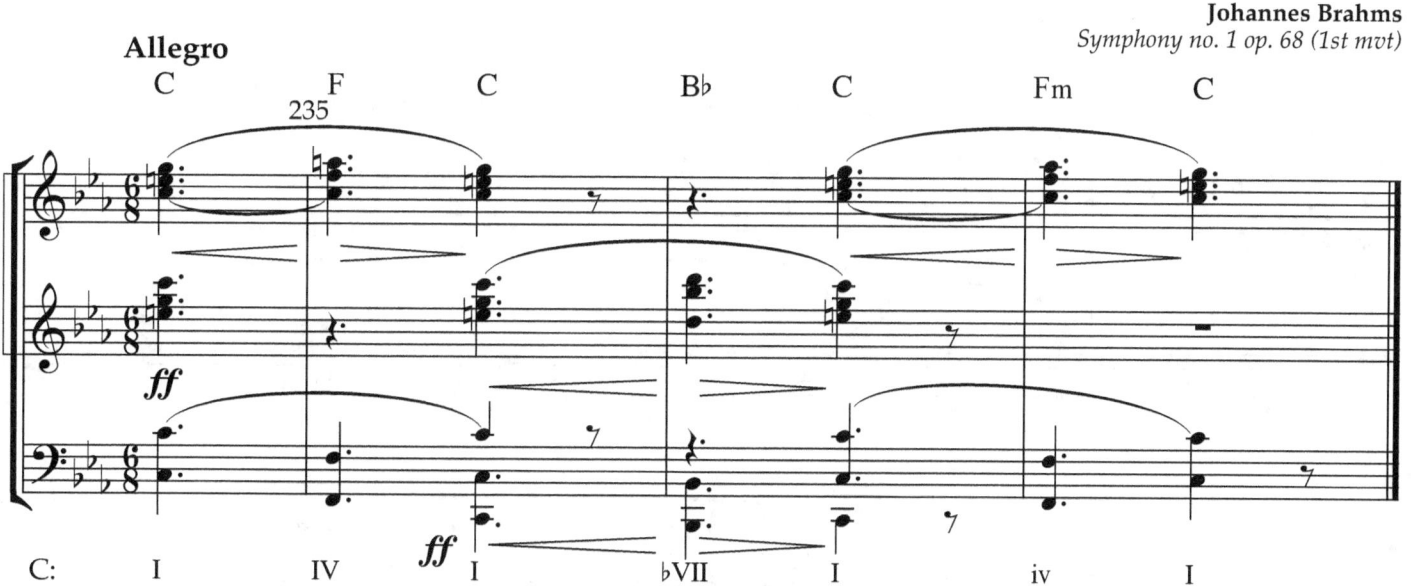

17. Complete the following progressions for four voices.

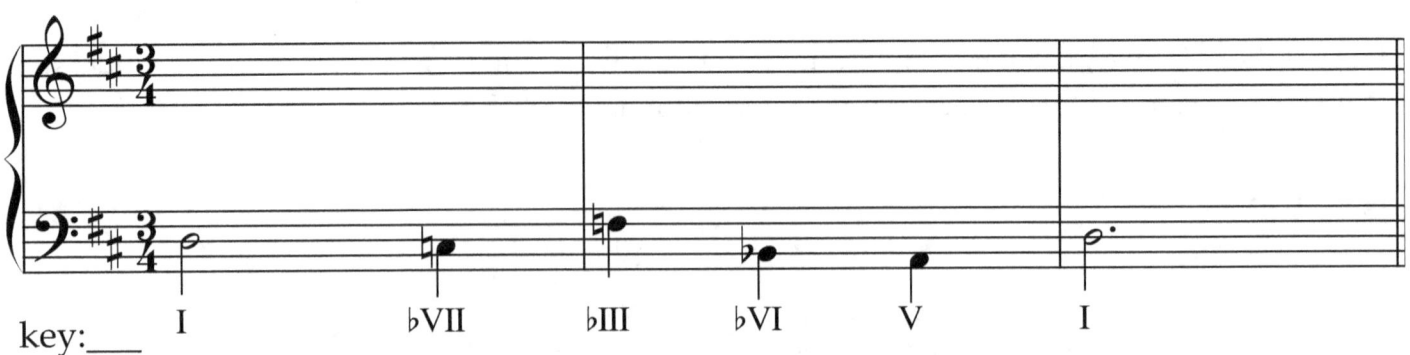

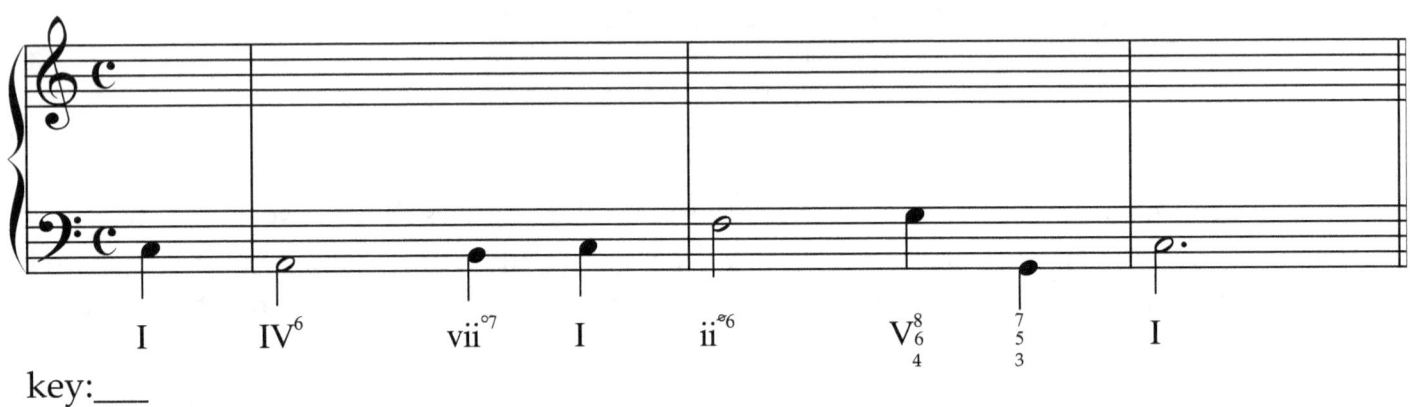

18. Provide a harmonic analysis of the following excerpt using functional chord symbols. Circle and identify any non-chord tones.

Frederic Chopin
Mazurka op. 7, no. 4

The Picardy Third

The most common borrowed chord in minor keys is the major tonic triad I, which contains a raised third. When this chord appears at the end of a piece in a minor key, it is called a **tierce de picardie** (or picardy third). Most scholars believe that the name comes from the Old French word, *picart*, meaning, sharp or pointed, rather than from Picardie, a region in France. Figure 1.27 comes from a chorale harmonization by J.S. Bach.

Figure 1.27

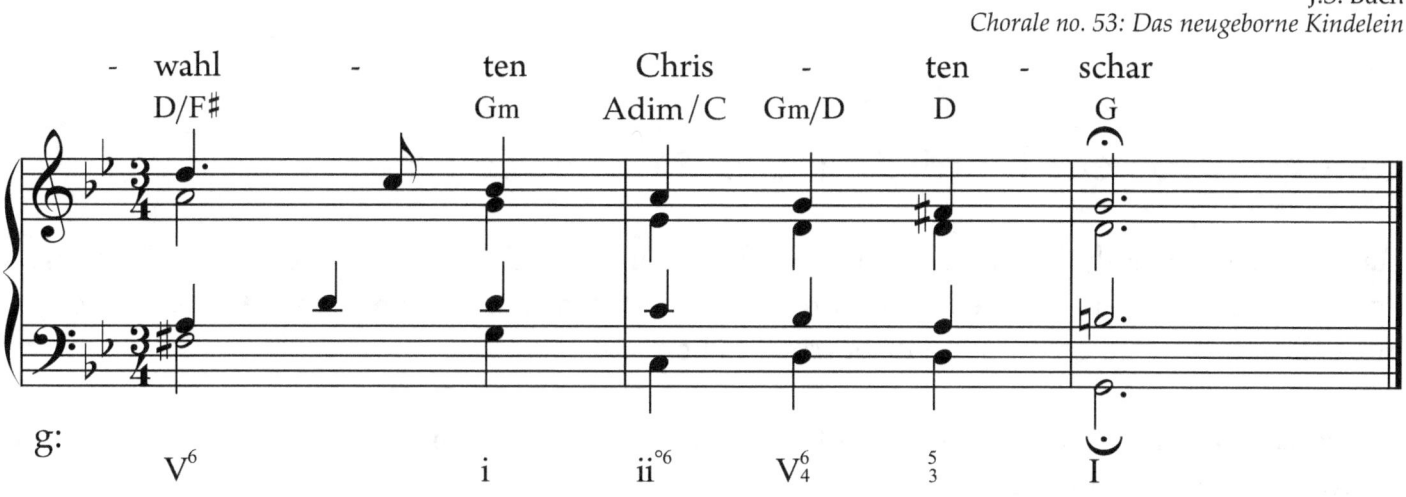

19. Provide a harmonic analysis of the following excerpt using functional chord symbols. Circle and identify any non-chord tones.

J.S. Bach
Chorale no. 48: Ach wie flüchtig, ach wie nichtig

20. Complete the following progressions for four voices.

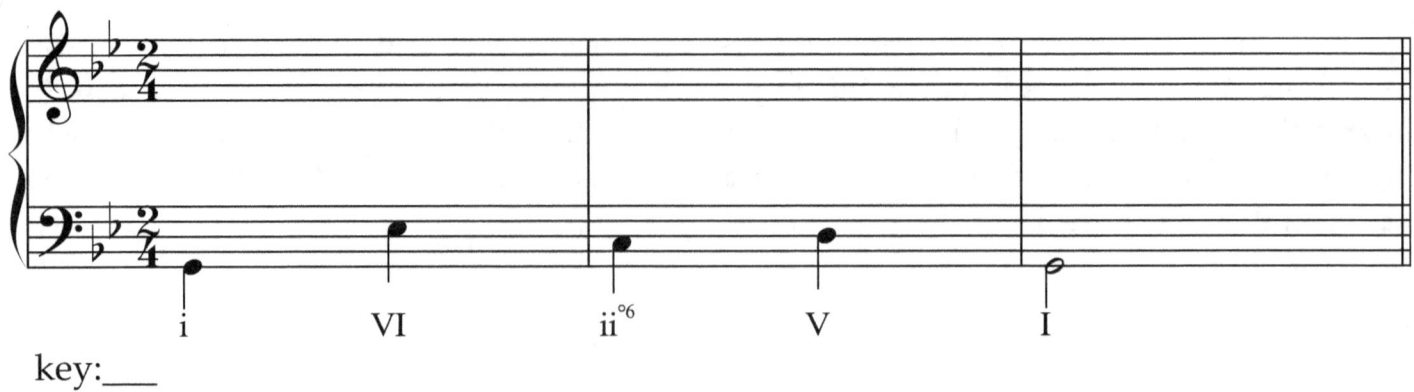

key:___

Using Borrowed Chords to Harmonize a Melody

Harmonizing a melody involves selecting chords that enrich and support a melodic line. Composers often draw from outside of the key to introduce variety, tension, and emotional depth. One of the most effective ways to do this is to use borrowed chords.

When harmonizing a melody, the goal is to support its motion and highlight its emotional content. Borrowed chords can be used to:

Introduce Contrast: borrowed chords create an immediate shift in color. For example, inserting an A♭ major chord into a passage in C major provides a striking contrast, due to its unexpected chromaticism and unexpected quality.

Express Emotion: Minor chords borrowed into a major key can enhance feelings of sadness, longing or mystery. A melody resting on the 4th degree of the scale (F in C major) might be harmonized with an F minor chord instead of the expected F major chord, adding depth and color.

Smooth Voice Leading: Borrowed chords can facilitate smoother transitions between chords. For example, moving from I to ♭VI (C to A♭ major) provides descending voice leading that feels natural and satisfying.

Highlight Pivotal Moments: Borrowed chords are effective when used sparingly at key moments in a phrase, perhaps at a cadence, or to set up a return to the tonic. For instance, using a ♭VII - IV - I progression (B♭ - F - C major) mimics the mixolydian mode and gives an interesting way to approach a final cadence.

Play the melody in Figure 1.28.

Figure 1.28

Now play the setting of the melody in Figure 1.29. The harmonization used here is entirely diatonic.

Figure 1.29

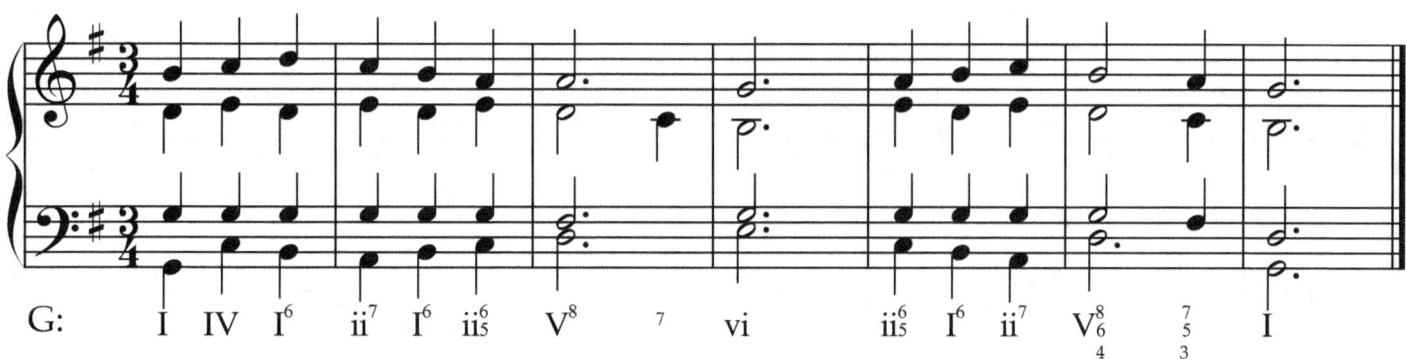

Now play the alternate setting in Figure 1.30. The addition of several borrowed chords adds chromatic and expressive interest to the setting. When using borrowed chords, it's important to ensure they align with the melody. Since these chords contain chromatic tones, check that the chord tones are either present in the melody or do not clash harshly. Additionally, use borrowed chords carefully. Too many can obscure the tonal centre and confuse the listener. They are most effective when used to highlight or intensify a particular moment.

Figure 1.30

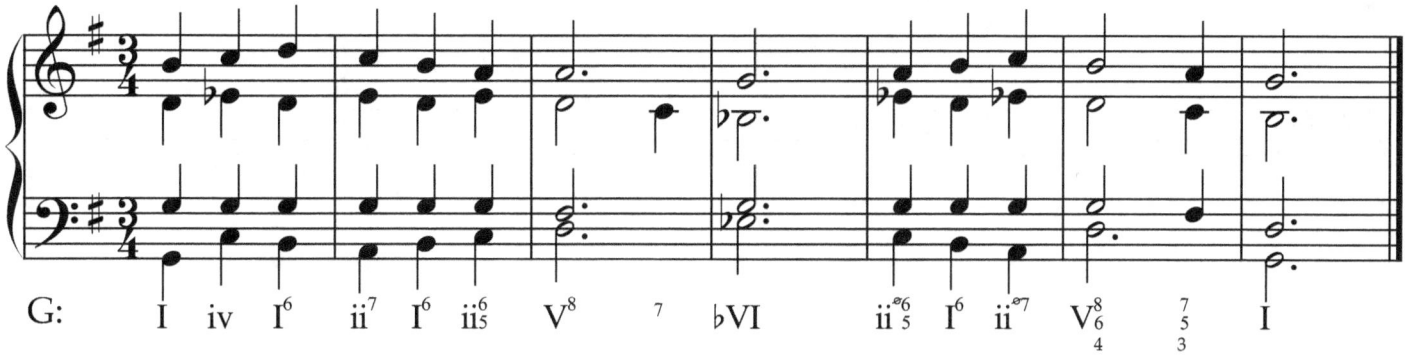

21. Harmonize the following melodic fragments in four parts, using borrowed chords were indicated. Complete each example with functional chord symbols.

22. Harmonize the following melody, using borrowed chords for the notes marked with asterisks (*). Complete each example with functional chord symbols.

23. Harmonize the following melody, using borrowed chords where appropriate to add color and interest. Complete each example with functional chord symbols.

key:___

SUMMARY

1. Borrowed chords are diatonic chords of one mode that may be used in a parallel mode. For example, chords belonging to the key of C minor maybe used to harmonize a melody in C major.

2. Borrowed chords function basically the same way as their unaltered (or diatonic) counterparts. For example, ii⁶ and IV often function as pre-dominant chords. The borrowed form of these chords ii°⁶ and iv may have the same pre-dominant function.

3. In major keys, the most common borrowed chords are ii° and ii°⁷ and their inversions, and ♭III, iv, ♭VI, and vii°⁷ and it's inversions.

4. In minor keys, the most common borrowed chord is I, using a raised 3rd.

2
The Neapolitan Chord

The **Neapolitan chord** is an altered supertonic triad that is associated with the "Neapolitan school" that included 18th century composers of opera, such as Alessandro Scarlatti, Giovanni Battista Pergolesi, and Domenico Cimarosa. The chord also appears in works of 17th century composers, including Arcangelo Corelli and Henry Purcell. This is a colourful and expressive chord. It is most commonly found in minor keys, and it adds a rich dramatic flavour to harmonic progressions. Despite its exotic name, the Neapolitan chord follows clear rules and serves an important function in harmony.

As this chord is almost always used in its first inversion, it is usually known as the **Neapolitan 6th**. Throughout this book, we will use the symbol N^6 to represent the Neapolitan 6th chord (that is, the first inversion of the triad), and the symbol N to represent this chord in it's (rarely used) root position.

The Neapolitan chord is a major chord built on the lowered second scale degree ($\flat\hat{2}$) of a key. In Roman numeral analysis it is often labelled N or $\flat$II. For example, in the key of C minor, the second scale degree is D and when it is lowered by a half step, it becomes D$\flat$. The Neapolitan chord in this key would therefore be a D$\flat$ major chord, consisting of the notes, D$\flat$, F, and A$\flat$.

The strong voice-leading tendency of this chord is created by the half step relationship between the root of the chord ($\flat\hat{2}$) and the first-degree ($\hat{1}$), a half step below. Note that a Neapolitan chord has the same sound in tonic major and minor keys.

- In minor keys, the only altered pitch of a Neapolitan chord is the root ($\flat\hat{2}$).
- In major keys, a Neapolitan chord has two altered pitches: the root ($\flat\hat{2}$) and the fifth ($\flat\hat{6}$).

Figure 2.1

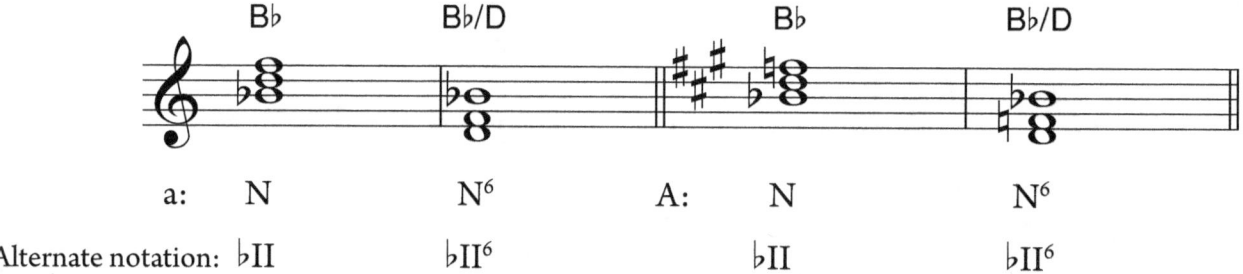

The Neapolitan 6th is most commonly found in minor keys. It often functions as a substitute for a diatonic pre-dominant chord (for example, iv or ii⁶.) In Figure 2.2, Chopin uses a N⁶ as a pre-dominant chord before V⁷ in a deceptive cadence.

Figure 2.2

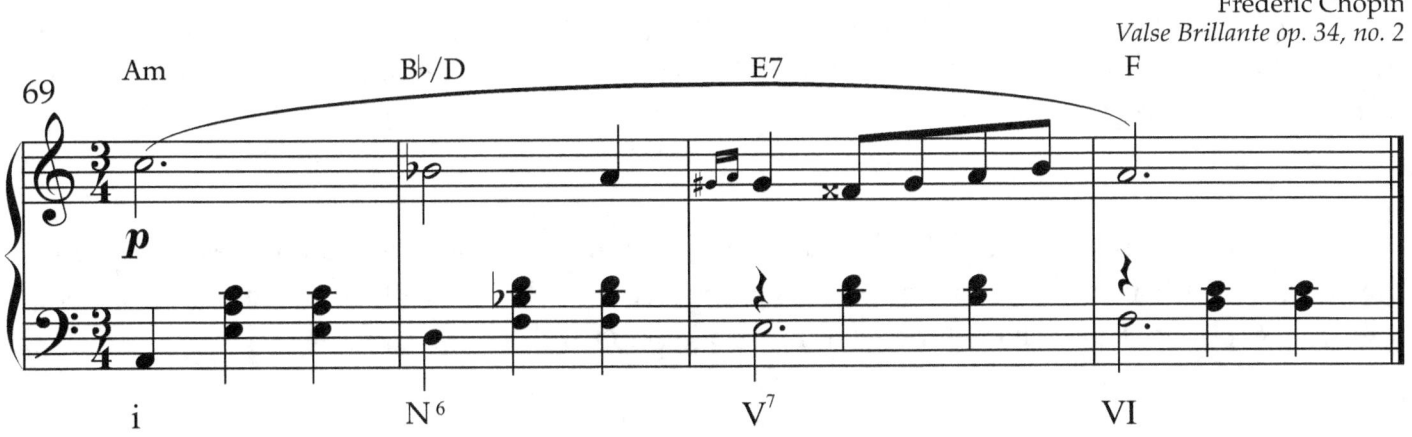

Figure 2.3 contains examples of N⁶ chords in major and minor keys.

Figure 2.3

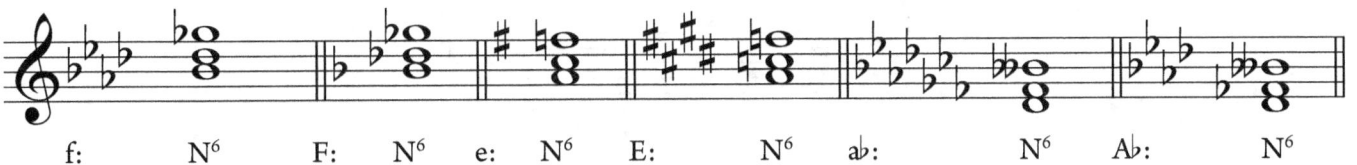

1. Write Neapolitan 6th chords in the following keys, using the correct key signatures, and any required accidentals.

Chapter 2: The Neapolitan Chord

Resolving a Neapolitan 6th Chord

Since the N⁶ chord is an altered supertonic chord, it is usually followed by a dominant chord (V), a dominant 7th (V⁷), or a cadential $^6_4$ (V$^{6-5}_{4-3}$). Note that you do not necessarily need an accidental in the melody in order to use a N⁶. In four-part texture, any note may be used in the soprano, although $\flat\hat{2}$ and $\hat{4}$ are the most common choices. Usually the third ($\hat{4}$) is doubled for the smoothest voice-leading. In the resolution of the chord, the sixth above the bass ($\flat\hat{2}$) falls a diminished 3rd, either directly or through another chord.

In Figure 2.4, the bass note is doubled by the tenor, and the $\flat\hat{2}$ in the soprano resolves downward to the leading tone. The false relation that occurs between the $\flat\hat{2}$ (B♭) of the N⁶ chord and the fifth of the following V chord (B♮) is characteristic of this progression and is not a fault.

Figure 2.4

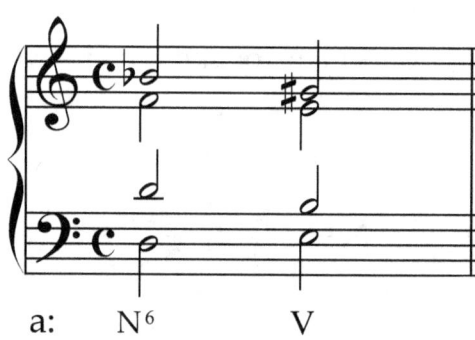

When N⁶ resolves to a dominant seventh, the V⁷ chord is typically incomplete. In this example, the root of V⁷ is doubled, and the fifth is omitted. In the resolution, the $\flat\hat{2}$ in the soprano falls to $\sharp\hat{7}$ (a melodic diminished 3rd), then rises to the tonic ($\hat{1}$). The path of the melody from a semitone above 1 to a semitone below creates a colorful tension that is characteristic of this progression.

Figure 2.5

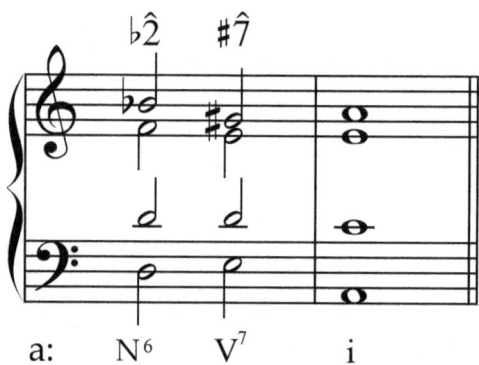

When N⁶ resolves to cadential $^6_4$, the false relation between $\flat\hat{2}$ and $\hat{2}$ does not occur. Here, the melodic diminished 3rd in the soprano between $\flat\hat{2}$ and $\sharp\hat{7}$ is filled by passing motion through the chord.

Figure 2.6

Pay careful attention to voice leading if $\flat\hat{2}$ and $\hat{2}$ are in the same voice in a resolution of N⁶ to V or V⁷, since errors may occur. In Figure 2.7, underneath the soprano, which moves from B-flat to B natural, there is a melodic augmented second in the alto (F – G sharp) and faulty parallel octaves between the tenor and bass.

Figure 2.7

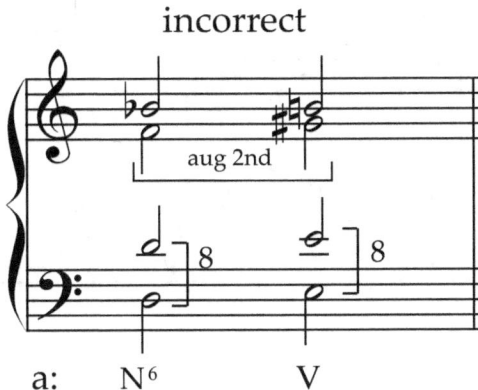

It is possible for a single voice to move from $\flat\hat{2}$ to $\hat{2}$. This occurs most often when the root of N⁶ is doubled. It is best to hide the shift from $\flat\hat{2}$ to $\hat{2}$ in an inner voice, as shown in Figure 2.8. However, such a treatment of a Neapolitan six with a doubled root is not normal procedure and is rarely seen.

Figure 2.8

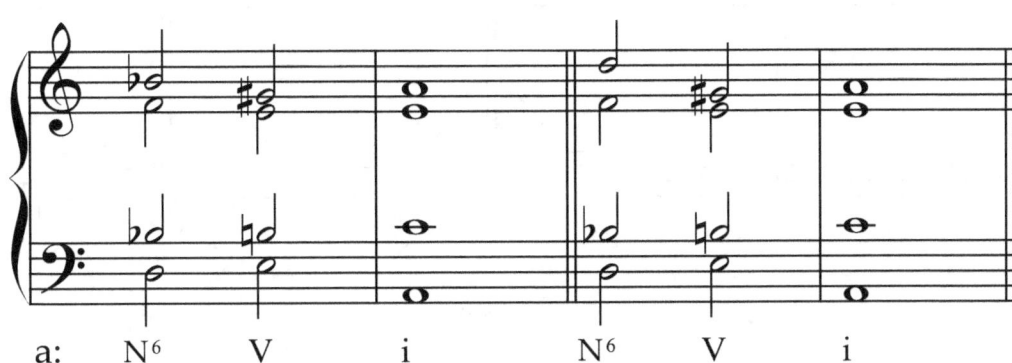

If ♭$\hat{2}$ occurs in an inner voice below $\hat{6}$, parallel 5ths may result when the N⁶ resolves to V$^6_4$. As long as ♭$\hat{2}$ is higher than $\hat{6}$ the voice leading will be fine, as demonstrated in Figure 2.9.

Figure 2.9

2. Resolve the following Neapolitan 6th chords.

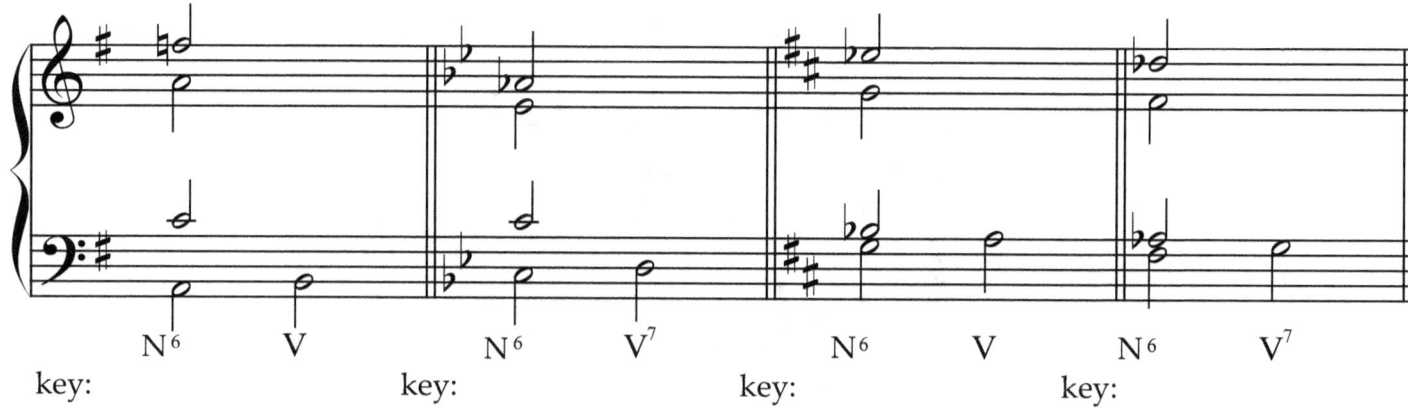

3. Name the keys and complete the following progressions in four parts.

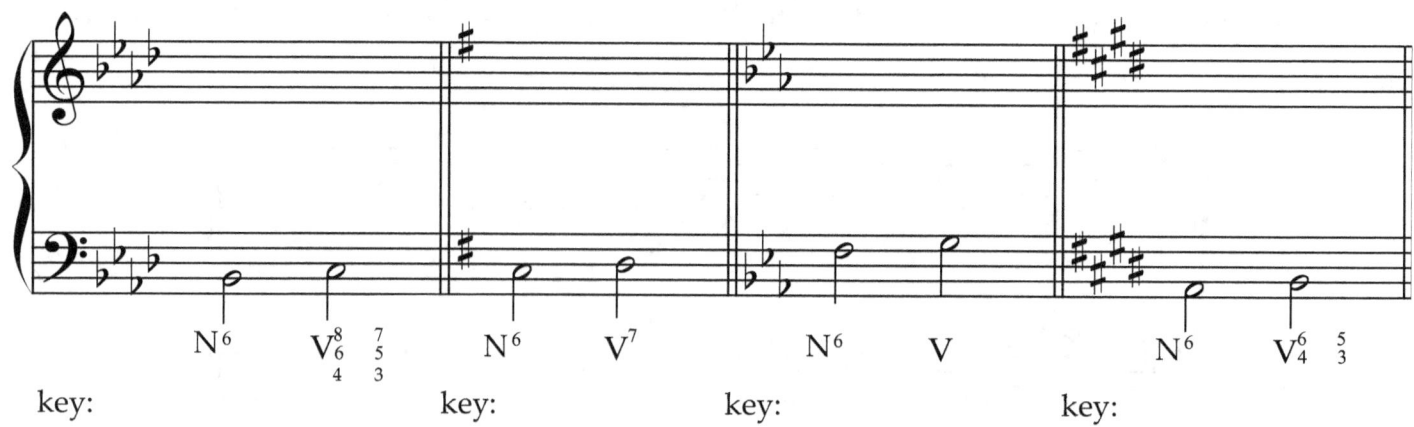

4. Complete the following progressions in four parts, using key signatures and any necessary accidentals.

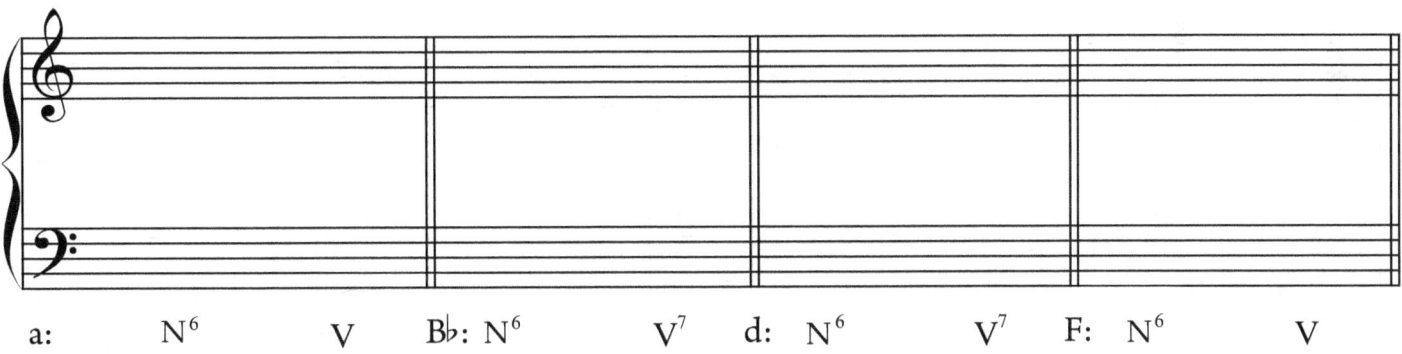

a: N⁶   V   B♭: N⁶   V⁷   d: N⁶   V⁷   F: N⁶   V

As shown in Figure 2.10, the Neapolitan 6th may resolve to an inversion of V⁷ (example a), a dominant function chord (example b), a secondary dominant (example c), or a leading tone seventh examples d and e). These progressions do not affect the voice-leading principles discussed earlier.

Figure 2.10

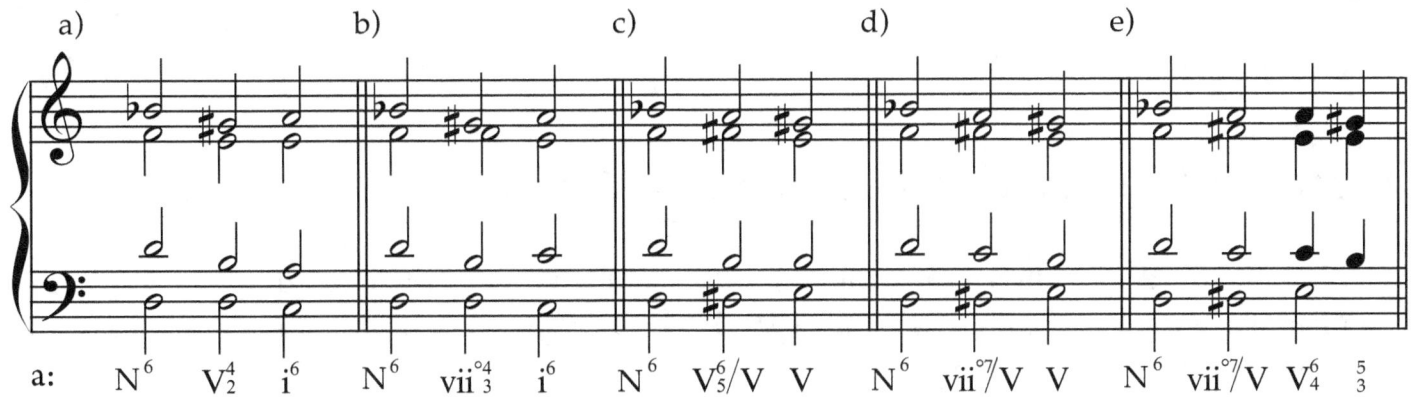

a: N⁶ V⁴₂ i⁶   N⁶ vii°⁴₃ i⁶   N⁶ V⁶₅/V V   N⁶ vii°⁷/V V   N⁶ vii°⁷/V V⁶₄ ⁵₃

In Figure 2.11, Mozart moves from N⁶ to vii°⁷/V, which acts as a passing chord before the cadential six-four progression.

Figure 2.11

Wolfgang Amadeus Mozart
Fantasia in C minor, K 475

c: N⁶   vii°⁷/V   V⁶₄ ⁵₃   i

Chapter 2: The Neapolitan Chord

5. Complete the following progressions in four parts, using key signatures and any necessary accidentals. Choose an appropriate time signature for each progression.

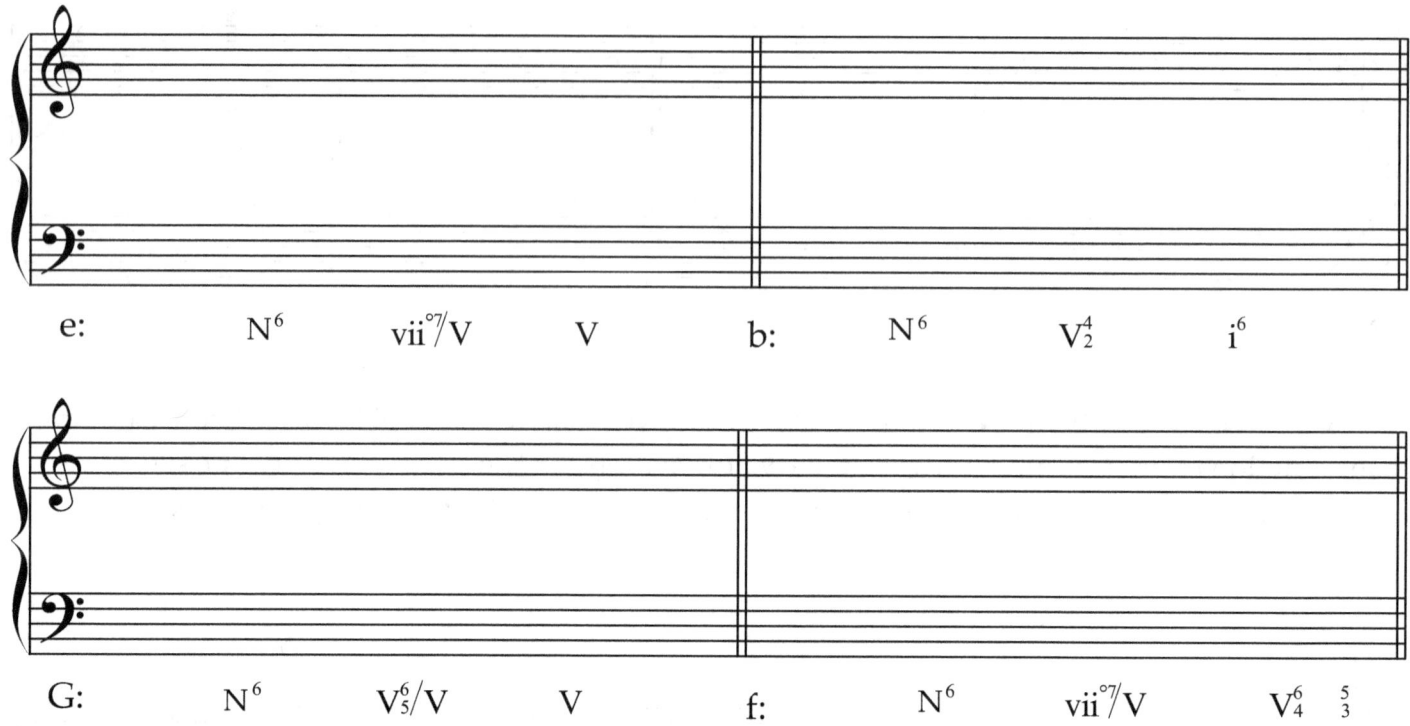

Approach Chords for the Neapolitan 6th

Since the N^6 chord is an altered supertonic chord, most harmonies that are used to proceed ii or ii^6 in a major key or ii^{o6} in a minor key are also good chords of approach for N^6. In minor keys, both i and i^6 are effective choices. An approach from i^6 allows stepwise motion in the bass (see Figure 2.12 a). If you use this progression in major keys, take care to avoid a melodic augmented interval in the approach to $\flat\hat{2}$. Note the incorrect and correct approaches to B flat in Figure 2.12 b.

Figure 2.12

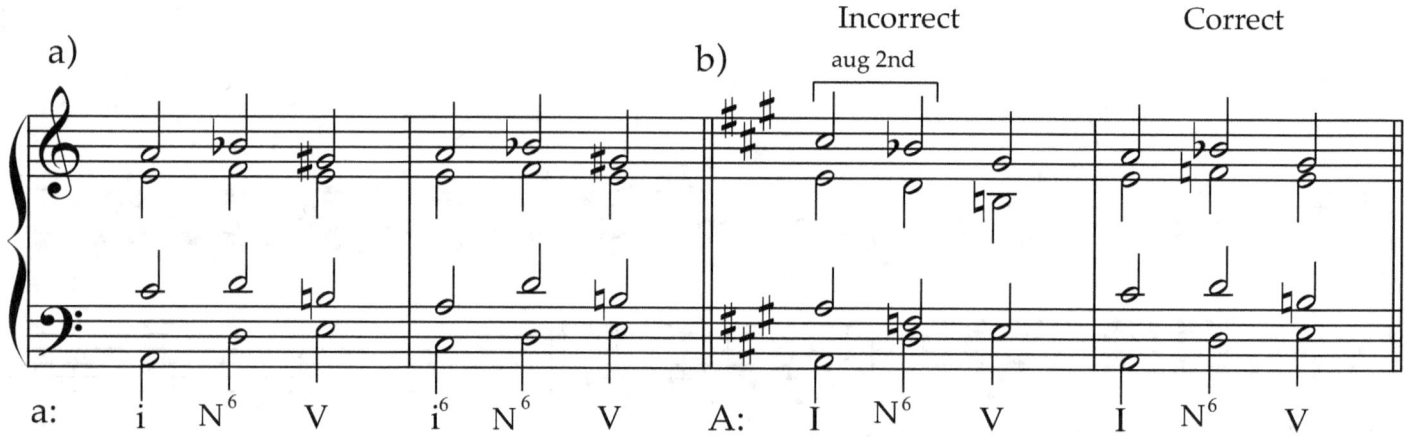

Chapter 2: The Neapolitan Chord

For the smoothest voice-leading from iv to N⁶, keep the two common tones (here, D and F) in the same voices.

Figure 2.13

The VI chord is another common approach chord to N⁶. In major keys, the harmonic color provided by the borrowed chord ♭VI is also an effective choice.

Figure 2.14

6. Complete the following progressions in four parts.

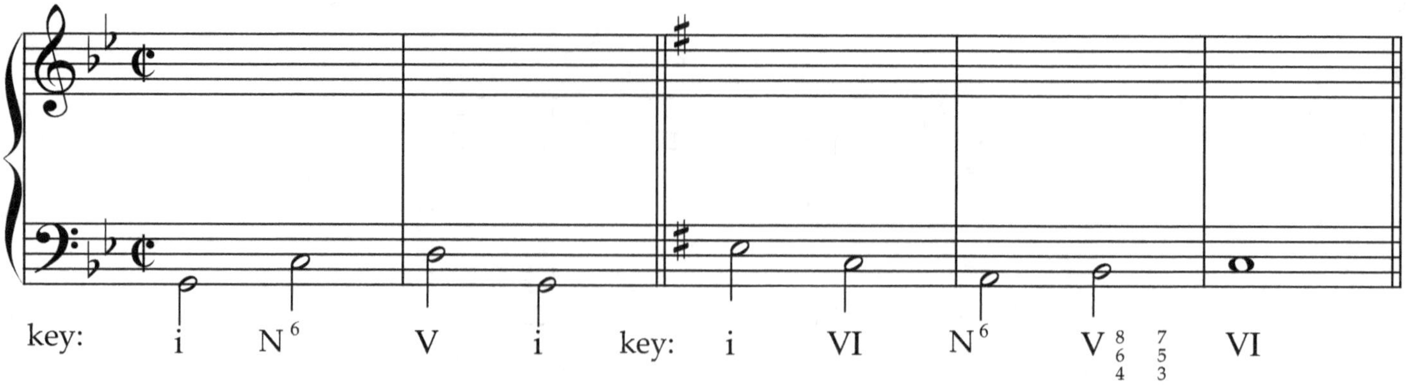

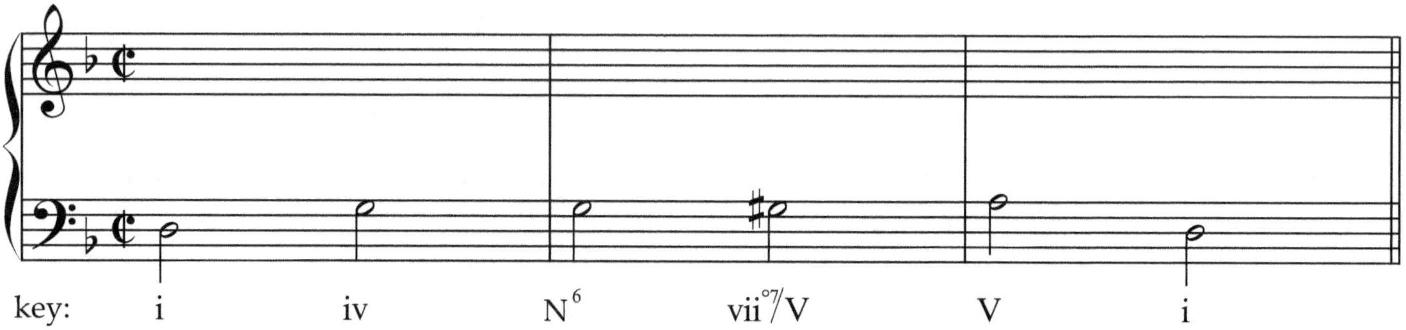

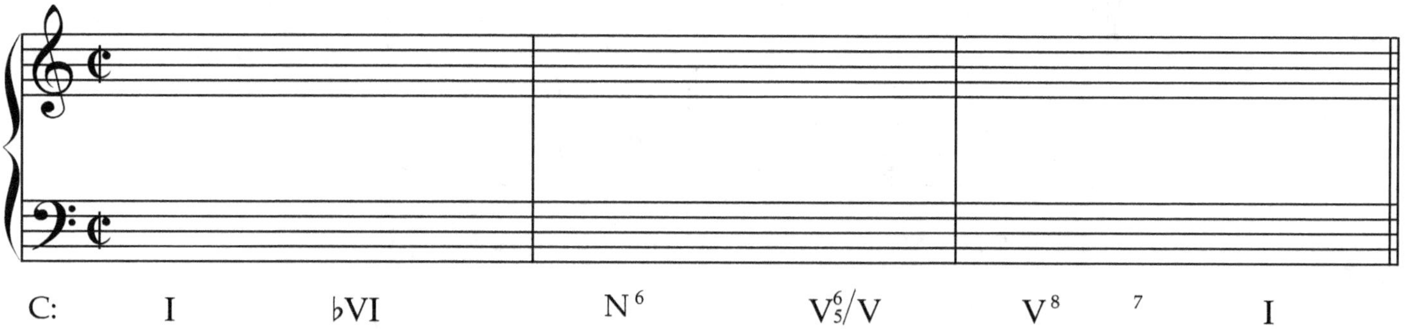

key: i   N⁶   V   i   key: i   VI   N⁶   V $^{8\ 7}_{6\ 5}_{4\ 3}$ VI

key: i   iv   N⁶   vii°⁷/V   V   i

C: I   ♭VI   N⁶   V$^6_5$/V   V⁸   ⁷   I

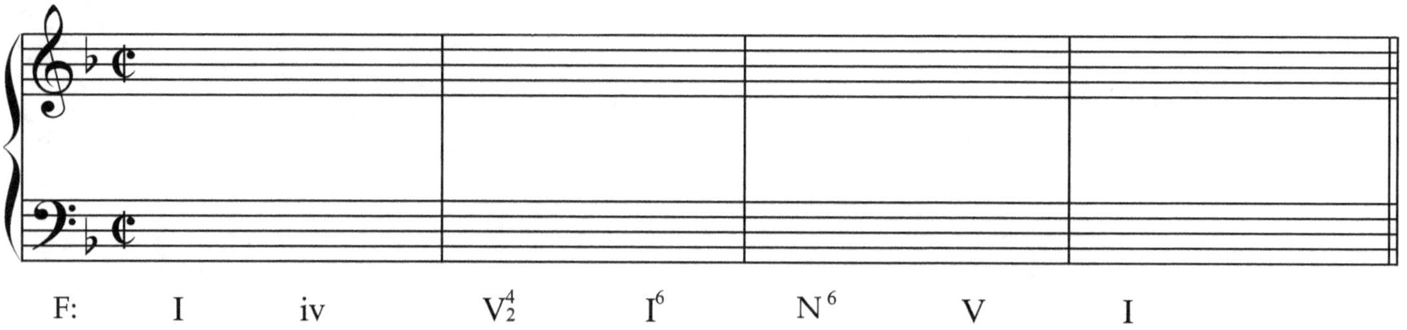

F: I   iv   V$^4_2$ I⁶   N⁶   V   I

Although the Neapolitan chord appears most often in first inversion, it is occasionally found in root position. When a root position N moves to V, the bass leaps an augmented 4th from ♭$\hat{2}$ to $\hat{5}$. Note the dissonant leap in the bass line (D flat to G) when Chopin uses this progression in the excerpt in Figure 2.15.

Figure 2.15

Frederic Chopin
Prelude in C minor op. 28, no. 20

[Musical excerpt: c: VI N V⁷ i i]

As a general rule, composers only use this progression for specific reasons: here, it is part of a descending 5th motive in the bass.

Tonicization of the Neapolitan Chord

Neapolitan chords, like other consonant triads, may be tonicized. The dominant of the Neapolitan chord is ♭VI in major keys, and VI in minor keys. Since the chord most often appears in first inversion (N⁶), it is usually tonicized by its own dominant 7th chord in third inversion, as Schubert has done in Figure 2.16.

Figure 2.16

Franz Schubert
An Mignon op. 19, no. 2, D 161

Chapter 2: The Neapolitan Chord

7. Provide a harmonic analysis of the following excerpts. Use functional and root/quality chord symbols. Circle and identify any non-chord tones.

Ludwig van Beethoven
Piano Sonata op. 27, no. 2 (1st mvt.)

key:___

Franz Schubert
Mass in G major D 167 (Sanctus)

D:

Richard Wagner
Die Walkure act 1, scene 2

Chapter 2: The Neapolitan Chord

Franz Schubert
Der Muller und der Bach
from Die schone Mullerin, op.25, D 795

key:___

Using the Neapolitan Chord to Harmonize a Melody

If a given melody contains ♭$\hat{2}$ or $\hat{4}$, you may use a Neapolitan chord in your harmonization. Remember that this chord often has a pre-dominant function, leading to a dominant chord or a cadential six-four. The Neapolitan 6th can be a striking addition to the harmony for a melody that descends by step from the dominant to the tonic, as shown in Figure 2.17.

Figure 2.17

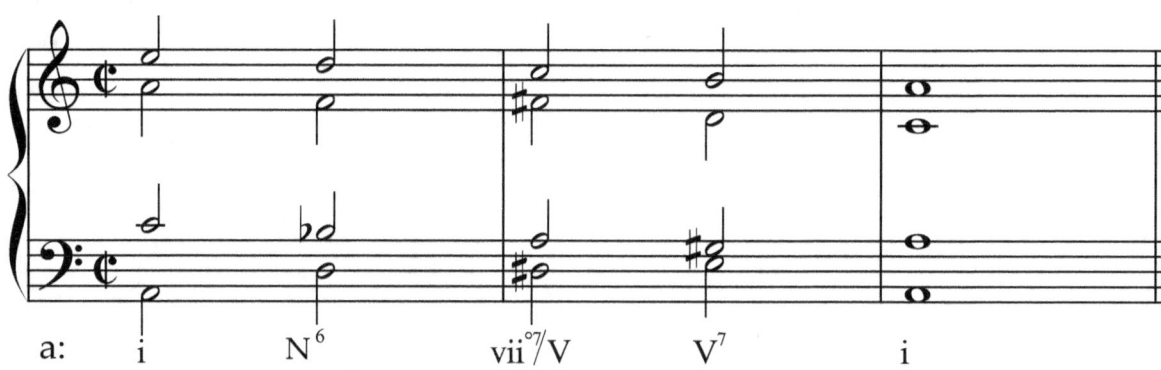

8. Harmonize the following melodies for four parts. Incorporate the indicated chords and use an appropriately placed Neapolitan chord in each melody. Complete each example with functional chord symbols.

SUMMARY

1. The Neapolitan 6th is an altered supertonic chord. It is a major triad built on the lowered second-degree of the scale (♭$\hat{2}$). The label 6th reflects the fact that it is most often used in first inversion. It is represented by the symbol N^6.

2. Since the N^6 is an altered supertonic chord, it usually resolves to dominant harmony, including V and V^7 (root position and inversions) and the cadential six-four progression. The N^6 can also resolve to other dominant function chords, secondary dominants, and leading tone 7ths.

3. Most chords that are used to approach other supertonic chords (ii, ii^6 in major keys, and ii^{o6} in minor keys), will work equally well with the Neapolitan 6th.

4. Although the Neapolitan chord is almost always used in first inversion, it can occasionally be found in root position. A Neapolitan chord in root position is represented by the symbol N.

3
Augmented 6th Chords

Augmented 6th chords are a special kind of pre-dominant chord used in classical harmony to build tension and lead smoothly to the dominant chord (V). What makes these chords special is the use of the interval of an augmented 6th, which gives the chord a very strong pull toward the dominant. The designation 6th refers *not* to the inversion of the chord, but rather to the augmented 6th interval that occurs within the chord.

Augmented 6th chords are most commonly built on the note that is a minor 6th above the tonic or a (half step above the dominant). In major keys, this note is ♭$\hat{6}$ and requires an accidental. In minor keys, no accidental is required because that note is part of the key.

Figure 3.1

In this lesson, we will examine three augmented 6th chords: the **Italian 6th** (It^6), the **German 6th** (Ger^6), and the **French 6th** (Fr^6). These national names are widely used, but have no political, geographical, or historical significance. Figure 3.2 illustrates the structure of these three chords. Note that they have two intervals in common: each chord contains both a major 3rd and an augmented 6th.

Figure 3.2

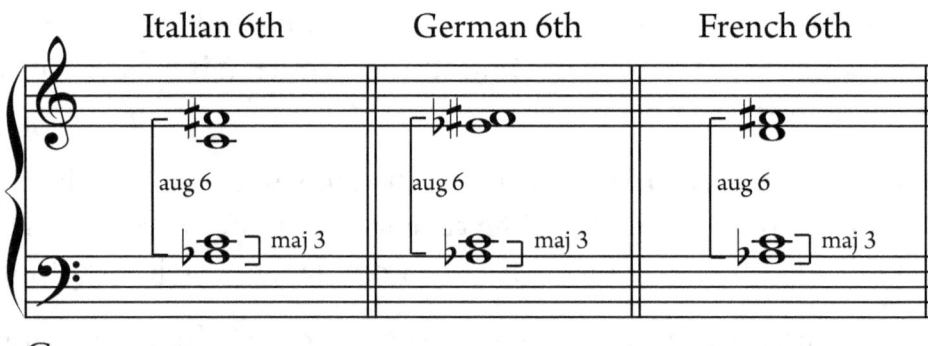

Augmented 6th are most commonly used as pre-dominant chords and are often found at important cadence points. Composers also use these chords to highlight a dramatic or intense moment within a piece. Play the excerpt in Figure 3.3 and note the placement and sonority of the German 6th chord.

Figure 3.3

Wolfgang Amadeus Mozart
Piano Sonata in F major
K 332 (1st mvt)

The Italian 6th

The Italian 6th consists of the intervals of a major 3rd and an augmented 6th above the bass. In four-part writing, the third above the bass (the tonic) is doubled. Note that this chord sounds the same in tonic major and minor keys. In both examples in Figure 3.4, the Italian 6th consists of a major third (C) and an augmented 6th (F sharp) above the bass note (A flat). The three different pitches are $\flat\hat{6}$, $\hat{1}$, and $\sharp\hat{4}$. In major keys, an accidental is required for $\flat\hat{6}$, but in minor keys this note is part of the key signature. In all keys, an accidental is required for $\sharp\hat{4}$. The Italian 6th is represented by the symbol It^6.

Figure 3.4

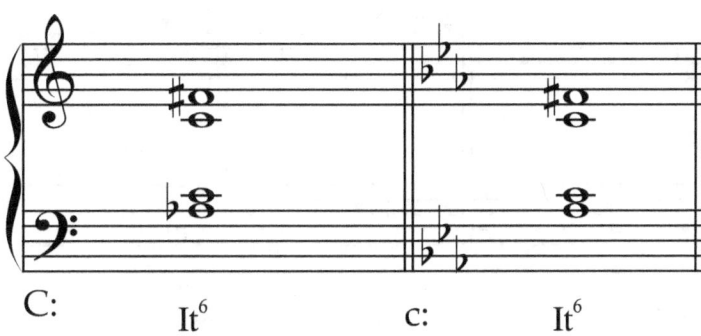

Chapter 3: Augmented 6th Chords

1. Name the keys and write Italian 6th chords above each bass note. Include chord symbols.

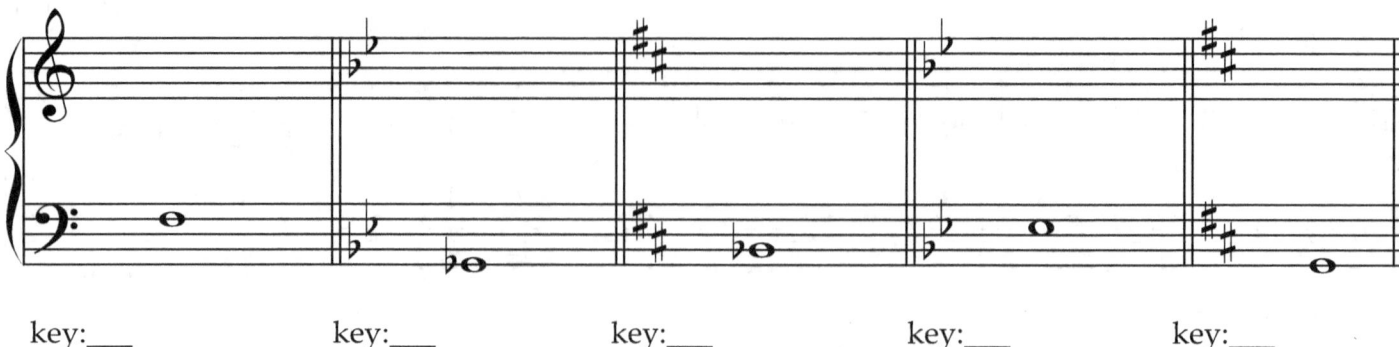

key:___   key:___   key:___   key:___   key:___

The German 6th

The German 6th is a four-note chord that consists of the intervals of a major 3rd, a perfect 5th, and an augmented 6th above the bass. Note that this chord sounds the same in tonic major and minor keys. In both examples in Figure 3.5, the German 6th consists of a major 3rd (C) a perfect 5th (E flat) and an augmented 6th (F sharp) above the bass note (A flat). The four pitches are ♭$\hat{6}$, $\hat{1}$, ♭$\hat{3}$, and ♯$\hat{4}$. In major keys, accidentals are required for ♭$\hat{6}$ and ♭$\hat{3}$, but in minor keys these notes are part of the key signature. In all keys, an accidental is required for ♯$\hat{4}$.

Figure 3.5

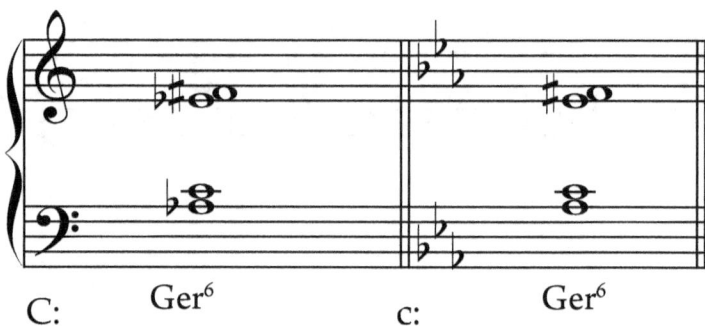

The German 6th is represented by the symbol Ger⁶. Note that the sonority of this chord is identical to a major-minor 7th that we hear most often as V⁷. Apart from the harmonic function, the difference between V⁷ and Ger⁶ is the spelling: V⁷ has a minor 7th while Ger⁶ has an augmented 6th.

2. Name the keys and write German 6th chords above each bass note. Include chord symbols.

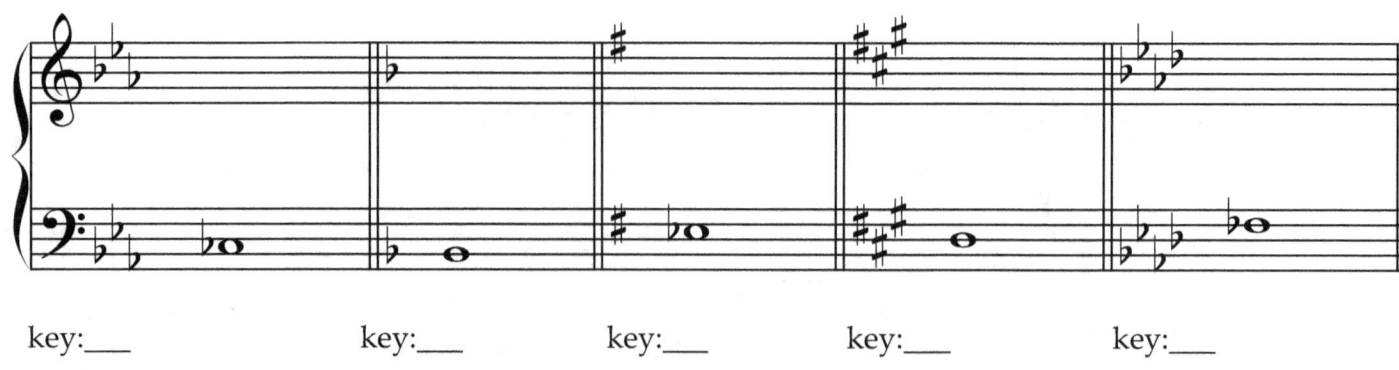

key:___   key:___   key:___   key:___   key:___

The French 6th

The French 6th is a four-note chord that consists of the intervals of a major 3rd, an augmented 4th, and an augmented 6th above the bass. Like it's Italian and German relatives, the French 6th sounds the same in tonic major and minor keys. In both examples in Figure 3.6, the French 6th consists of a major 3rd (C), an augmented 4th (D), and an augmented 6th (F sharp) above the bass note (A flat). The four pitches are $\flat\hat{6}$, $\hat{1}$, $\hat{2}$, and $\sharp\hat{4}$. In major keys, an accidental is required for $\flat\hat{6}$, but in minor keys this note is part of the key signature. In all keys, an accidental is required for $\sharp\hat{4}$. The French 6th is symbolized by Fr⁶.

Figure 3.6

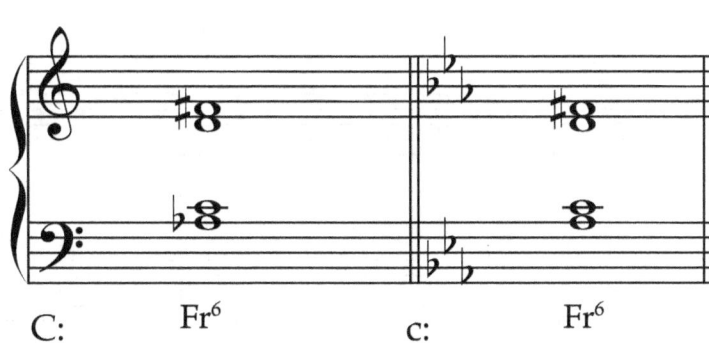

3. Name the keys and write French 6th chords above each bass note. Include chord symbols.

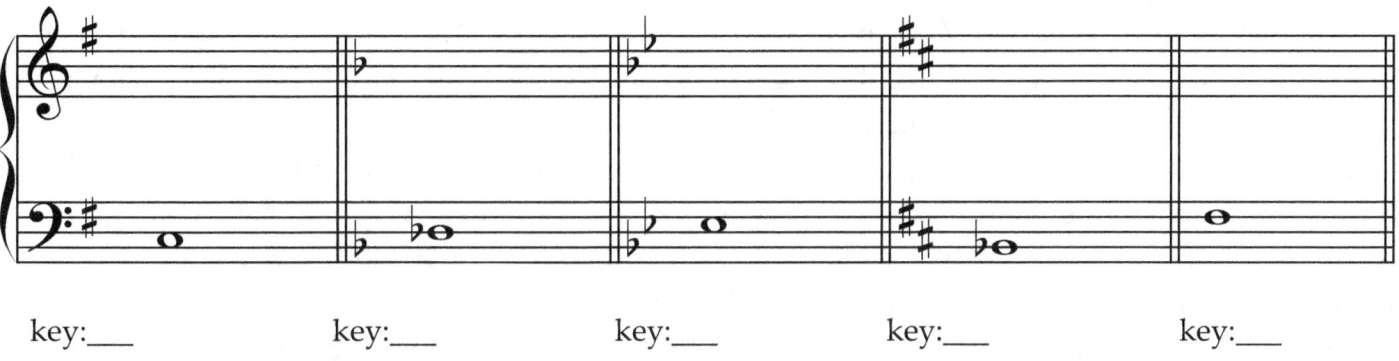

key:___   key:___   key:___   key:___   key:___

4. Name the keys and identify the following augmented 6th chords as It⁶, Ger⁶, or Fr⁶.

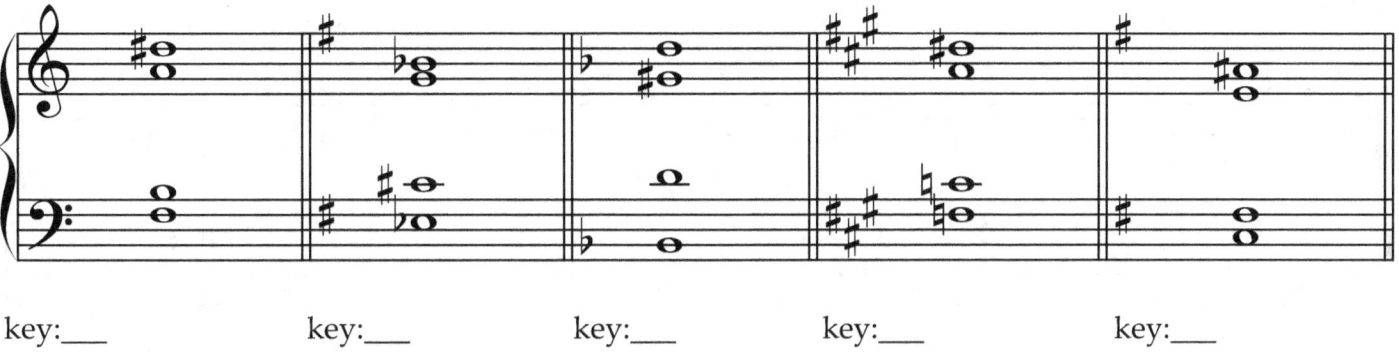

key:___   key:___   key:___   key:___   key:___

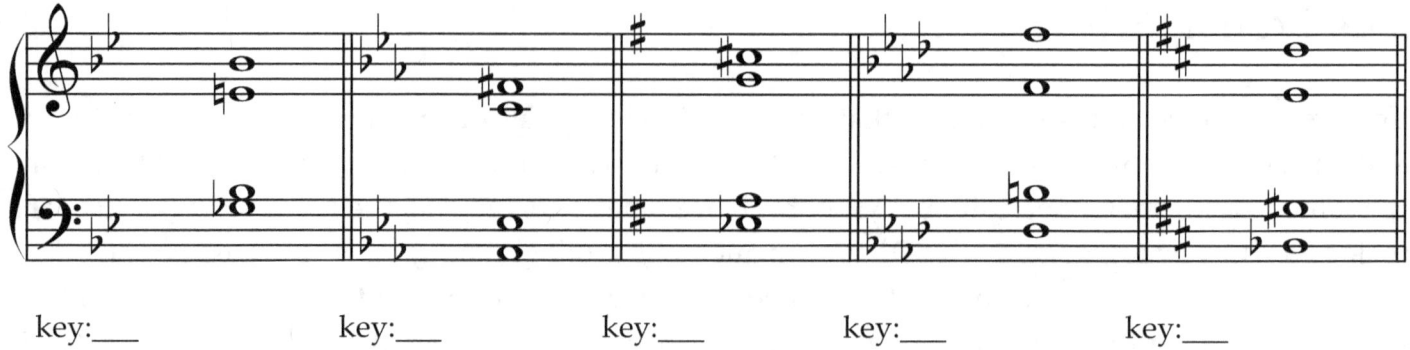

key:___   key:___   key:___   key:___   key:___

5. Write the following augmented 6th chords, using the correct key signature and any required accidentals.

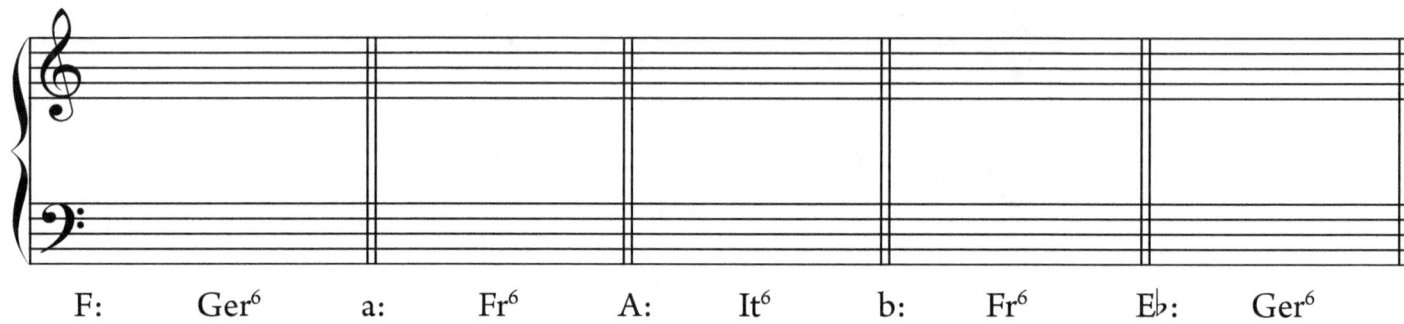

F: Ger⁶   a: Fr⁶   A: It⁶   b: Fr⁶   E♭: Ger⁶

Root/Quality Chord Symbols and Augmented 6th Chords

The functional chord symbols for augmented six chords are: It⁶, Fr⁶, and Ger⁶. These symbols are not used as root/quality chord symbols. Root/quality chord symbols do not tell us the function of the chord. They simply state the root and the quality of the chord.

The It⁶ and the Ger⁶ sound like major-minor seventh chords. Figure 3.7 shows the root/quality symbols for these two chords. The Ger⁶ and It⁶ in C major and C minor are labeled A♭⁷. This reflects the root of the chord (A♭) and its quality (major-minor 7th). The Fr⁶ chord is like a major-minor 7th chord with a lowered fifth (spelled enharmonically). The root/quality symbol for this chord in C major and C minor is A♭⁷⁽♭⁵⁾. Here, (♭5) is used to reflect the lowered 5th. ♭5 is always used in this figuration to indicate the lowered 5th, no matter what accidental (or note) is used in the chord. Here, the D sounds like the 5th above the root (E♭) has been lowered a half step.

Figure 3.7

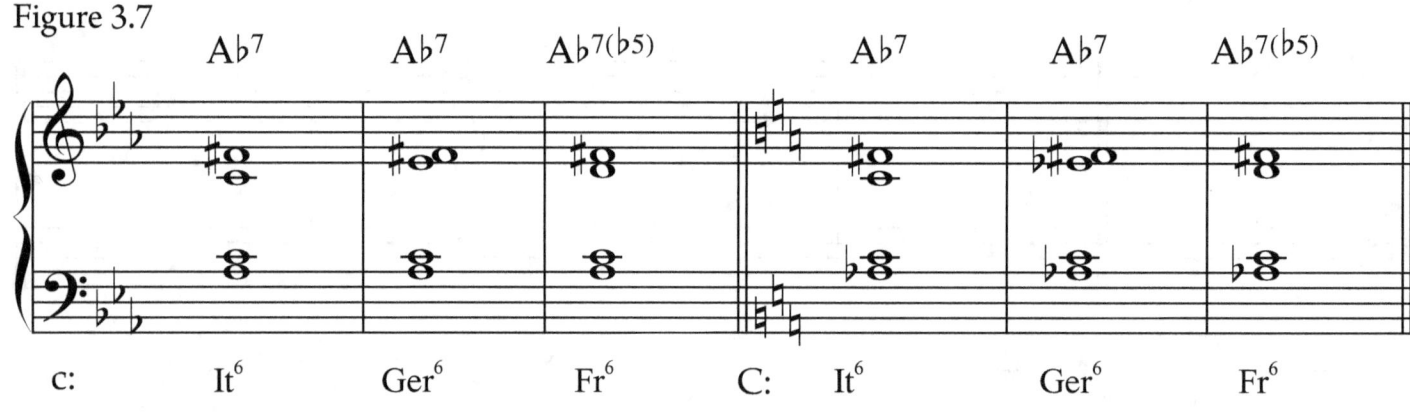

c: It⁶   Ger⁶   Fr⁶   C: It⁶   Ger⁶   Fr⁶

Resolving Augmented 6th Chords

As a general rule, augmented 6th chords resolve to the chord that has a root a half step below the bass of the augmented 6th chord. Thus, augmented 6th chords built on ♭$\hat{6}$ in major keys, and $\hat{6}$ in minor keys function as pre-dominant chords and resolve to dominant harmony (V, V^7, and cadential six-four).

When an augmented 6th chord resolves to V, the augmented 6th interval should always resolve outward to the dominant octave ($\hat{6}$ to $\hat{5}$ and ♯$\hat{4}$ to $\hat{5}$). The two other notes move in stepwise motion to the remaining notes of the V chord.

Figure 3.8

When an Italian 6th resolves to V, the doubled third should resolve by step in contrary motion in order to avoid parallel octaves. In Figure 3.9 the two A's move to G sharp and B respectively, while the augmented 6th F to D sharp resolves outward to the dominant octave E.

Figure 3.9

The resolution of a German 6th to V can sometimes involve parallel 5ths. In Figure 3.10 a, parallel perfect 5ths between the tenor and the bass are acceptable. However, parallel perfect 5ths between the bass and the soprano are considered incorrect (see 3.10 b). The option most commonly used to avoid faulty parallel 5ths is to introduce a cadential six-four into the progression as shown in example 3.10 c. A cadential six-four is often found following a German 6th *even* when the 5ths are not in the outer voices.

Figure 3.10

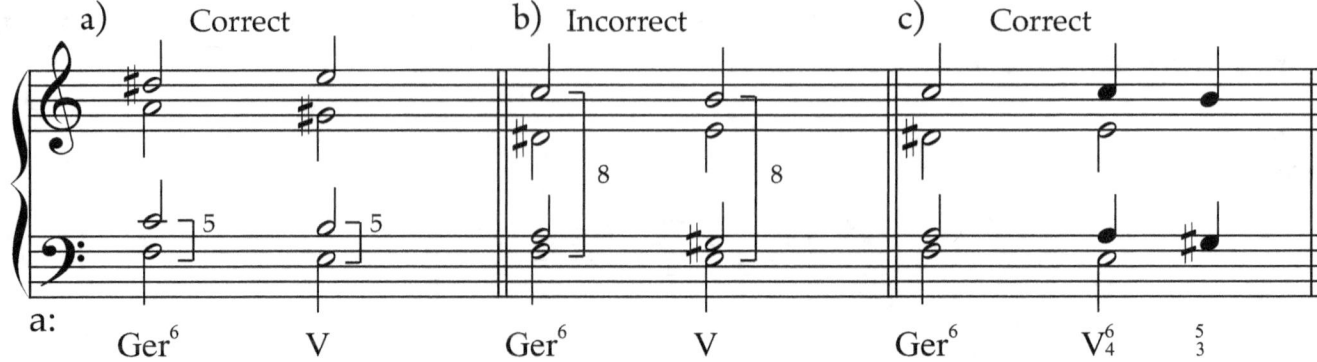

As with the other augmented 6th chords, when a French 6th resolves to V, the augmented 6th resolves outward to the dominant octave (see Figure 3.11). The third of the chord falls to the leading tone (here, A to G sharp) and the fourth (B) remains as a common tone.

Figure 3.11

Italian and French 6ths may also resolve to a cadential six-four, as shown in Figure 3.12. In each case, the augmented 6th resolves outward to the dominant octave.

Figure 3.12

It is also possible to combine two augmented 6th chords. In Figure 3.13, the alto moves from E flat to D changing the harmony from a Ger⁶ to a Fr⁶. However, two other interpretations are possible, depending on the rhythmic context. The progression might be analyzed as a Ger⁶ with the alto quarter note D described as an anticipation, or as a Fr⁶ with the alto E flat described as a suspension.

Figure 3.13

An augmented 6th chord may also resolve to V⁷. The most common resolution occurs when the augmented 6th moves through V the on the way (with the figuration 8-7 as in Figure 3.14a). If the augmented 6th resolves directly to a dominant seventh, the $\sharp\hat{4}$ should not rise to $\hat{5}$ but instead fall to $\natural\hat{4}$, which is the seventh of V⁷, keeping the chromatic half-step in the same voice (Figure 3.14b).

Figure 3.14

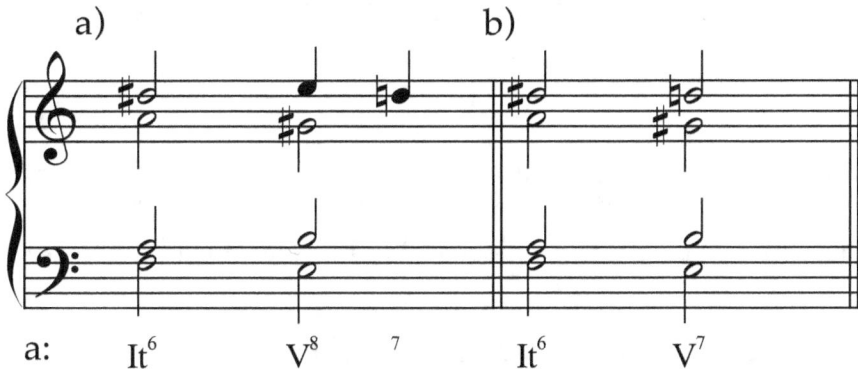

The four progressions in Figure 3.15 contain augmented 6th chords. Play each progression, listen for the unique chromatic sound these augmented chords provide, and note how each one resolves.

Figure 3.15

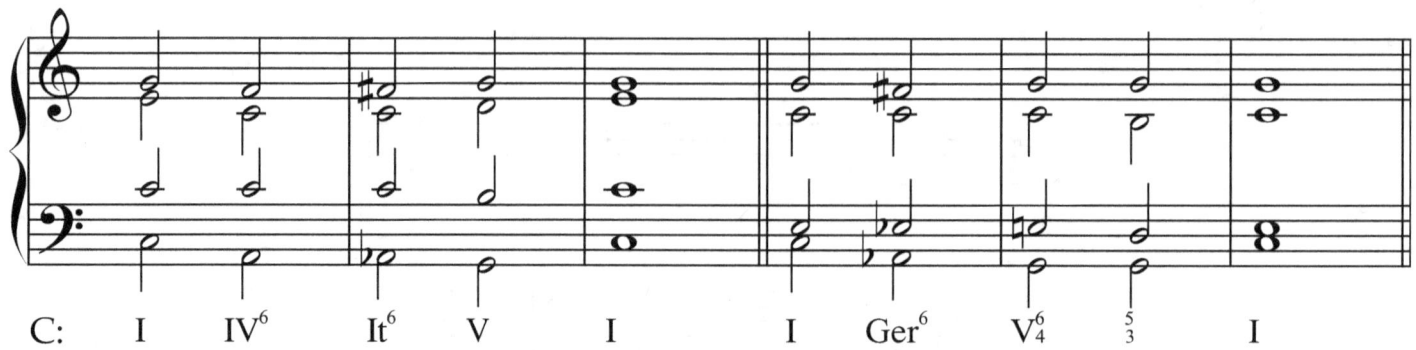

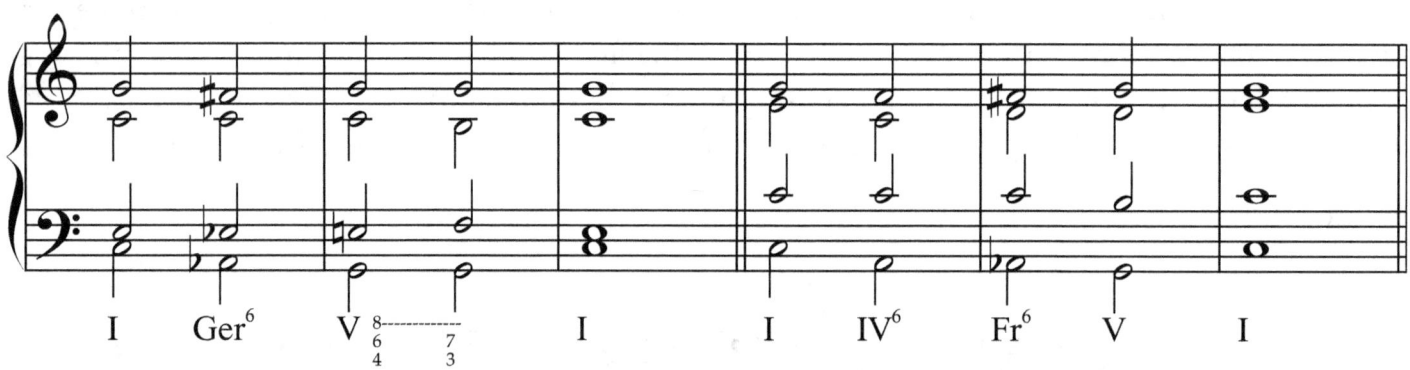

The excerpts in Figures 3.16 and 3.17 demonstrate a number of common feature features of augmented 6th chords. Find at least one example or excerpt that illustrates each of the following points.

1. Augmented 6th chords occur in both major and minor keys.
2. The Italian 6th contains three pitches; the German and French 6th both contain four pitches.
3. Augmented 6th chords are usually built on $\flat\hat{6}$, which is the bass note. All augmented chords contain the interval of an augmented 6th, which occurs between $\flat\hat{6}$ and $\sharp\hat{4}$.
4. All three forms of the augmented 6th chord, Italian, German, and French, contain a major 3rd above the bass.
5. There is only one note that differs among these three chords. The Italian 6th contains $\flat\hat{6}$, $\hat{1}$, and $\sharp\hat{4}$. The German six contains $\flat\hat{6}$, $\hat{1}$, $\flat\hat{3}$, and $\sharp\hat{4}$. The French six contains $\flat\hat{6}$, $\hat{1}$, $\hat{2}$, and $\sharp\hat{4}$.
6. Augmented 6th chords built on $\flat\hat{6}$ may resolve to V, V^7, or to a cadential six-four.
7. Both $\flat\hat{6}$ and $\sharp\hat{4}$ resolve to $\hat{5}$ by contrary motion. The exception to this rule occurs in progressions where an augmented 6th moves to V^7. In such cases $\sharp\hat{4}$ resolves to $\natural\hat{4}$.

Figure 3.16

Wolfgang Amadeus Mozart
Piano Sonata in D major
K 284 (3rd mvt.)

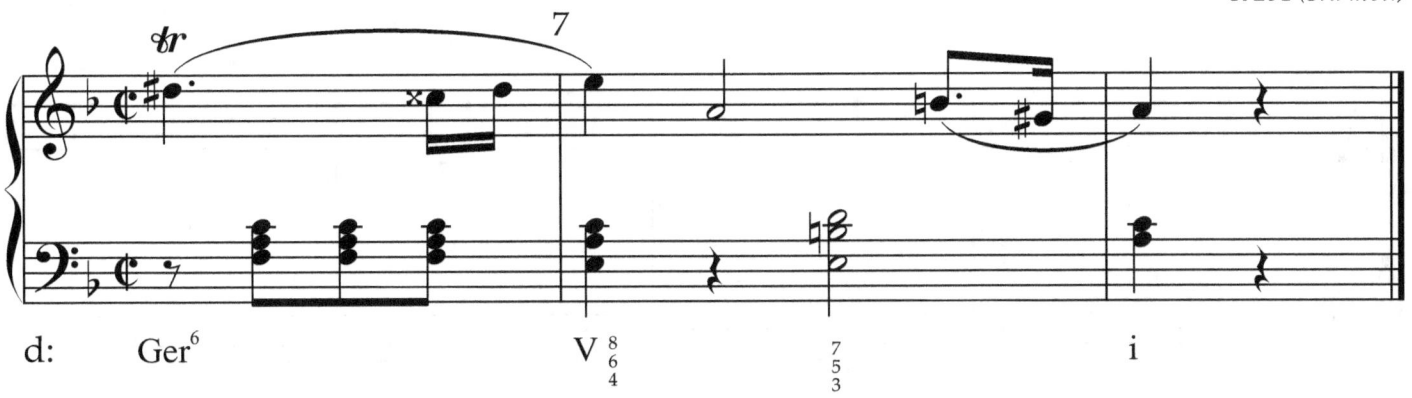

Figure 3.17

Ludwig van Beethoven
Piano Sonata in C minor
op. 13 (3rd mvt.)

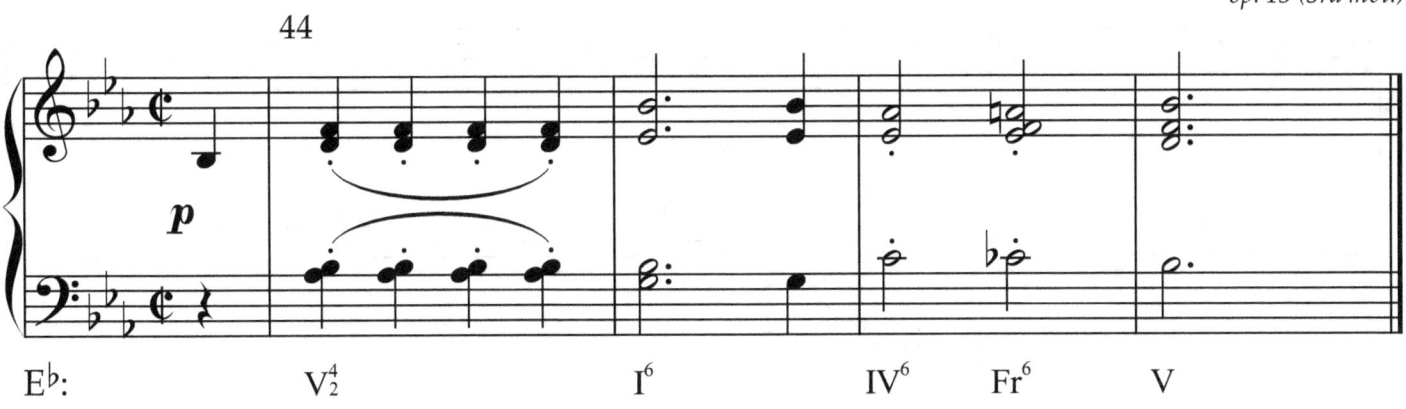

6. Name the keys and resolve the following augmented 6th chords. Resolve the interval of the augmented 6th outward to an octave in each example.

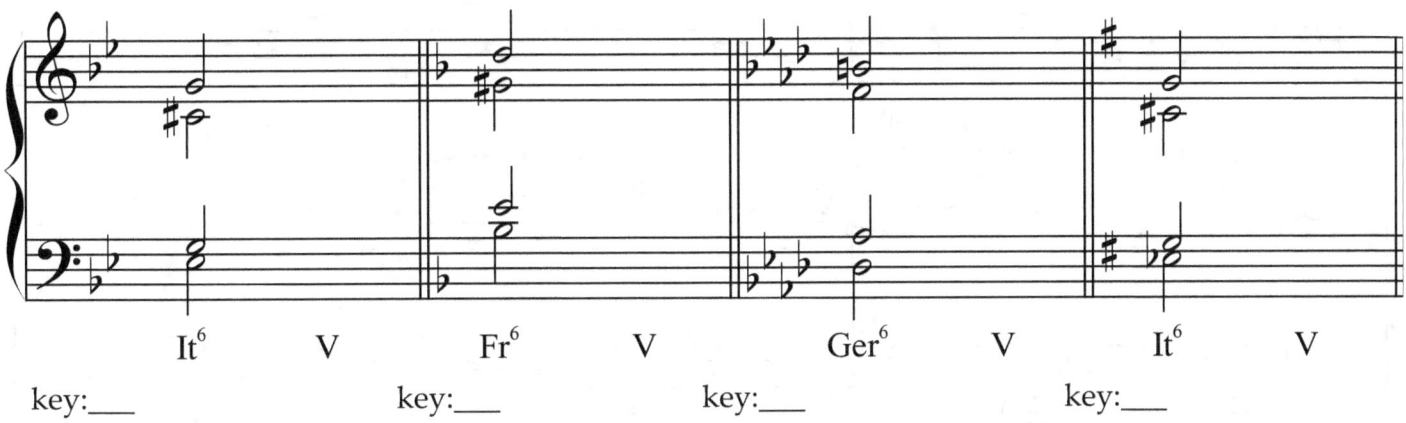

57   Chapter 3: Augmented 6th Chords

7. Write the following augmented 6th chords with resolutions, using the correct key signatures, and any required accidentals. Add root/quality chord symbols.

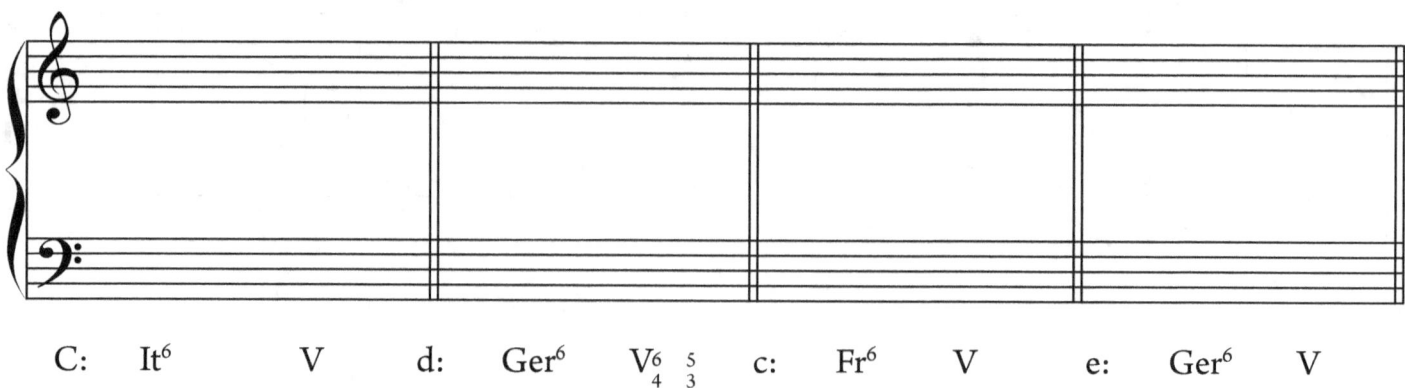

C: It⁶ V   d: Ger⁶ V⁶₄ ⁵₃   c: Fr⁶ V   e: Ger⁶ V

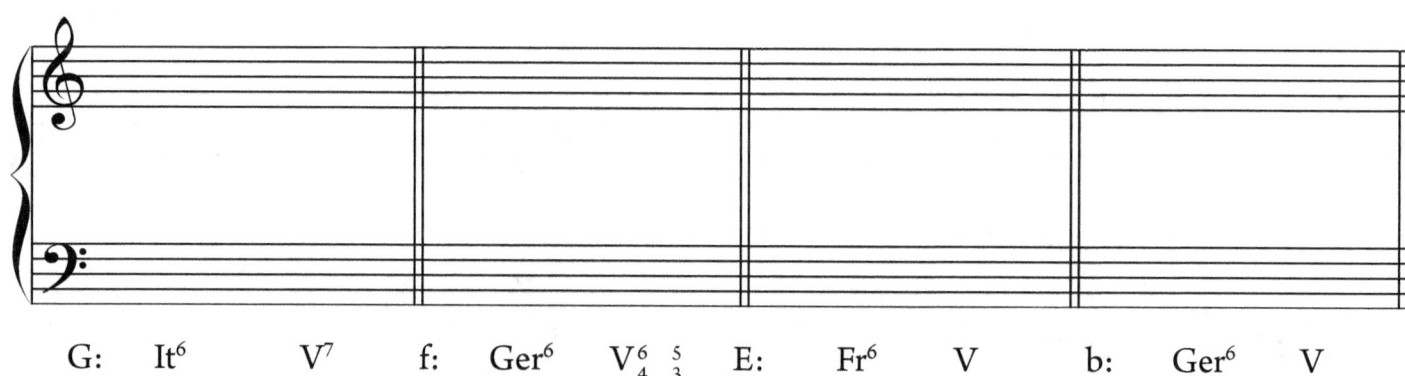

G: It⁶ V⁷   f: Ger⁶ V⁶₄ ⁵₃   E: Fr⁶ V   b: Ger⁶ V

8. Provide a harmonic analysis of the following excerpts. Use both functional and root/quality chord symbols. Circle and identify any non-chord tones.

Franz Schubert
Der Doppelganger
from Schwanengesang, D 957

key:___

Franz Schubert
Mass in G major D 167 (Sanctus)

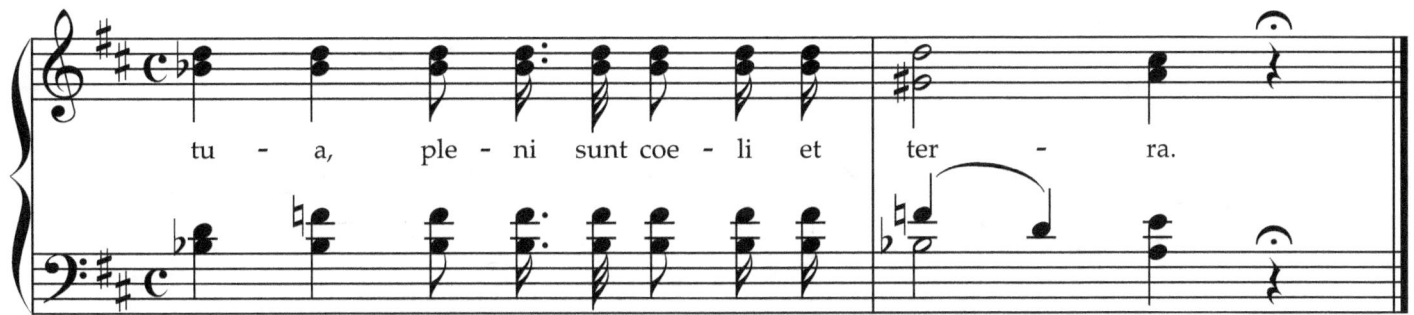

key:___

Approaching Augmented 6th Chords

The following examples show some of the chords most commonly used to approach an augmented 6th chord. You may, however, encounter other chords of approach, and occasionally you may find an augmented 6th at the beginning of a piece, with no chord of approach.

Augmented 6th chords are often approached from IV⁶ (or iv⁶). In major keys, they may also be approached by a borrowed chord, such as iv⁶ or ♭VI, both of which introduce ♭$\hat{6}$ in the bass. Composers often take advantage of the chromatic sound of an augmented 6th chord to emphasize the appearance of the dominant. As you can see from the examples, the chromatic nature of augmented 6th chords often gives them a linear, rather than vertical, character.

The most common approach to the augmented 6th chord is the pre-dominant IV or IV⁶. In Figure 3.18, the Fr⁶ has the effect of chromatically intensifying the subdominant harmony leading to V. Note the chromatic motion in the tenor ($\hat{4}$ - #$\hat{4}$ - $\hat{5}$) and bass ($\hat{6}$ - ♭$\hat{6}$ - $\hat{5}$).

Figure 3.18

In major keys, iv⁶, a borrowed chord from the tonic minor, is also an effective approach to an augmented 6th. The bass note of iv⁶ is a common tone with the bass note of the augmented 6th, allowing for smooth voice leading (see Figure 3.19).

Figure 3.19

Sometimes an augmented 6th may be approached from IV through a six-four chord in a chromatic voice exchange. In Figure 3.19, the exchange occurs between the bass (D-E-F) and the soprano (F-E-D sharp).

Figure 3.20

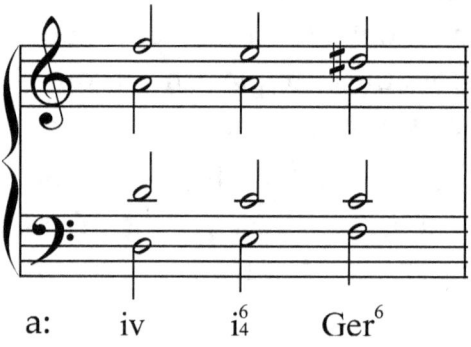

9. Name the keys and complete the following progressions.

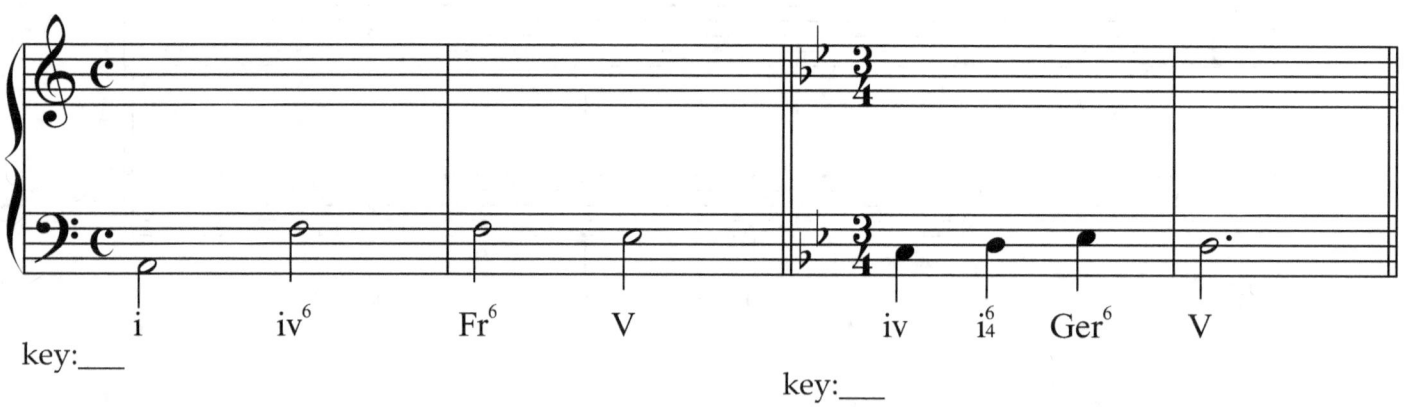

The supertonic chords, ii, ii⁶, and ii⁷ (and inversions) are good choices for approaching an augmented 6th chord. In Figure 3.21a the common tone (F) between ii$^{ø4}_3$ and It⁶ is in the bass, allowing for smooth voice leading. Here, the augmented 6th chord delays the resolution of the seventh of ii$^4_3$ (the alto A). This note remains in the alto and resolves downward by step when V arrives.

The tonic chords i and i⁶ are also effective chords to proceed an augmented sixth, as shown in Figure 3.21b.

Figure 3.21

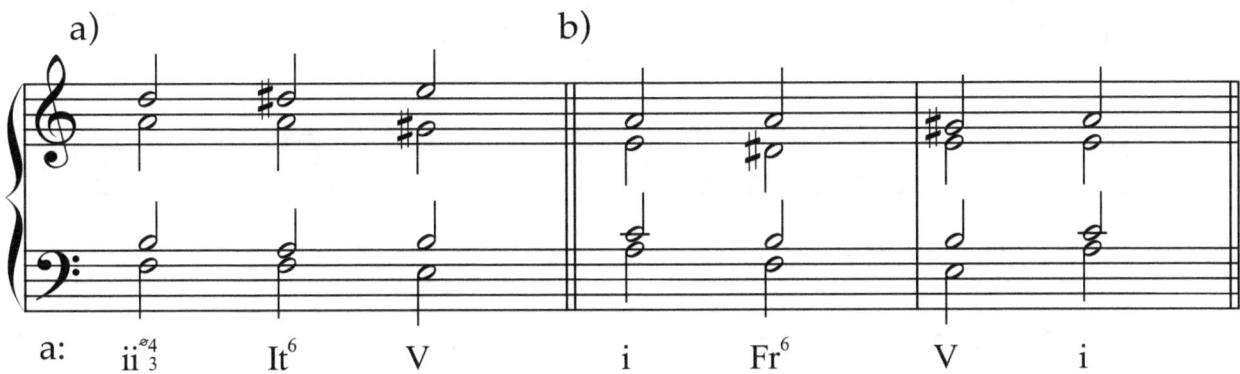

In minor keys, VI is also a common chord of approach for an augmented 6th chord. The addition of $\sharp\hat{4}$ to VI creates a German 6th chord (see Figure 3.22a). In major keys, the borrowed chord ♭VI may also function as a chord of approach (see Figure 3.22b).

Figure 3.22

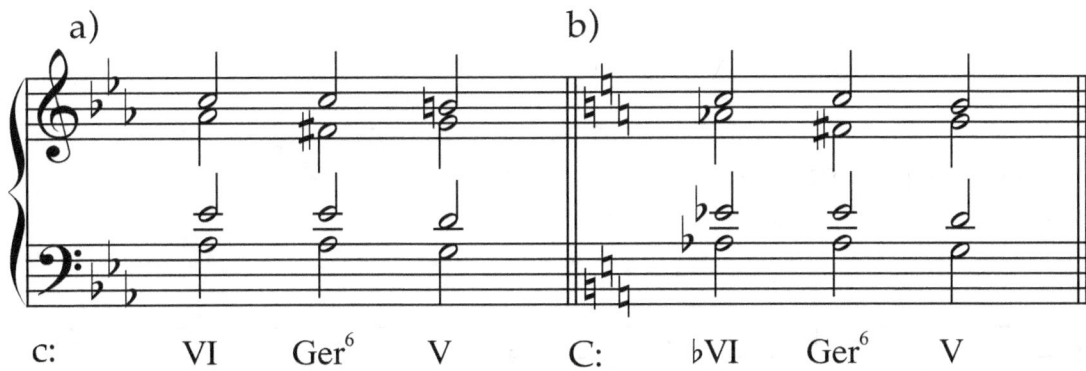

Chapter 3: Augmented 6th Chords

In Figure 3.23a, the Italian 6th chord is approached by a melodic augmented 2nd (C - D sharp) in the alto. Up to this point, augmented melodic intervals have been avoided, but in this context, the augmented 2nd is not only permitted, but also highly effective. The melodic augmented interval can, however, be avoided by moving the alto to the root of VI (C - F - D sharp), as shown in 3.23b.

Figure 3.23

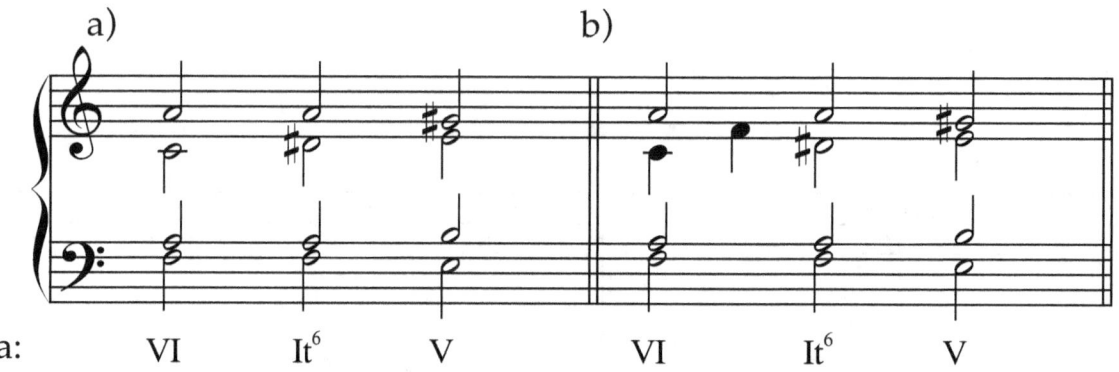

Finally, the augmented 6th may be approached from V. Since it also resolves to V, the augmented 6th in this progression acts as a neighbour chord to V in a prolongation of dominant harmony (see Figure 3.24).

Figure 3.24

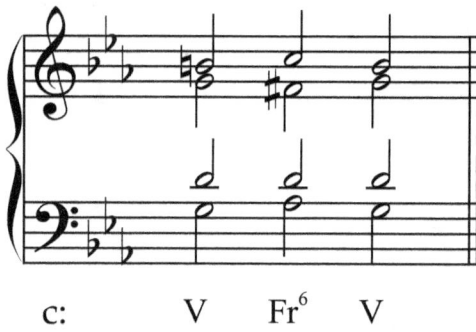

10. Write the following progressions.

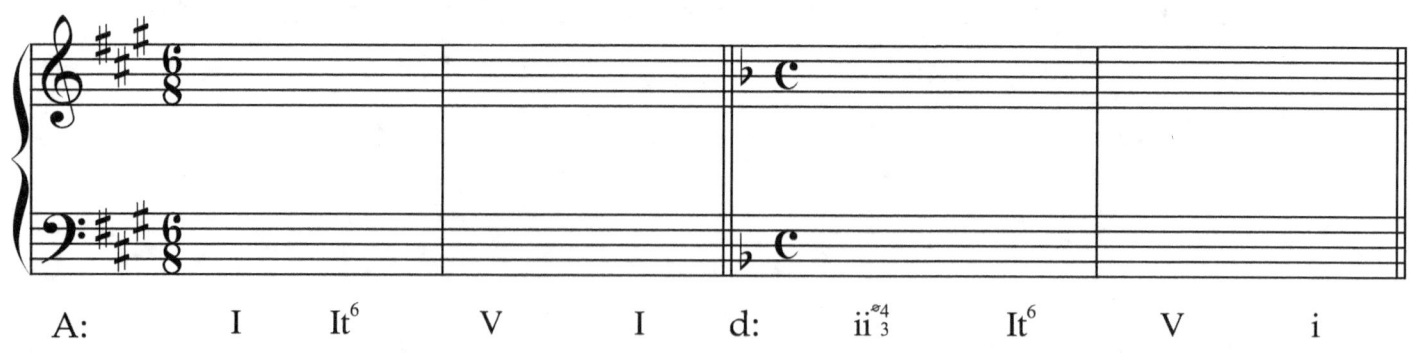

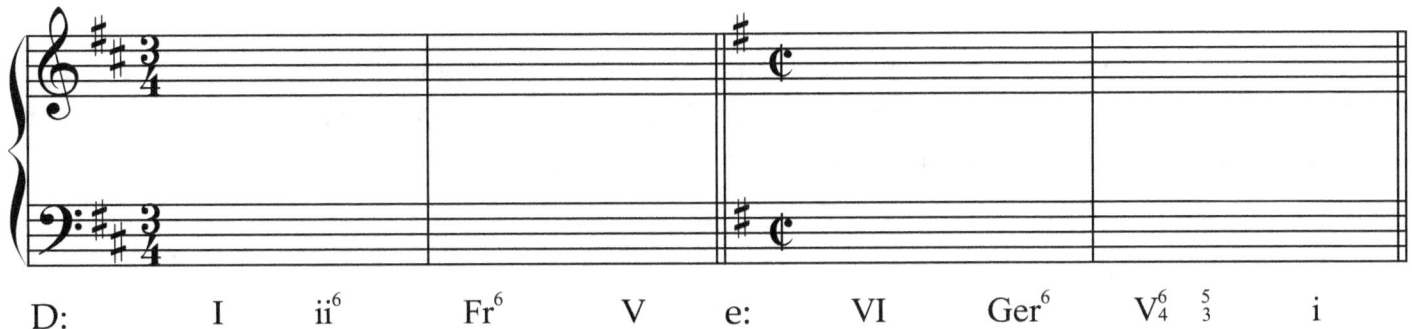

D: I ii⁶ Fr⁶ V   e: VI Ger⁶ V$^6_4$ $^5_3$ i

11. Provide a harmonic analysis of the following excerpts using functional chord symbols. Circle and identify any non-chord tones.

Frederic Chopin
Lento con gran espressione
WN 37

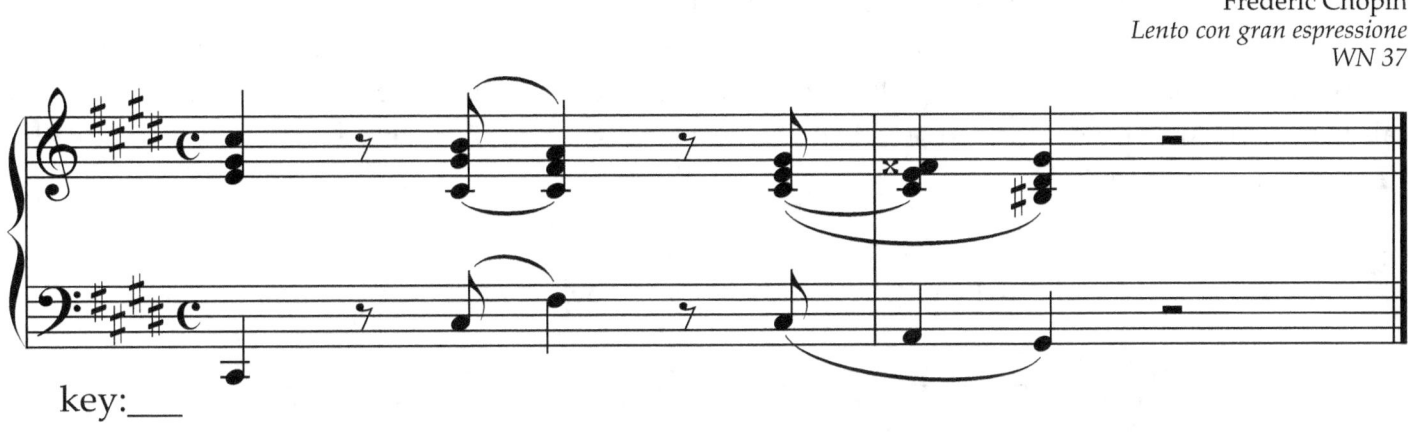

key:___

Ludwig van Beethoven
Piano Sonata in C minor
op. 13 (3rd mvt.)

Double Augmented 4th Chords

The interval of a perfect 5th can be re-spelled enharmonically as a double augmented 4th. For example, the perfect 5th E flat to B flat can be spelled as E flat to A sharp. Since the interval E flat to A is an augmented 4th, the interval E flat to A sharp is a double augmented 4th.

Figure 3.25

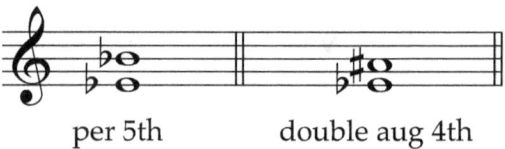

per 5th   double aug 4th

When the German 6th chord is written in major keys and progresses to a six-four chord, an alternate spelling may be used: the ♭$\hat{3}$ may be written as ♯$\hat{2}$. The resulting chord is sometimes called a **double augmented 4th chord** and may be symbolized with an AA4th, although the symbol Ger⁶ based on its function rather than it spelling is preferred. It contains the intervals of an augmented 6th, a major 3rd, and a double augmented 4th (♭$\hat{6}$ - ♯$\hat{2}$).

Composers sometimes use this spelling of a German 6th in order to avoid the visually awkward voice leading when a German 6th moves to a cadential six-four (♭$\hat{3}$ - ♮$\hat{3}$ becomes ♯$\hat{2}$ - ♮$\hat{3}$). In Figure 3.26, the B-flat of the German 6th is respelled enharmonically as A sharp in the AA4th. As a general rule, raised notes resolve upward and lowered notes, resolve downward. With this enharmonic spelling, the ♯$\hat{2}$ resolves upward to $\hat{3}$.

Figure 3.26

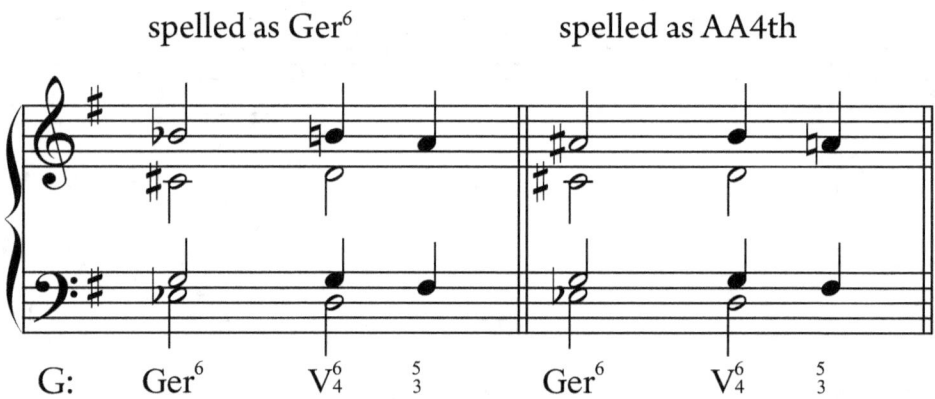

Do not confuse the AA4th chord with a French 6th, which has an augmented 4th. When analyzing an augmented 4th chord, pay attention to the quality of the intervals rather than their numeric size.

12. Provide a harmonic analysis of the following excerpts using functional chord symbols. Circle and identify any non-chord tones.

The Diminished 3rd Chord

In most augmented 6th chords, the interval of the augmented 6th occurs between the bass and one of the upper voices. However, occasionally, you will find an augmented 6th chord with $\sharp\hat{4}$ in the bass. In such cases, the augmented 6th interval is inverted, becoming a diminished 3rd (F sharp to A flat in Figure 3.27a). This chord, known as a **diminished 3rd chord** has a strong tendency towards V. Diminished 3rd chords are symbolized by the figuration ^{o3}, following the name of the augmented 6th chord (Ger^{o3} in example 3.27a). The French diminished 3rd chord (Fr^{o3}) is also seen (Figure 3.27b), but the Italian diminished 3rd (It^{o3}) is uncommon.

Figure 3.27

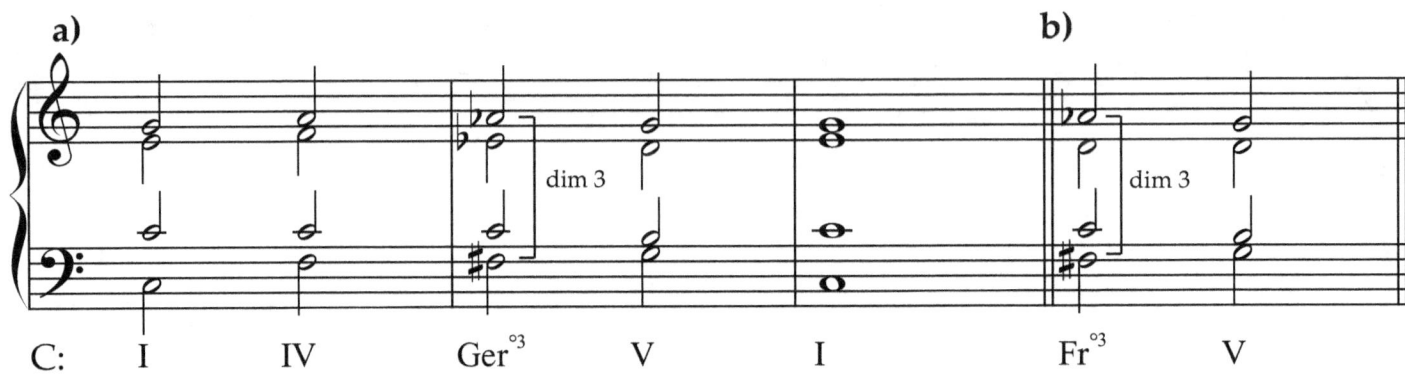

In the excerpt in Figure 3.28, Chopin uses a German 6th with $\sharp\hat{4}$ in the bass. The interval between $\sharp\hat{4}$ and $\natural\hat{6}$ (D sharp - F natural) is a diminished 3rd.

Figure 3.28

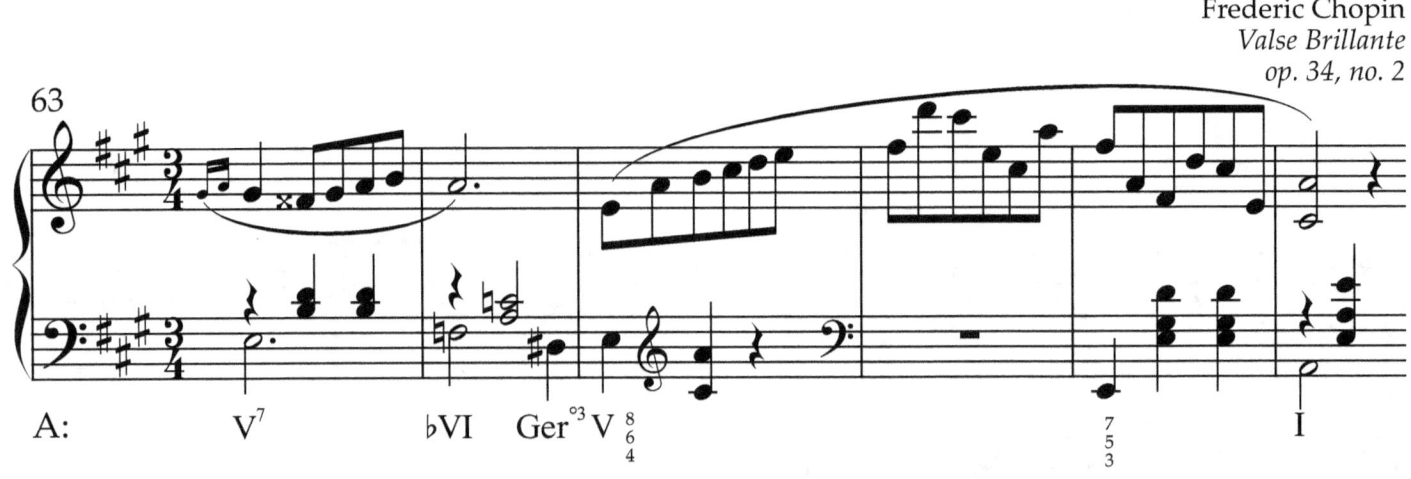

Frederic Chopin
Valse Brillante
op. 34, no. 2

13. Provide a harmonic analysis of the following excerpt. Add functional chord symbols. Circle and identify any non-chord tones.

Pyotr Il'yich Tchaikovsky
Eugene Onegin
act 2, scene 2

key:___

14. Write the following progressions in four parts.

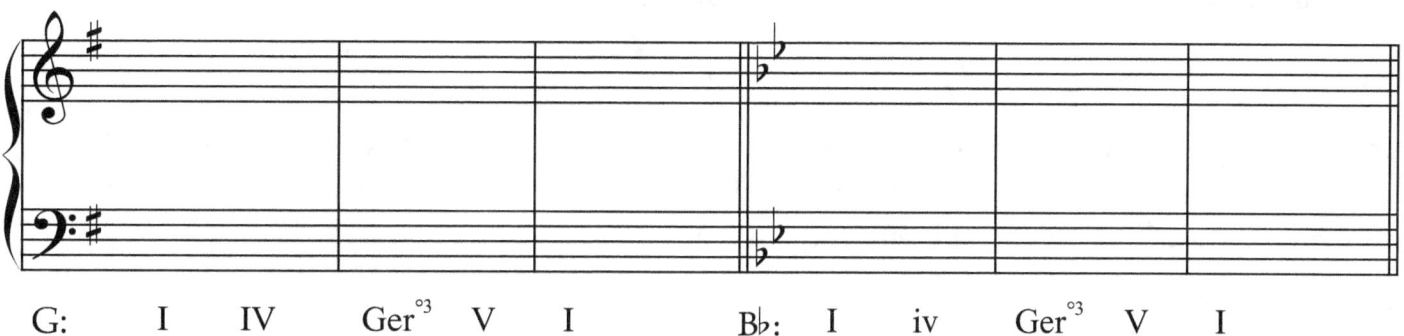

G: I   IV   Ger⁶₃   V   I   B♭: I   iv   Ger⁶₃   V   I

Secondary Augmented 6th Chords

Augmented 6th chords usually resolve to the chord a half step below the note on which they are built. We have already examined augmented six chords built on ♭$\hat{6}$ (major keys), and $\hat{6}$ (minor keys), that act as predominant chords and resolve to dominant harmony. Secondary dominants may also be preceded by their own augmented 6th chords. In other words, the notes of a progression moving from an augmented 6th to V may be transposed to other keys.

In Figure 3.29, the secondary dominant V/vi is proceeded by two augmented 6th chords, Ger⁶ and Fr⁶. These two chords are part of the secondary key area and function as pre-dominant chords to the secondary dominant.

Figure 3.29

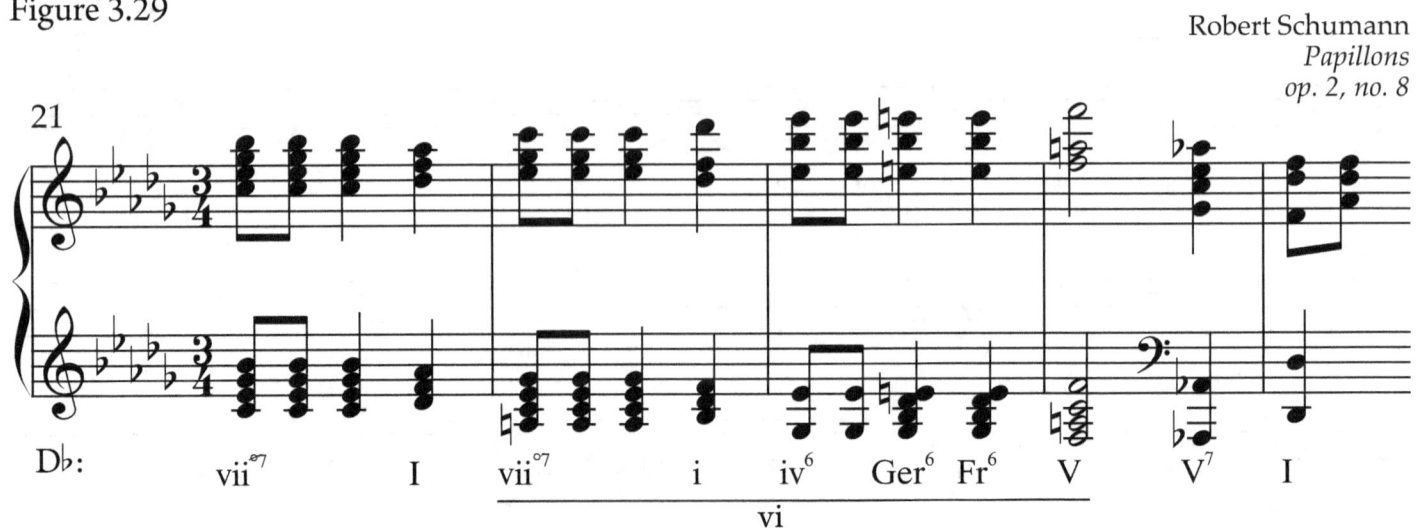

Robert Schumann
Papillons
op. 2, no. 8

Augmented 6th Chords Built on Other Scale Degrees

Augmented 6th chords built on scale degrees ♭$\hat{6}$ (major keys) or $\hat{6}$ (minor keys) have a pre-dominant function. Augmented 6th chords may also be built on other scale degrees. The most commonly used scale degrees are the lowered second degree (♭$\hat{2}$) in major and minor keys, and the fourth scale degree ($\hat{4}$) in major keys. These augmented 6th chords contain the same intervals as those built on ♭$\hat{6}$ and $\hat{6}$.

Augmented 6th Chords Built on ♭$\hat{2}$

The scale degree ♭$\hat{2}$ has a strong tendency to resolve downward to 1. Thus, an augmented 6th chord built on ♭$\hat{2}$ has a dominant function because it contains the leading tone and it moves to the tonic. The excerpt in Figure 3.30 contains a French 6th built on ♭$\hat{2}$.

Figure 3.30

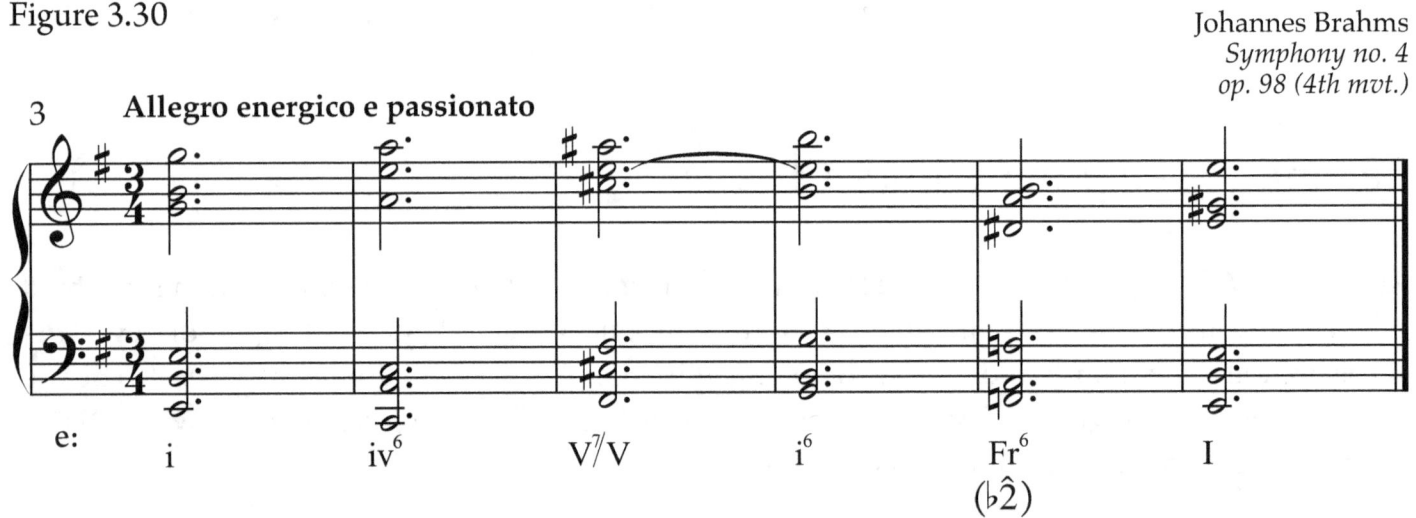

Johannes Brahms
Symphony no. 4
op. 98 (4th mvt.)

Augmented 6th chords built on $\flat\hat{2}$ resolve to a root position tonic chord. Figure 3.31 shows the resolution of three augmented 6th chords built on $\flat\hat{2}$. Play each one and note the sound of the chord and it's resolution.

Figure 3.31

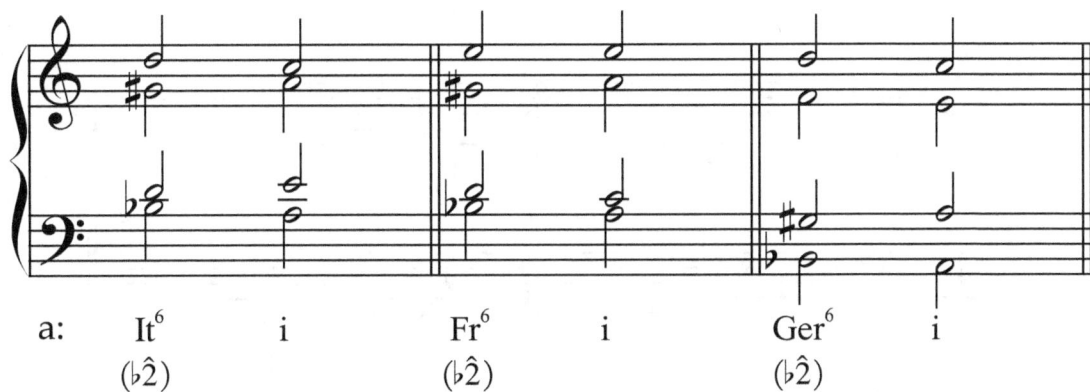

These chords contain the same intervals as an augmented 6th built on $\flat\hat{6}$ or $\hat{6}$, and they resolve in a similar way. However, here the augmented sixth interval expands outward to a tonic octave rather than a dominant octave. Since these chords resolve to I, they have a dominant function and are often used at cadences.

15. Name the keys, write the following augmented 6th chords, and resolve them as indicated.

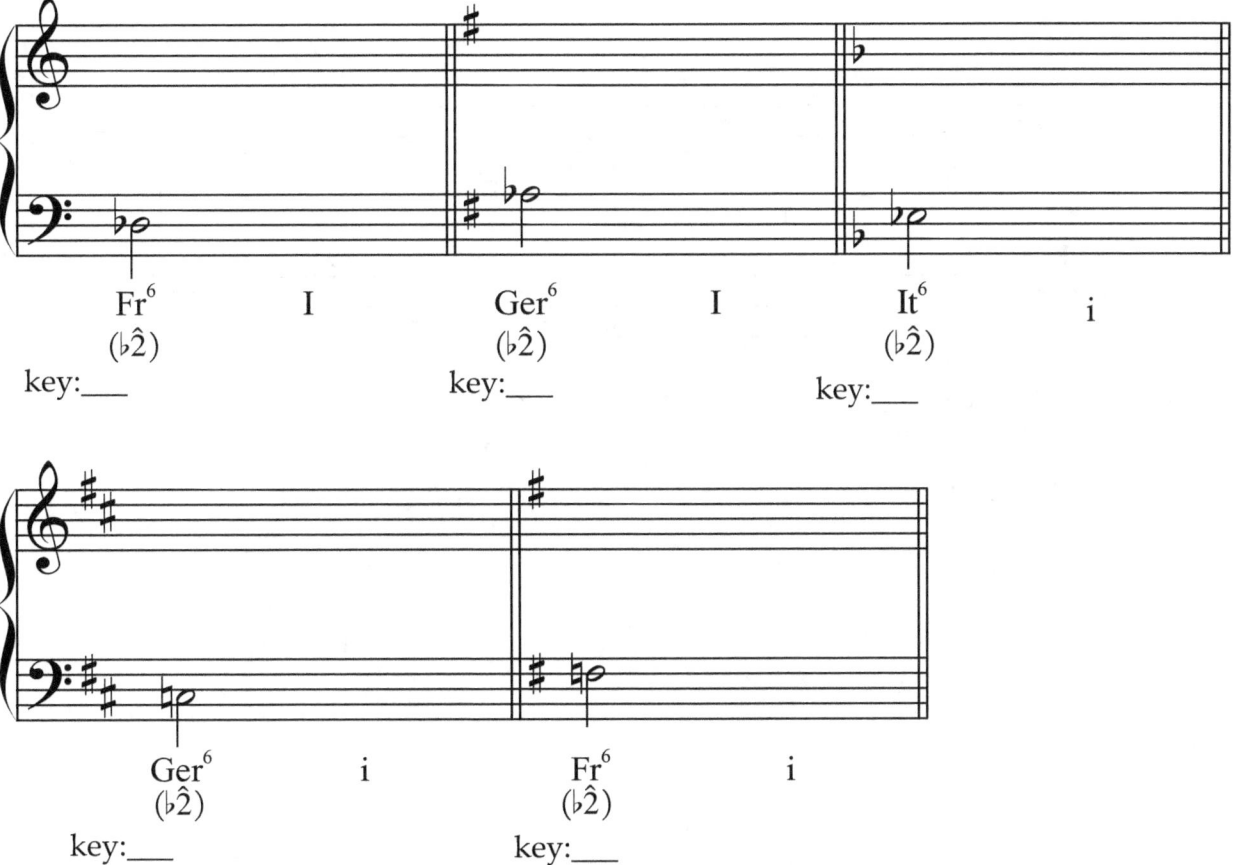

Chapter 3: Augmented 6th Chords

Inversions of augmented 6th chords built on ♭$\hat{2}$ are rarely seen in musical literature. We can, however, discuss three examples. A Fr⁶ built on ♭$\hat{2}$ is sometimes found in first inversion. In Figure 3.32, note the resolution of the augmented 6th (D flat - B) to the tonic octave (C).

Figure 3.32

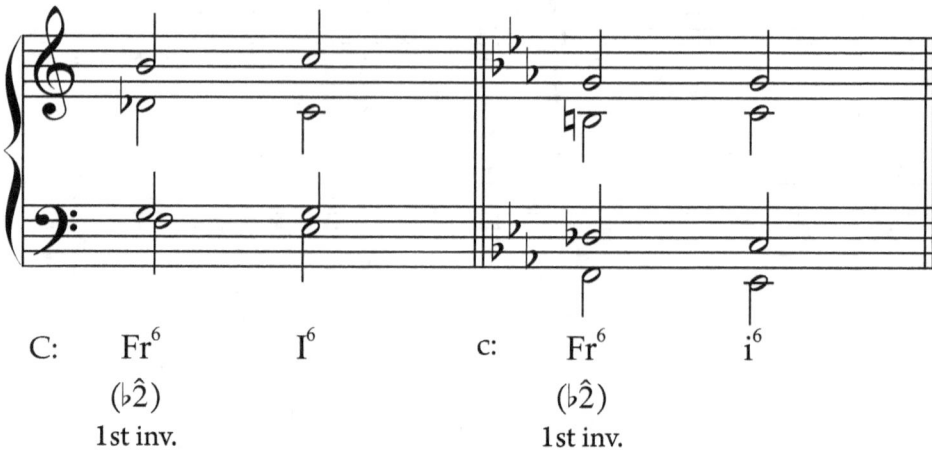

In Figure 3.33, a second inversion Ger⁶ built on ♭$\hat{2}$ resolves to I$^6_4$. Note the doubled root in the six-four chord.

Figure 3.33

In Figure 3.34, a third inversion Ger⁶ built on ♭2̂ resolve to I. Since the augmented 6th interval is inverted to a diminished 3rd, this chord is known as a **German diminished 3rd chord** (Ger°³).

Figure 3.34

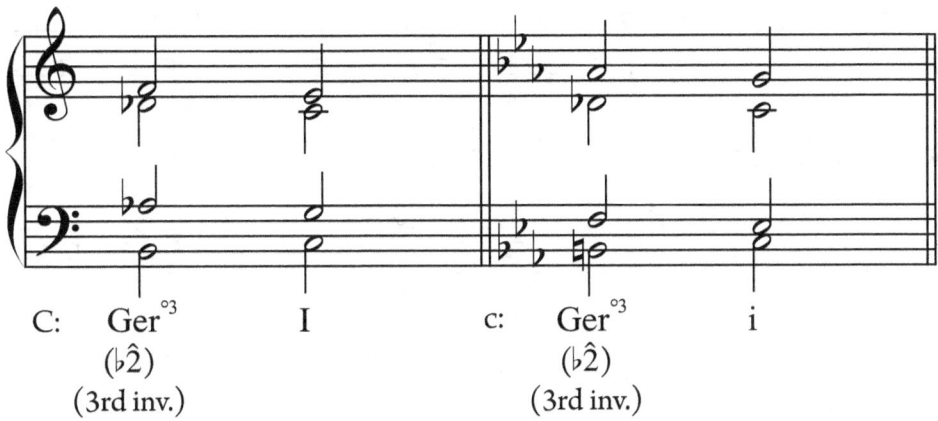

16. Provide a harmonic analysis of the following excerpt. Add functional chord symbols. Circle and identify all non-chord tones.

Pyotr Il'yich Tchaikowsky
Le matin en hiver
from Album for the Young, op. 39

Augmented 6th Chords Built on 4̂

In major keys, augmented 6th chords may be built on 4̂, and resolve to I or I⁶. The harmonic function of an augmented 6th chord built on the fourth degree of the scale is different from those built on ♭6̂ or ♭2̂. When the augmented 6th built on 4̂ progresses to I, the augmented sixth interval does not resolve. Play the excerpt in Figure 3.35 and examine Gounod's treatment of the German 6th built on 4̂. Here, the progression of Ger⁶ to I has the effect of a plagal cadence.

Figure 3.35

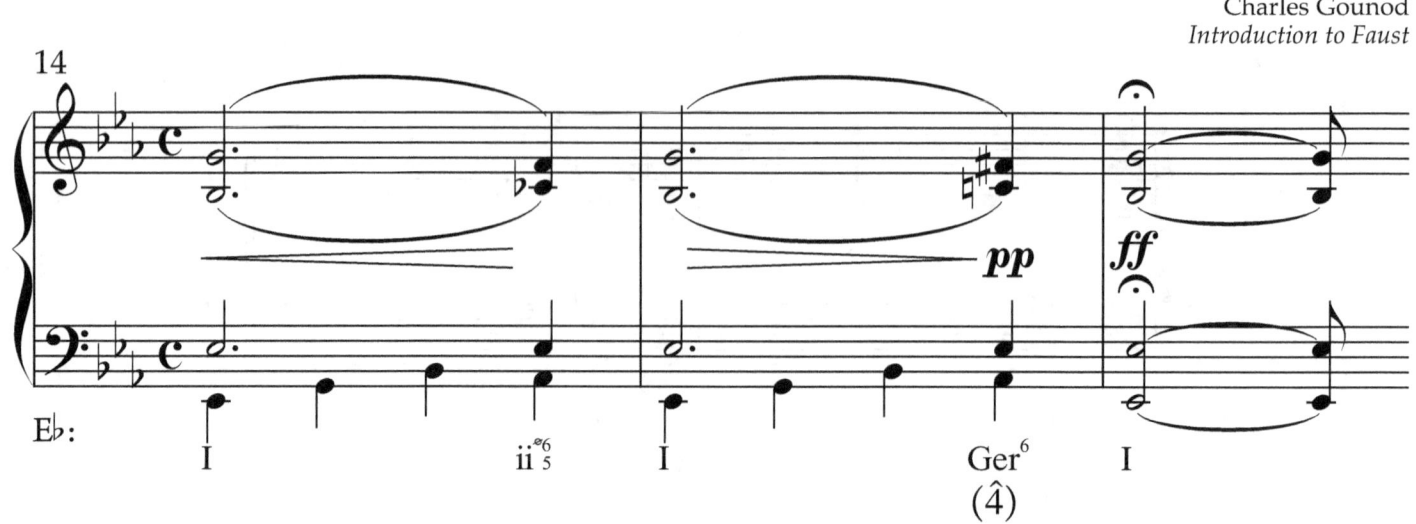

17. Provide a harmonic analysis of the following excerpt. Add functional chord symbols. Circle and identify all non-chord tones.

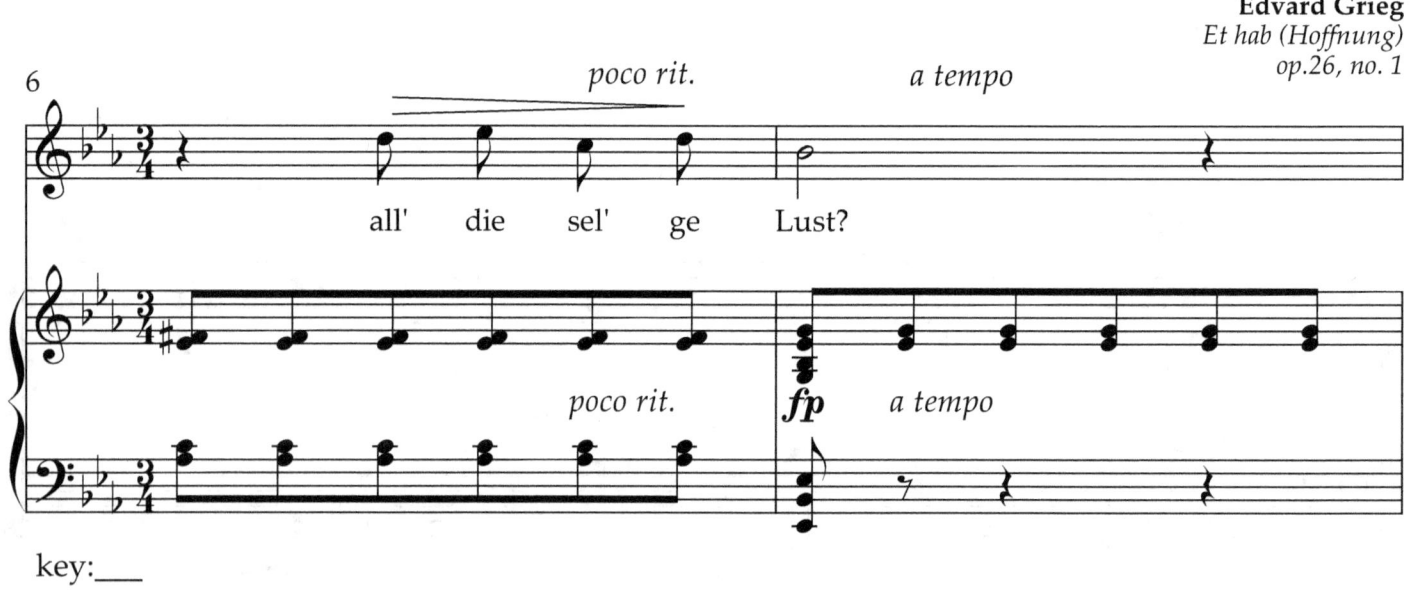

Ludwig van Beethoven
Sonata for Violin and Piano
Op. 23 (3rd mvt.)

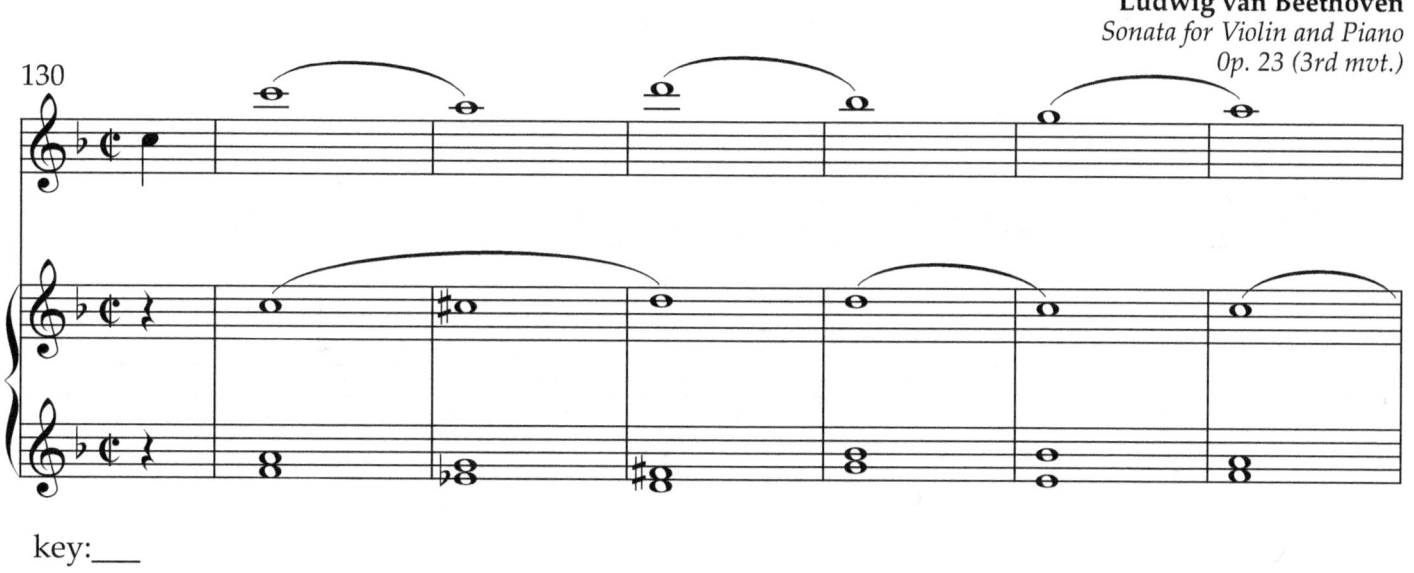

key:___

18. Harmonize the following bass fragments using augmented 6th chords in the places marked by asterisks*. Complete the examples with functional chord symbols.

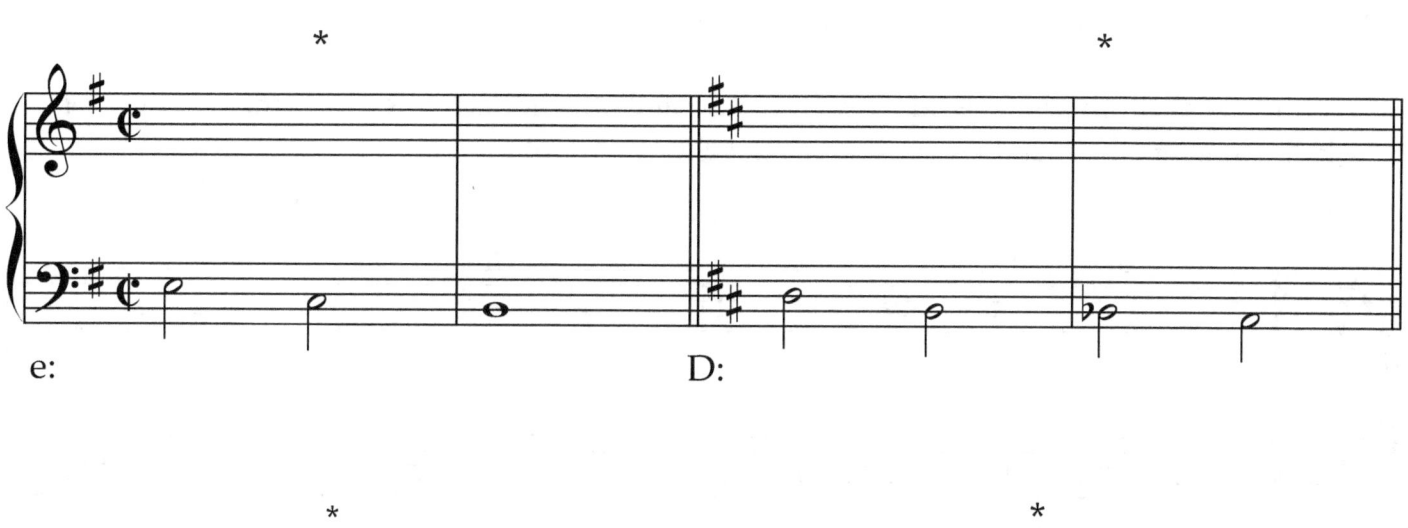

e: D:

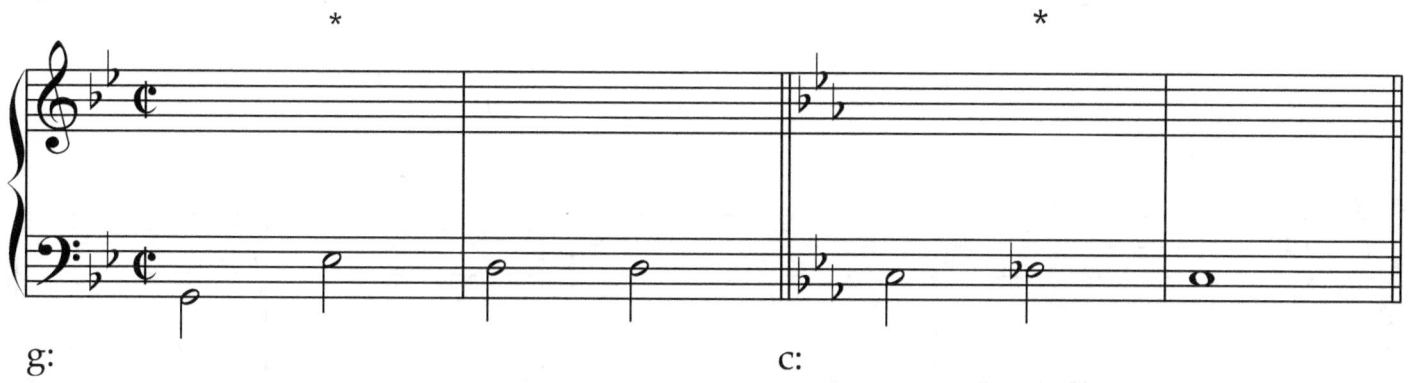

g: c:

19. Harmonize the following melodic fragments using augmented 6th chords in the places marked by asterisks*. Complete the examples with functional chord symbols.

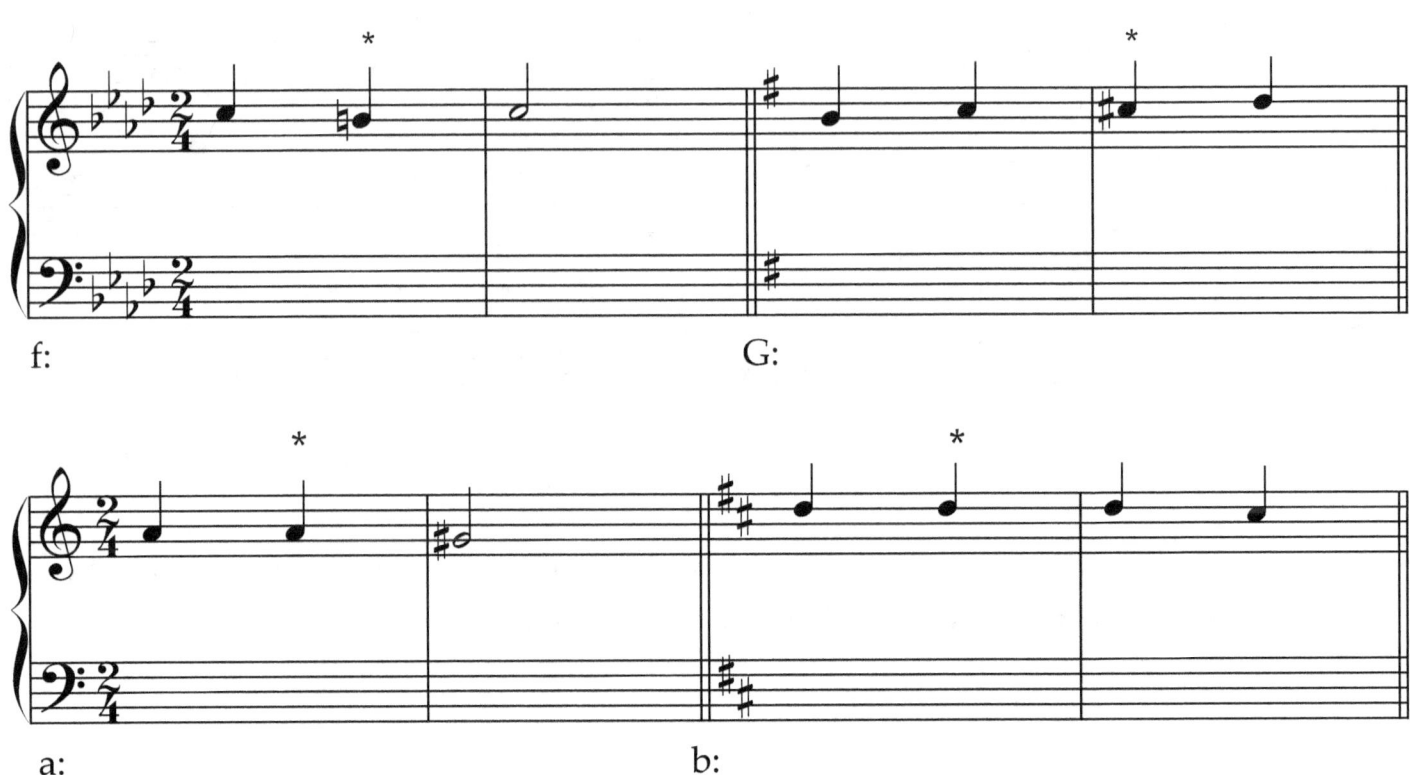

f:

G:

a:

b:

20. Harmonize the following melodies using augmented 6th chords in the places marked by asterisks*. Complete the examples with functional chord symbols.

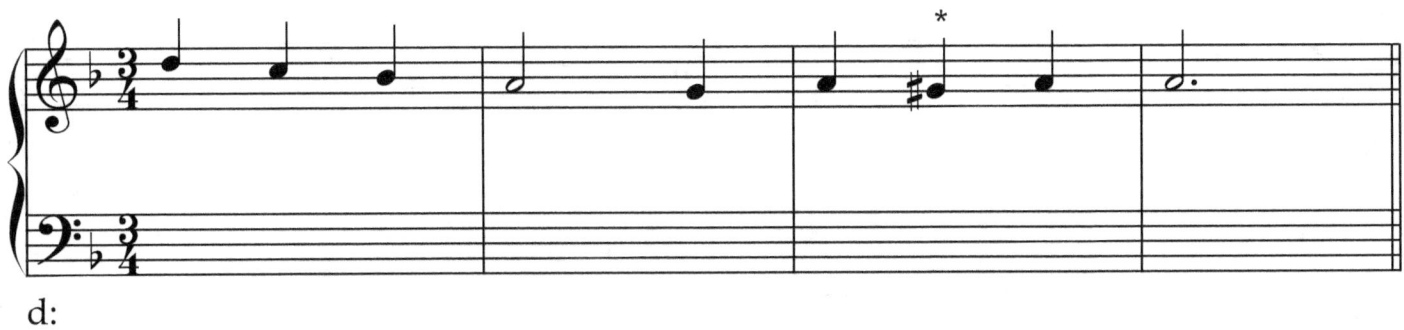

d:

g:

Chapter 3: Augmented 6th Chords

21. Harmonize the following bass lines using augmented 6th chords where appropriate. Complete the examples with functional chord symbols.

22. Harmonize the following descending chromatic bass line according to the chord symbols.

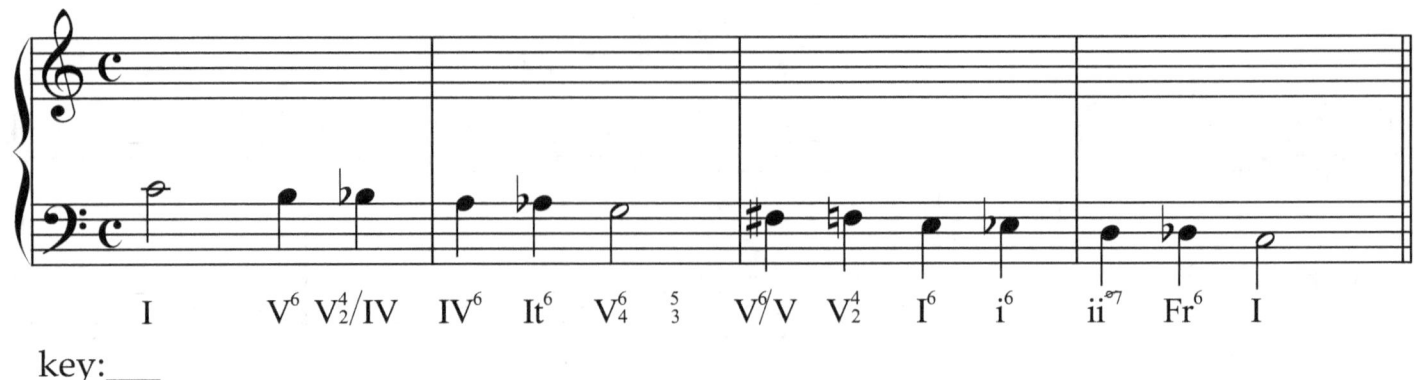

key:___

SUMMARY

1. All augmented 6th chords contain the intervals of an augmented 6th and a major 3rd.

2. The Italian 6th (It^6) consists of a major 3rd and an augmented 6th above the bass. The major 3rd is doubled.

3. The German 6th (Ger^6) consists of a major 3rd, an augmented 6th, and a perfect 5th above the bass.

4. The French 6th (Fr^6) consists of a major 3rd, an augmented 6th, and an augmented 4th above the bass.

5. Augmented 6th chords built on $\flat\hat{6}$ (major keys), and $\hat{6}$ (minor keys) resolve to dominant harmony.

6. Augmented 6th chords built on $\flat\hat{2}$ resolve to the tonic chord in root position.

7. Augmented 6th chords built on $\hat{4}$ (major keys) resolve to I or I^6.

8. In major keys, when a German 6th progresses to a six-four chord, an alternate spelling may be used: $\flat\hat{3}$ may be written as $\sharp\hat{2}$. This chord is sometimes called a double augmented 4th chord because it contains the interval of a double augmented 4th.

9. In most augmented chords, the augmented 6th occurs between the bass and a higher voice. However, in some cases, the augmented 6th is inverted so that $\sharp\hat{4}$ is in the bass and the augmented 6th interval becomes a diminished 3rd. The resulting chord is called a German diminished 3rd chord and as symbolized as Ger^{o3}.

10. Augmented 6th chords usually resolve to the chord a half step below the note on which they are built. Augmented 6th chords may also function like secondary dominants, and resolve to other diatonic chords, altered chords, or secondary dominants.

4
Chromatically Altered Chords

Composers use a number of chromatically altered chords to decorate, prolong, or take the place of diatonic chords in a harmonic progression. These chords can create surprise or tension, smoothly transition between keys during modulation, add expressive color to a harmonic progression, and lead more powerfully into a resolution, especially at cadences.

Augmented Triads

Composers in the romantic era often altered the fifth of a triad chromatically. If the fifth of the major triad is raised a half step, the result is in augmented triad. Chords built on an augmented triad are sometimes called raised 5th chords because the fifth of the chord is raised chromatically.

Augmented triads in either major or minor keys require an accidental. They usually occur as a result of chromatic voice leading, and are rarely seen alone as an independent harmony. The most common augmented triads are I$^+$ and V$^+$. The symbol + indicates that the triad is augmented. Some systems use the symbol x to indicate an augmented triad. Chromatically raised tones usually resolved by rising. Thus, the altered fifth of an augmented triad resolves upward. In four part writing, the raised fifth of the chord is not doubled.

The tonic augmented triad (I$^+$) occurs in major keys only. Although it may be preceded by other chords, it sounds best when proceeded by I. When this chord resolves to IV, the raised fifth of I$^+$ rises to the third of IV. In Figure 4.1a, the augmented triad (I$^+$) occurs as a result of chromatic passing motion between I and IV. The tonic augmented 5th triad may also be used in first inversion (I^{+6}) as shown in Figure 4.1b.

Figure 4.1

As stated above, I⁺ is not used in minor keys. Figure 4.2a demonstrates the unusual harmonic quality created by ♯5 by in the minor mode: a triad with a minor 3rd and an augmented 5th (C – E flat – G sharp). Since ♯5 (G sharp) is the enharmonic equivalent of the third of iv (A flat), this note sounds like an anticipation rather than a passing note, and the chord looks as if it is misspelled. In Figure of 4.2b, the A flat is analyzed as an anticipation.

Figure 4.2

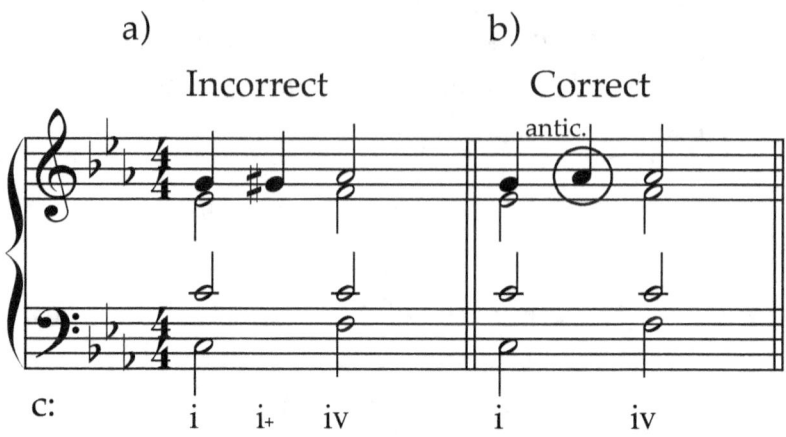

In the excerpt in Figure 4.3, the altered triad occurs as a result of chromatic linear motion in the left hand part (C – C sharp – D). The passing tone, C sharp, turns the tonic chord into an augmented triad.

Figure 4.3

Chromatically Altered Dominant Chords

When we alter one or more chord tones of V or V^7 using accidentals (chromatic notes) we get altered dominant chords. These chords still function as dominants, but with added color and tension. Figure 4.4 shows the dominant and dominant 7th chords with raised fifths. In both of these examples, the fifth is raised a half step resulting in an augmented triad (V^+) or in the case of the dominant 7th an augmented minor seventh chord (V^{+7}). The plus sign (+) next to the Roman numeral refers to the augmented quality of the triad. Note the root/quality chord symbols for these chords. In the resolution of these chords the chromatically altered 5th resolves upwardly to the 3rd of chord I. In the resolution of V^{+7} the G sharp resolves up to A and the 7th (B) must resolve down to A resulting in a I chord with a doubled 3rd.

Figure 4.4

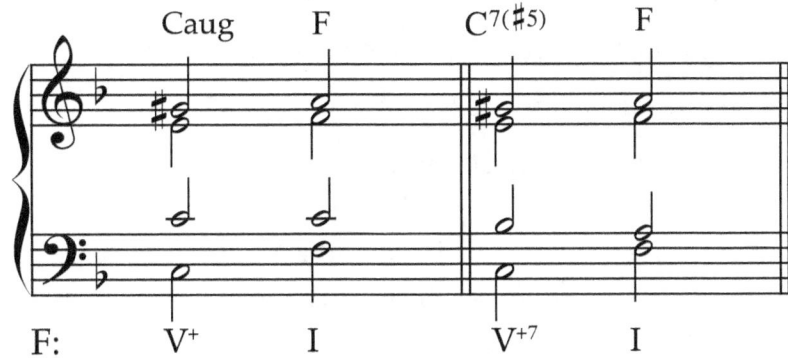

1. Provide a harmonic analysis of the following excerpt. Use both functional and root/quality chord symbols. Circle and identify any non-chord tones.

Johannes Brahms
Piano Concerto no. 2
op. 83 (4th mvt.)

2. Write the following progressions for four voices. All progressions are in major keys.

| I | I+ | IV | I | I+ | IV | V | V+ | I | V | V+ | I |

The fifth of a dominant 7th chord can be raised chromatically to create an altered dominant seventh chord. This chord is used in major keys only and normally resolves to a tonic major triad. The altered-dominant 7th with a raised fifth contains three active tones:

- the third (the leading tone), which tends to resolves upward by step
- the raised fifth, which resolves upward by step
- the seventh, which resolves downward by step

Altered dominant 7ths may be used in root position and all inversions, and should always be written as a complete chord using the root, third, raised fifth, and seventh.

In Figure 4.5 a and b, the fifth of V^7 is raised, creating an augmented minor 7th chord (an augmented trial with a minor 7th). Since chromatically raised notes tend to resolve upward, the raised fifth of V^7 rises to the third of I. In example a, the seventh falls, and the third (the leading tone) rises, creating a tonic chord in which both the root and third are doubled. An example b, the third falls (B – G), creating a tonic chord with a double third. This is OK as long as the leading-tone is in an inner voice. If the leading-tone is in an outter voice, it must rise to the tonic.

In example c, the altered dominant is used in third inversion and resolves to a I^6 chord.

Figure 4.5

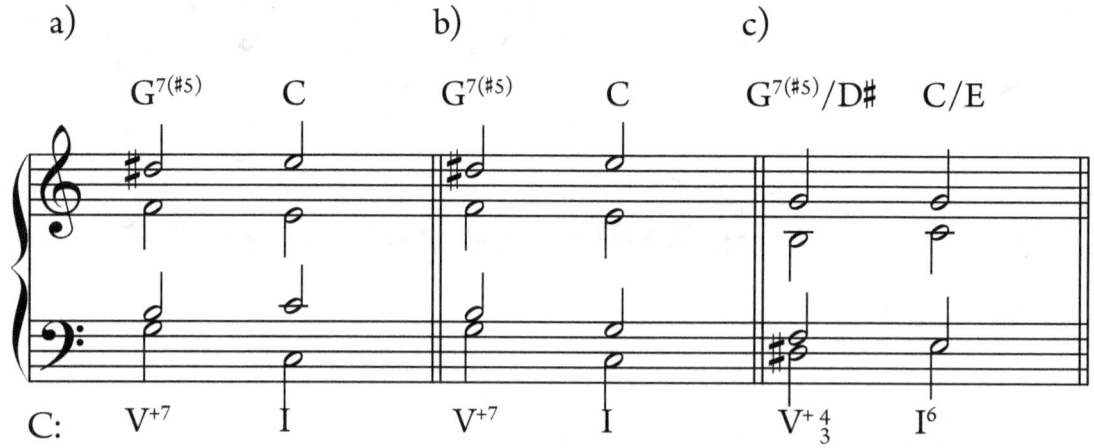

Chapter 4: Chromatically Altered Chords

3. Write and resolve the following altered dominant 7th chords.

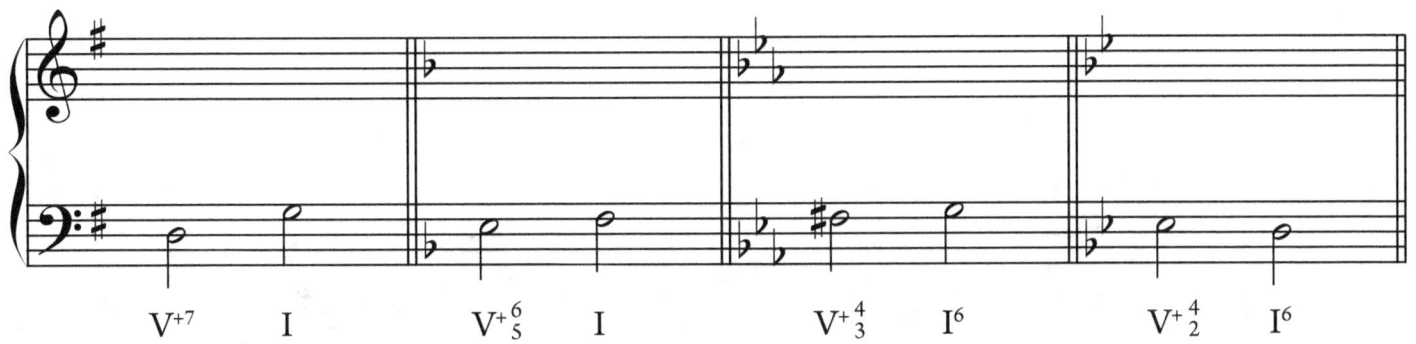

4. Provide a harmonic analysis of the following excerpt using functional chord symbols. Circle and identify any non-chord tones.

Franz Schubert
Erlkonig
op.1, D 328

key:___

Altered dominant 7ths may be used as secondary dominants in tonicization or modulation. In the excerpt in Figure 4.6, IV is tonicized by an altered secondary dominant.

Figure 4.6

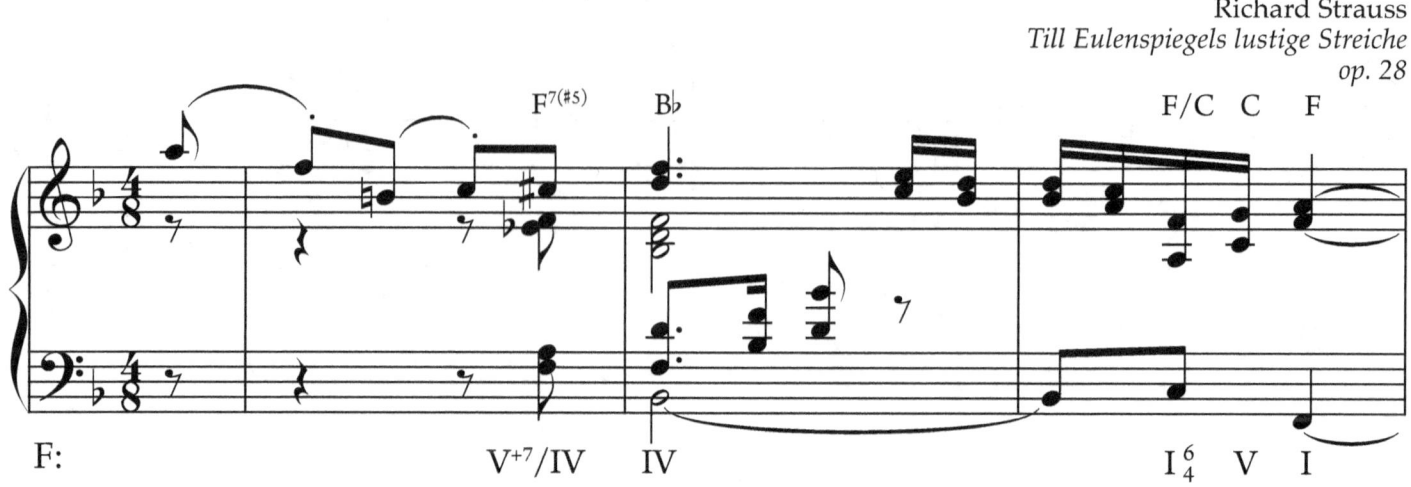

Lowered Fifth Chords

The fifth of a dominant triad or a dominant 7th chord may also be lowered chromatically. Since the resulting chord is not one of the four diatonic triads, there is no symbol to represent its quality. In this text, we will use an uppercase Roman numeral (V) and indicate the lowered fifth in the figuration ($V^{\flat 5}$ and $V^{6}_{\flat}$). Dominant triads and dominant 7ths with a lowered fifth may be used in both major and minor keys and normally resolve to a tonic triad.

Chromatically lowered notes tend to resolve by falling. The dominant triads in Figure 4.7a and b resolve to a tonic triad, with the lowered fifth falling to the root of I.

Figure 4.7

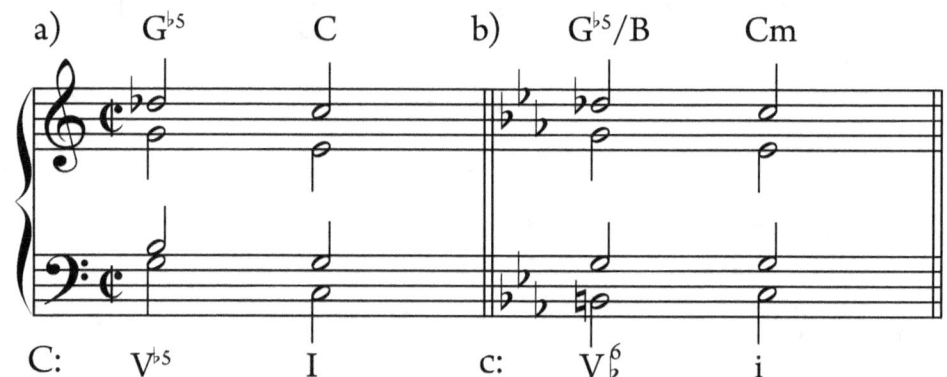

A dominant 7th chord with a lowered fifth may occur in root position and all three inversions. As in the dominant chord, the lowered fifth resolves downward to the root of I. The altered 5th is shown in the functional chord symbols. In Figure 4.8c, the ♭1 shows in the chord symbols because D flat is the altered tone. Note that the second inversion chord shown in 4.8c could also be analyzed as a Fr⁶ built on $\flat\hat{2}$: in most contexts, this would be the preferred analysis for this chord.

Figure 4.8

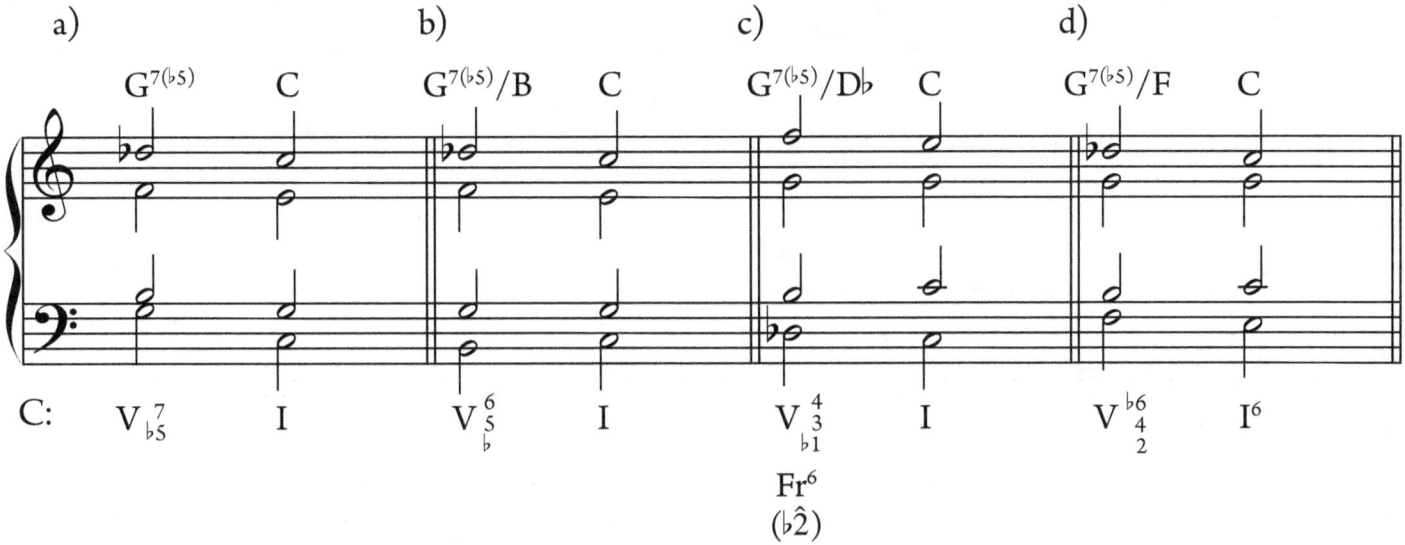

5. Write the following progressions for four voices.

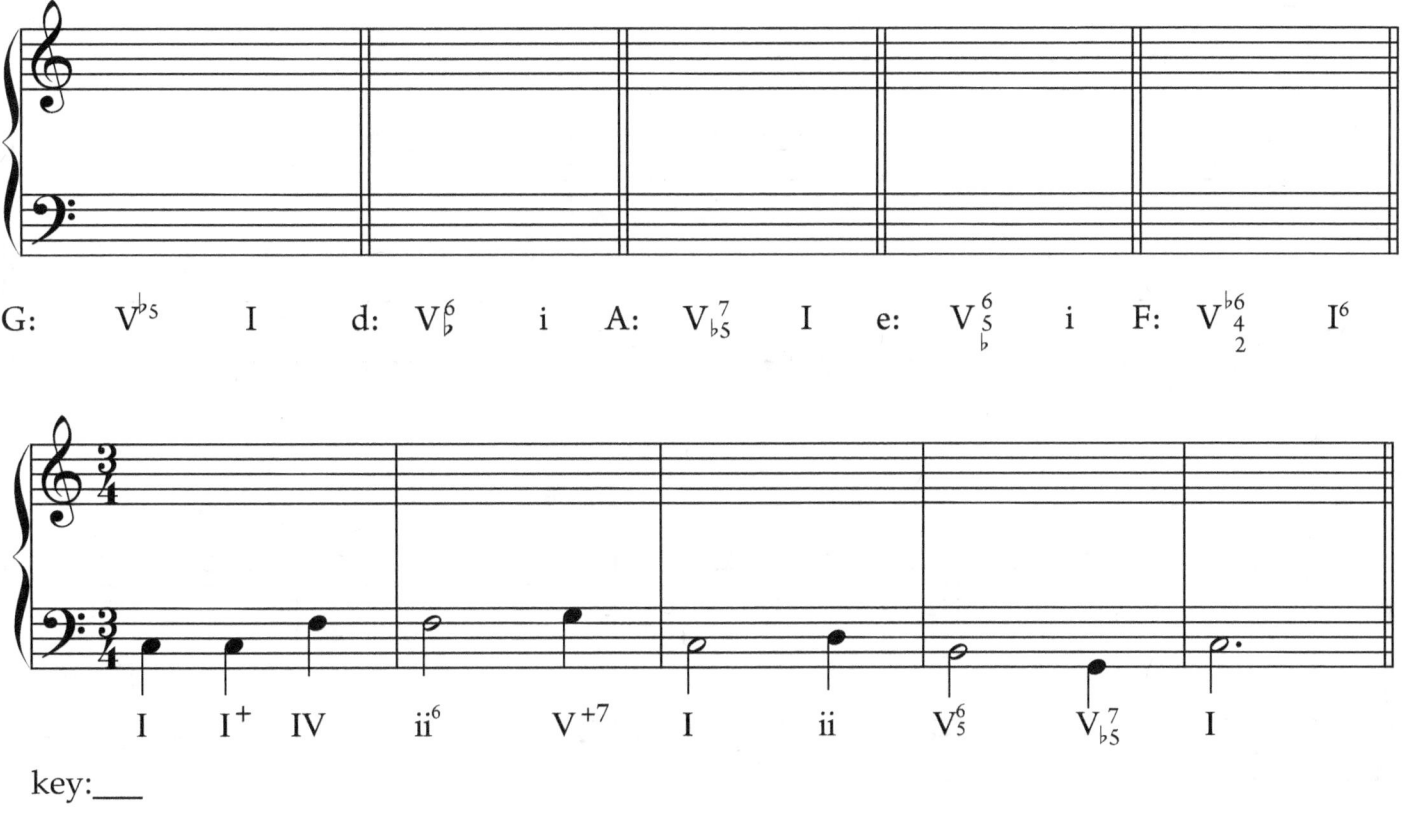

6. Harmonize the following melodic fragments using altered triads or altered dominant 7ths where appropriate. Add functional chord symbols.

7. Provide a harmonic analysis of the following excerpt using functional chord symbols. Circle and identify any non-chord tones.

Frederic Chopin
Nocturne
op. 27, no. 1

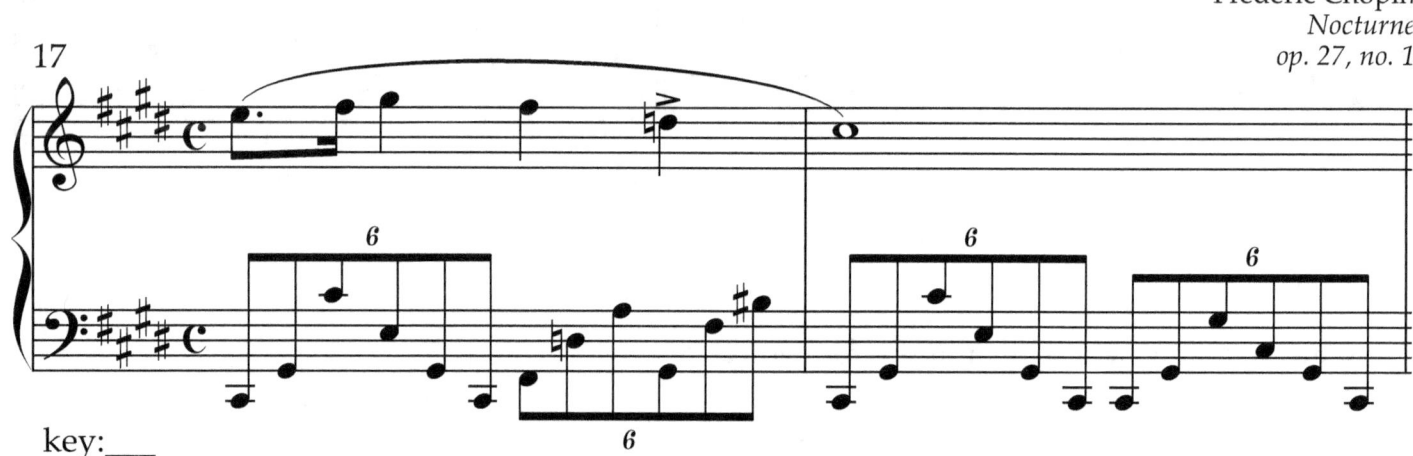

key:___

8. Complete the following for four voices.

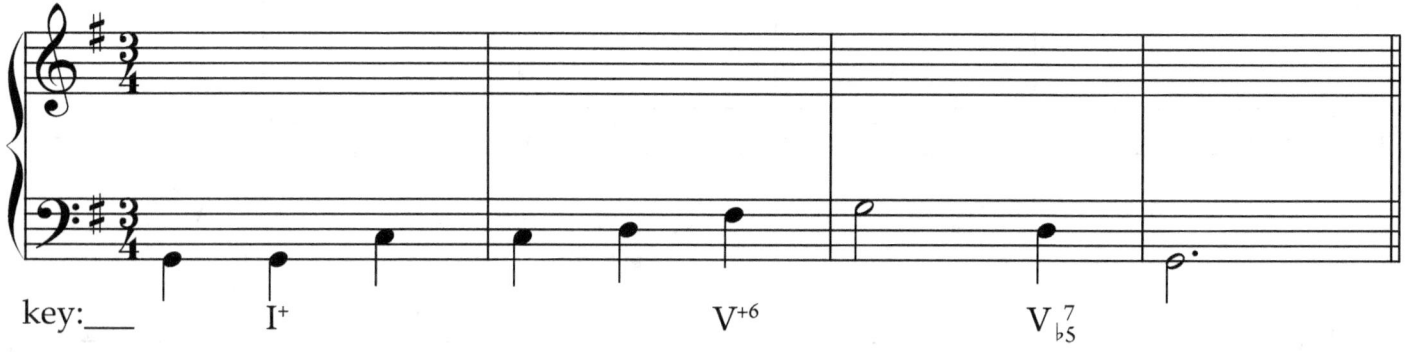

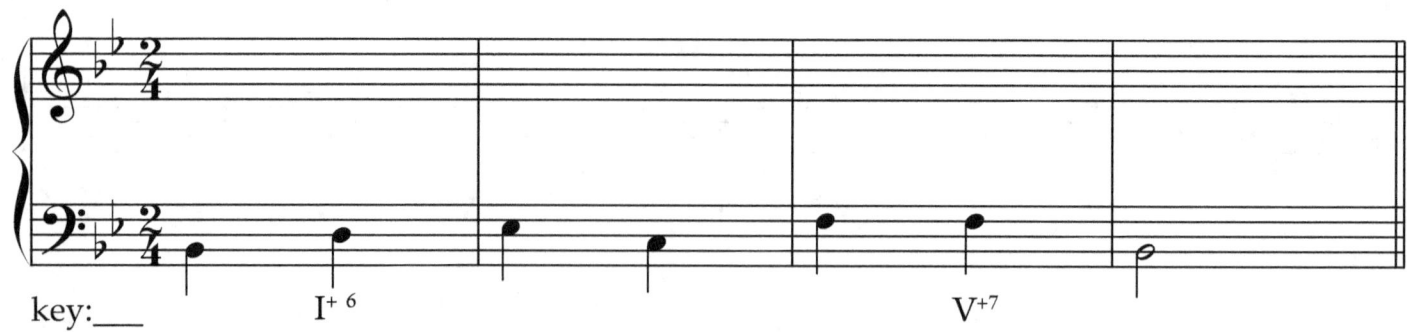

84 Chapter 4: Chromatically Altered Chords

9. Harmonize the following melodies using altered chords where appropriate.

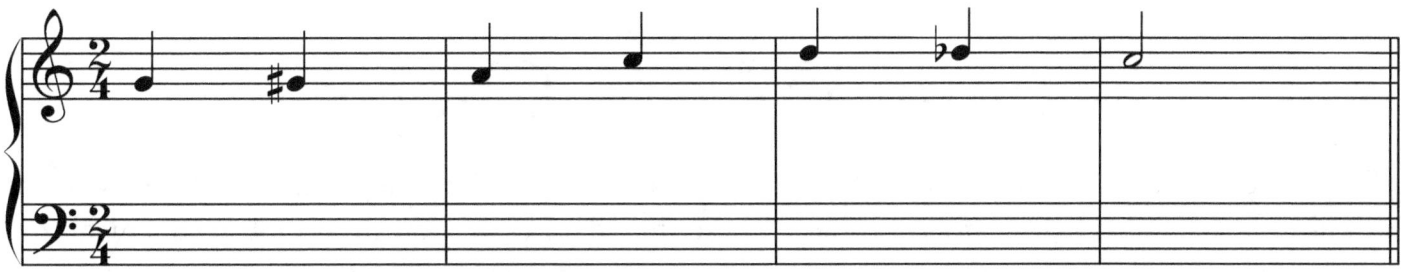

SUMMARY

1. When the fifth of a major triad is raised chromatically, the resulting chord is called an augmented triad. Since the fifth is raised chromatically, these chords are also known as raised 5th chords.

2. Chords with a raised fifth require an accidental in both major and minor keys.

3. Tonic and dominant augmented triads (I$^+$ and V$^+$) are used in major keys only and can occur in root position and first inversion.

4. I$^+$ usually resolves to IV, with the altered fifth rising to the third of IV.

5. V$^+$ usually resolves to I, with the altered fifth rising to the third of I.

6. When the fifth of a dominant triad is lowered chromatically, the resulting chord is symbolized as V$^{\flat 5}$. This chord can be used in both major and minor keys.

7. A V$^{\flat 5}$ resolves to I, with the lowered fifth falling to the root of I.

8. When the fifth of a dominant 7th is raised chromatically, the resulting chord (V^{+7}) resolves to I: the raised fifth resolves upward by step and the 7th resolves downward by step.

9. When the fifth of a dominant 7th is lowered chromatically, the resulting chord (V$^7_{\flat 5}$) resolves to I: the lowered 5th falls to the root of I and the 7th falls to the third of I.

10. Altered V^7 chords may be used in root position and all three inversions.

5
Common-Tone Chords

Common-tone chords are chords that share one or more of the same notes, or tones, with the chords that come before and after them. These shared notes help create smooth and logical connections between different harmonies. Composers use common tone chords to create a sense of unity, blend, and flow in a musical progression.

The Common-Tone Diminished 7th Chord

The common-tone diminished 7th is a diminished 7th chord that embellishes or decorates another chord. The name of this chord comes from the fact that the root of the chord that is embellished must be a common tone with the diminished 7th. We will give the symbol CT^{o7} to the common-tone diminished 7th chord. Common-tone diminished 7ths usually embellish I or V.

In most uses, the seventh of a CT^{o7} becomes the root of the chord to which it resolves. In Figure 5.1a and b, the CT^{o7} (D sharp– F sharp – A– C) that embellishes I in C Major is built on $\sharp\hat{2}$ (D sharp). The seventh of this chord C is also the root of I. In Figure 5.1a, the CT^{o7} decorates I by means of a common tone C and three neighbour tones (G –F sharp, E – D sharp, and G – A). In Figure 5.1c, which is in C minor, both the fifth and the seventh of the CT^{o7} are common tones. Here, the CT^{o7} (F Sharp – A natural– C – E flat) is built on $\sharp\hat{4}$.

Figure 5.1

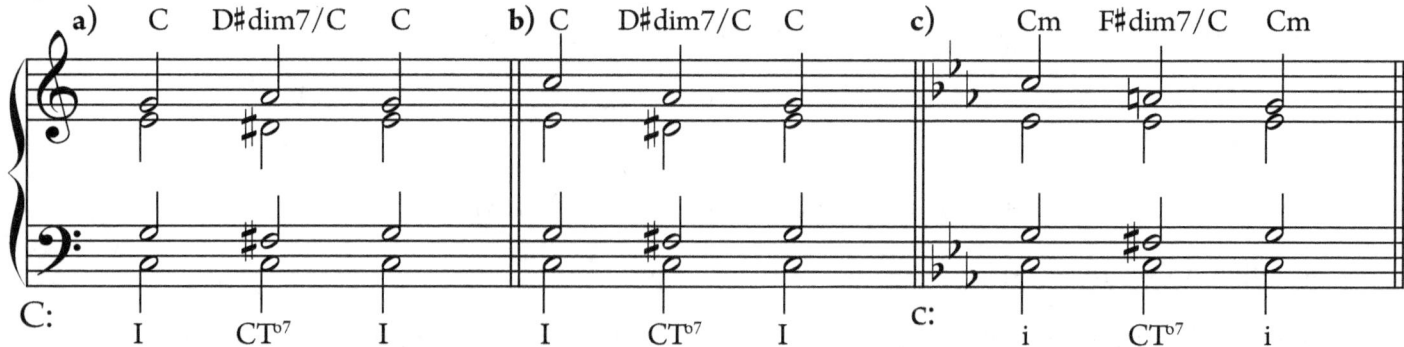

The CT^{o7} differs from other diminished 7th chords that we have studied. First of all, because the seventh of the CT^{o7} is the common tone, it does not resolve downward by step. Also, since the CT^{o7} is an embellishing chord, it has a weak harmonic function. Although this chord can embellish any major or minor triad, it usually moves to either I in major keys or V or V^7 in major or minor keys. A CT^{o7} usually functions as a neighbour chord or a passing chord. Note that because it has no functional root, inversions are not indicated in the figuration.

The root/quality chord symbols, identify the root of these chords by their letter name and state the quality and position of the chord. They do not indicate the key or the function of the chords within the key.

How to Identify a Common-Tone Diminished 7th

1. **Look for a diminished 7th chord.**
   - The diminished 7th is built of stacked minor thirds. For example B-D-F-A♭.
   - This chord usually doesn't belong to the key and is chromatically altered.

2. **Check what chord comes before and after it.**
   - Common-tone diminished 7ths usually appear between two identical or related chords.
   - Most often, they decorate a tonic or dominant chord.

3. **Find the common tone.**
   - See if one note from the diminished 7th chord is also found in the chord it resolves to (or comes from).
   - That common tone is often held or appears in the same voice.

4. **Check if it acts as embellishment.**
   - If the diminished 7th chord resolves back to or prepares a familiar chord and shares a tone with it, it's likely functioning as a common-tone diminished 7th, not a leading tone chord.

In the excerpt in Figure 5.2, Mendelssohn uses a CT°7 as a neighbor chord to I in a prolongation of the opening tonic harmony. The common tone (E) is the root of I and the seventh of the diminished 7th (F double sharp – A sharp – C sharp – E) built on ♯$\hat{2}$.

Figure 5.2

Felix Mendelssohn
Andante and Rondo capriccioso
op. 14

As stated earlier, in this text, we describe these chords as common-tone diminished 7ths and label them as CT°7. This terminology illustrates their relationship with the chords that they embellish. However, since common-tone diminished 7ths are often built on ♯$\hat{2}$ or ♯$\hat{6}$, other textbooks, sometimes label them as ♯ii°7 or ♯vi°7. Note that the roots of these chords do not have the same function as the roots of normal ii or vi chords. (For example, these chords cannot serve as pre-dominants or links). They function only as decorations of other chords, and are created as a result of linear movement.

1. Provide a harmonic analysis of the following excerpts. Use both functional and root/quality chord symbols. Circle and identify all non-chord tones.

Wolfgang Amadeus Mozart
Piano Sonata
K 545 (2nd. mvt)

Frederic Chopin
Grande valse brillante
op. 18

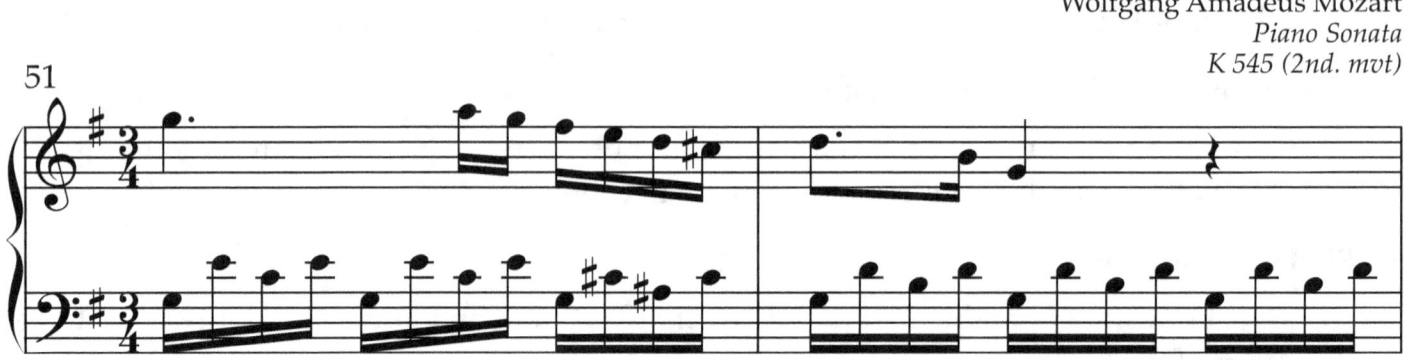

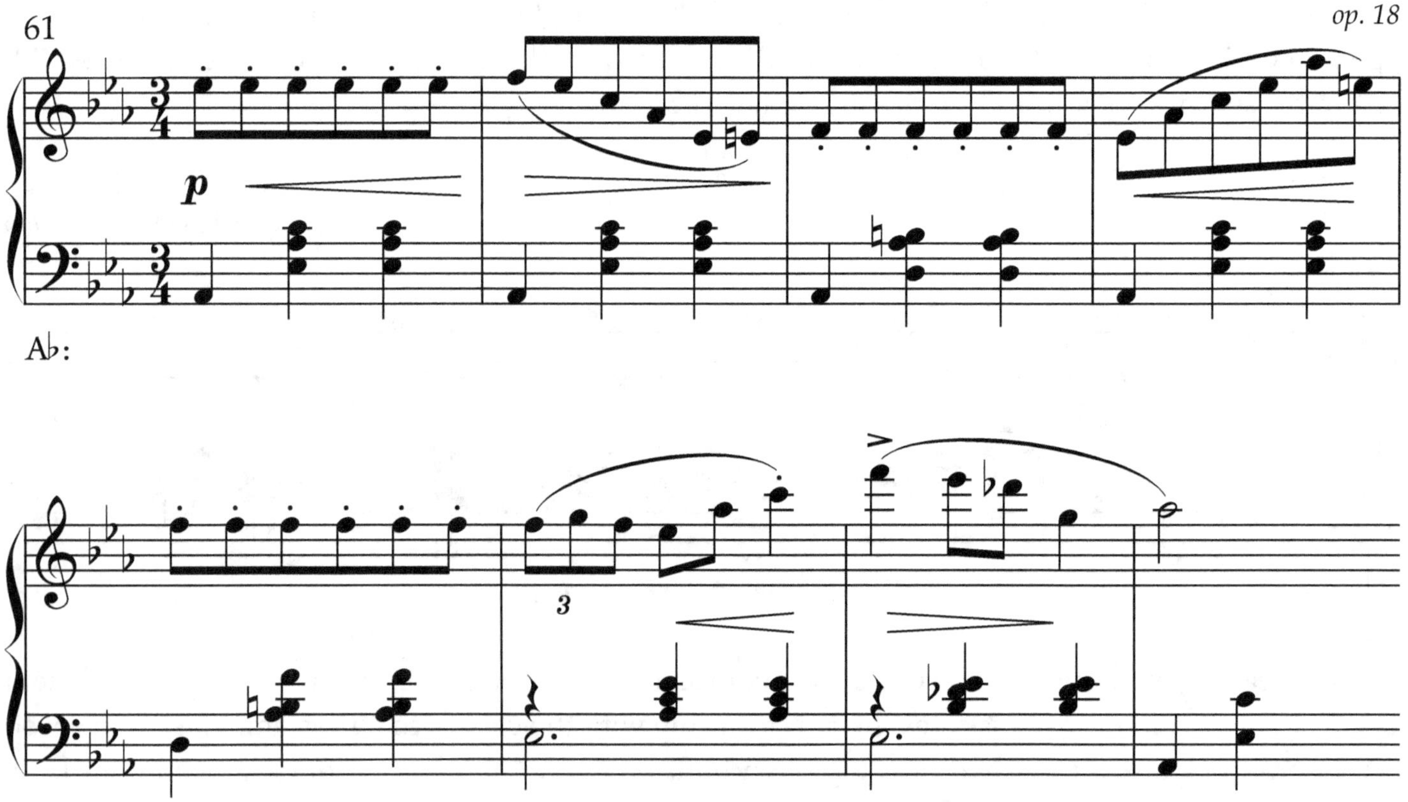

2. Complete the following progressions in four parts. All examples are in major keys.

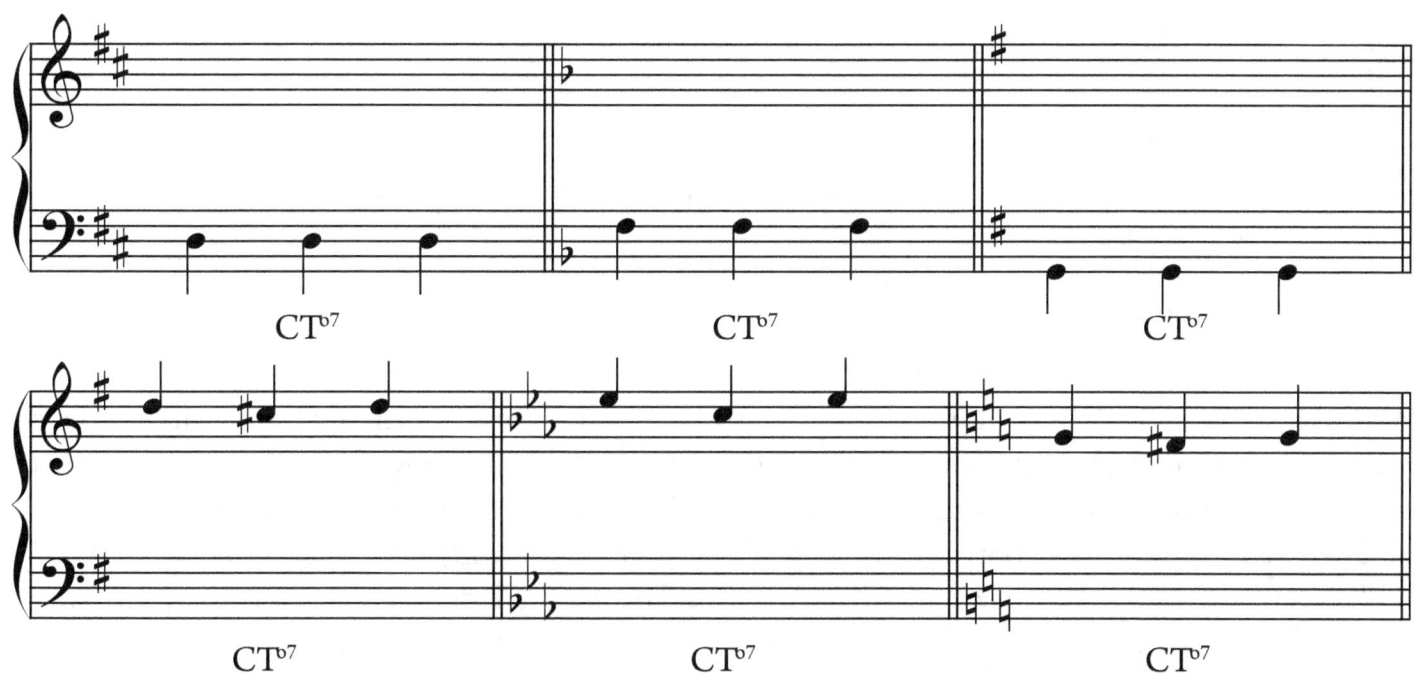

In a CT°7 progression, the common tone may occur in any voice. In Figure 5.3a, it appears in the alto. A CT°7 may embellish an inverted triad, as shown in 5.3b. Here, the common tone occurs in the tenor.

Figure 5.3

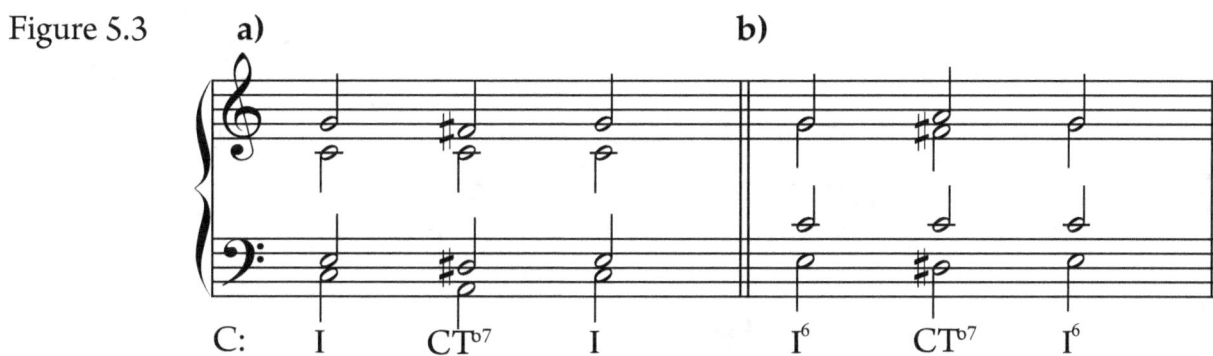

A CT°7 may also be approached by a chord other than I. In Figure 5.4a, the chord of approach is vi and the common tone (C) is in the alto. Figures 5.4b and c illustrate a CT°7 built on #$\hat{6}$ (A sharp – C sharp – E – G) embellishing the chords V and V7. The common tone (G) is the root of V and the 7th of CT°7.

Figure 5.4

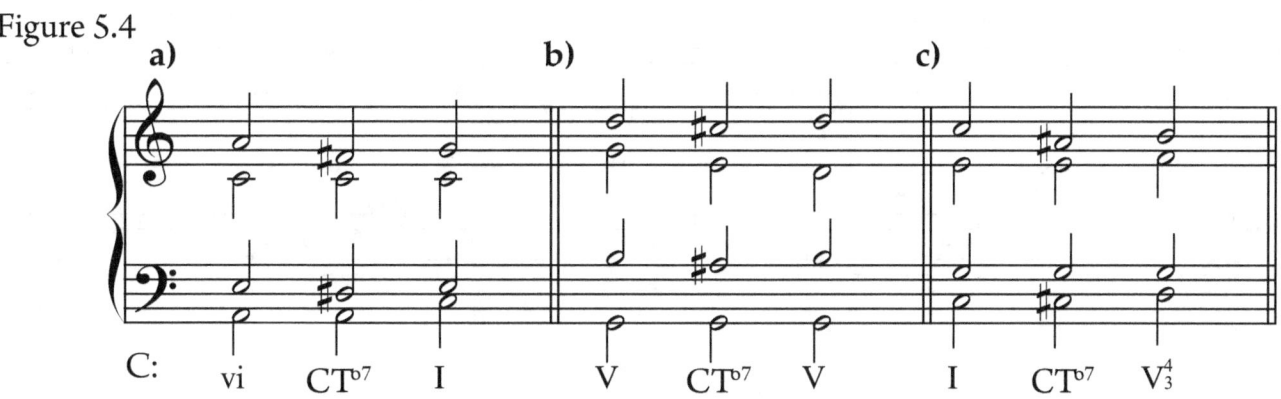

3. Complete the following progressions in four parts.

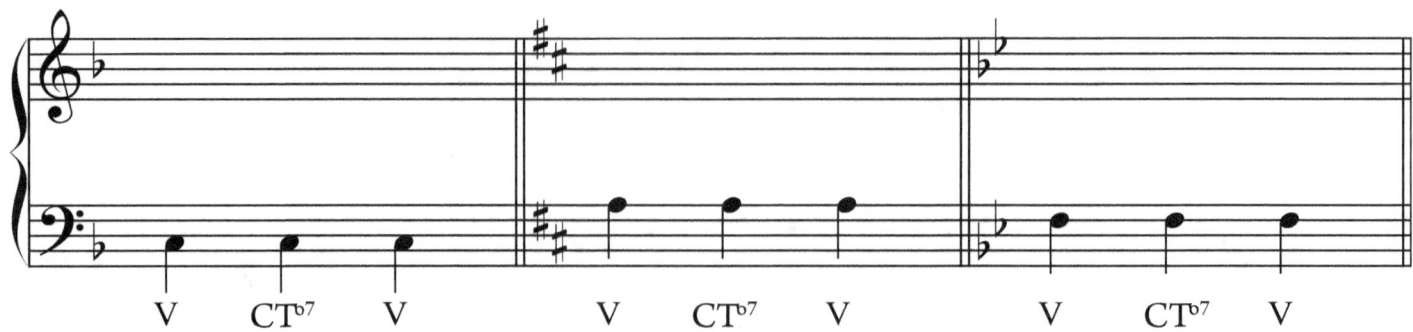

Alternate spellings of CT⁰⁷ chords are sometimes found. Since these chords are the results of contrapuntal decoration and have no functional root, their spelling may be changed as convenient. Compare the CT⁰⁷ chord that Tchaikovsky uses in mm. 2 and 4 in Figure 5.5 with the examples in Figure 5.4b and c on the previous page. Both are CT⁰⁷ chords built on #$\hat{6}$: the difference is in the spelling. A CT⁰⁷ built on #$\hat{6}$ and used to embellish V⁷ of A major would be spelled F double sharp – A sharp – C sharp – E, but here, Tchaikovsky has written G natural rather than F double sharp. The root seems to change from #$\hat{6}$ (F double sharp) to #$\hat{1}$ (A sharp), but since the CT⁰⁷ does not have a functional root, the apparent change does not affect the function of the chord.

Figure 5.5

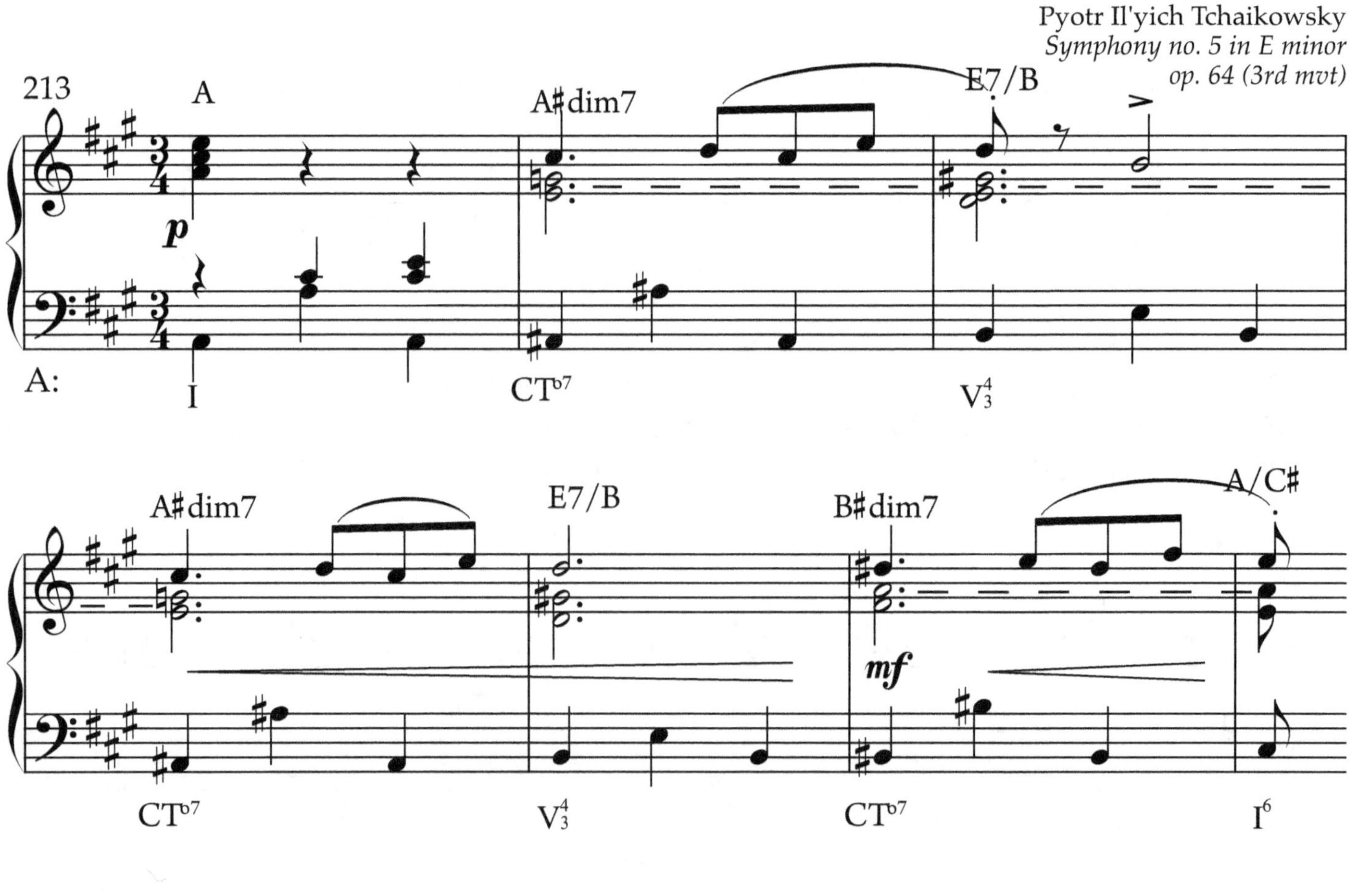

Pyotr Il'yich Tchaikowsky
Symphony no. 5 in E minor op. 64 (3rd mvt)

Chapter 5: Common-tone Chords

Most common-tone diminished 7ths are built on #$\hat{2}$ and #$\hat{6}$ but other degrees are also possible. In the excerpt in Figure 5.6, Schubert uses a CT°7 built on #$\hat{4}$. This chord could be also analyzed as a CT°7 built on #$\hat{2}$ and respelled enharmonically (E flat – D sharp).

Figure 5.6

Franz Schubert
String Quartet in C major
op. posth. 163, D 956 (1st mvt.)

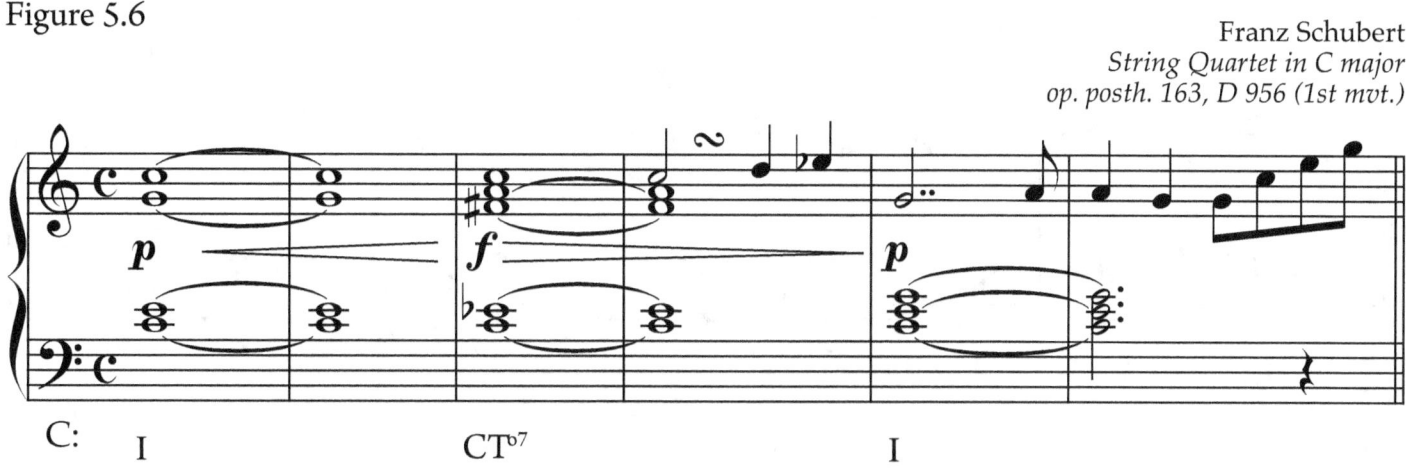

In Figure 5.7, Donizetti uses the CT°7 to connect I and V$^6_5$. The CT°7 (A sharp – C sharp – E – G) is built on #$\hat{6}$ and the common tone (G) is the root of V. The CT°7 functions as a passing chord, harmonizing the chromatic movement of the melody notes C – C sharp – D.

Figure 5.7

Gaetano Donizetti
A sposo!
from Don Pasquale, act 3, scene 2

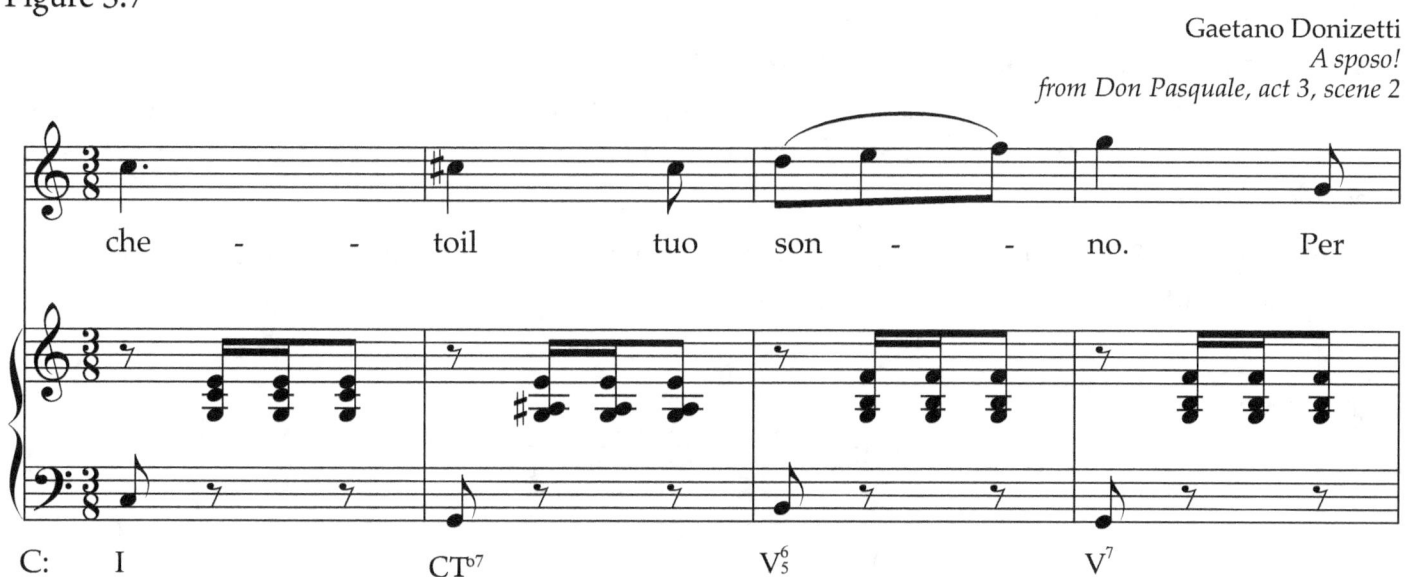

Chapter 5: Common-tone Chords

4. Provide a harmonic analysis of the following excerpt using functional chord symbols. Circle and identify any non-chord tones.

Robert Schumann
Papillons
op. 2, no. 10

key:___

The Common-Tone German 6th

The common-tone German 6th is a voice-leading variation of the regular German 6th. It is so named because it shares a common-tone with the chord that follows it - usually the tonic chord in second inversion. This approach creates a smoother, more expressive connection between the German 6th and the tonic chord. In this version, one tone, typically the tonic note remains constant between the German 6th and the I$^6_4$ chord.

A German sixth built on $\flat\hat{6}$ has two common tones with the tonic chord (i) in minor keys, and one common tone, the tonic chord (I) in major keys. We will symbolize this chord as CTGer^6. Here is a step-by-step comparison of a German 6th (Ger^6) chord with the predominant function and a common-tone German 6th (CTGer^6). Note the difference in the resolution of the augmented 6th interval in each example.

In a German 6th chord built on $\flat\hat{6}$, the augmented 6th interval resolves outward to the dominant octave ($\flat\hat{6}$ to $\hat{5}$ and $\sharp\hat{4}$ to $\hat{5}$) as shown in Figure 5.8.

Figure 5.8

C:
aug 6th on $\flat\hat{6}$ resolves to $\hat{5}$

In Figure 5.9, a German 6th with a predominant function moves to V. The augmented 6th between ♭$\hat{6}$ and ♯$\hat{4}$ resolves to $\hat{5}$, which becomes the root of the dominant chord (V, V^7, V$^6_4$, etc.). As previously noted, parallel 5ths between the tenor and bass are acceptable in this case

Figure 5.9

C: Ger^6 V

In Figure 5.10, the CTGer^6 chord moves to I. The augmented 6th between ♭$\hat{6}$ and ♯$\hat{4}$ resolves to $\hat{5}$, which becomes to the fifth of the tonic chord. The common tone is $\hat{1}$. In major keys ♭$\hat{3}$ (here, E flat) is often respelled as ♯$\hat{2}$ (here, D sharp), since it resolves upward to ♮$\hat{3}$.

Figure 5.10

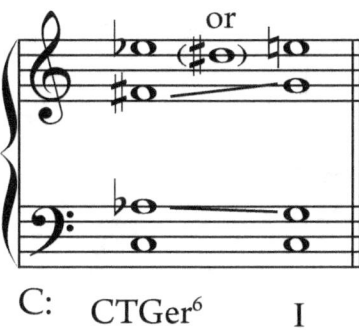

C: CTGer^6 I

In Figure 5.11, the tonic chord (i) is in root position and the CTGer^6 is in first inversion. In this progression, there are two common-tones (A and C) and two neighbour tones (E-D sharp and E-F). Because the augmented 6th interval resolves to $\hat{5}$, the tonic chord has a doubled fifth. German 6th chords are not normally inverted, so this chord does not function as a normal German 6th. Here, it is a linear chord created by a common-tone relationship with the tonic chord (i).

Figure 5.11

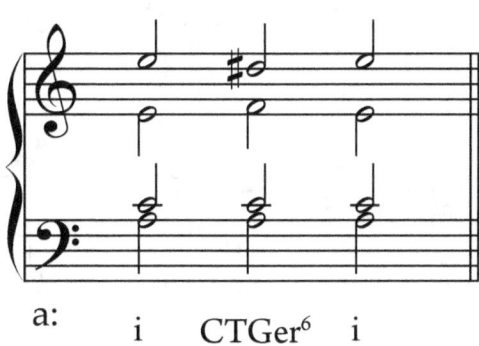

a: i CTGer^6 i

5. Complete the following progressions in four parts.

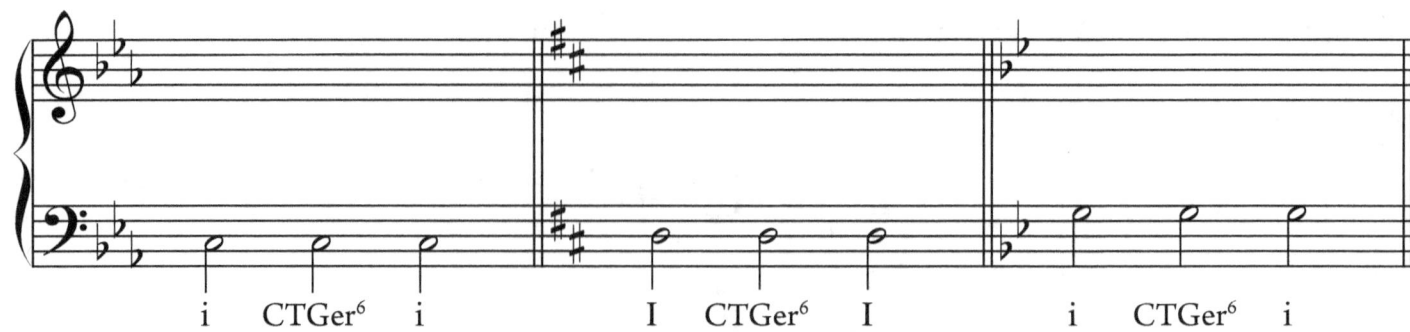

| i CTGer⁶ i | I CTGer⁶ I | i CTGer⁶ i |

In the late 19th century, composers occasionally allowed the bass to leap in a CTGer⁶ progression. In Figure 5.12, both i and CTGer⁶ are in root position. There are two common tones and one neighbor tone. The bass falls a 3rd. Note the different resolution of the augmented 6th: #$\hat{4}$ rises to $\hat{5}$ and $\hat{6}$ skips to $\hat{1}$.

Figure 5.12

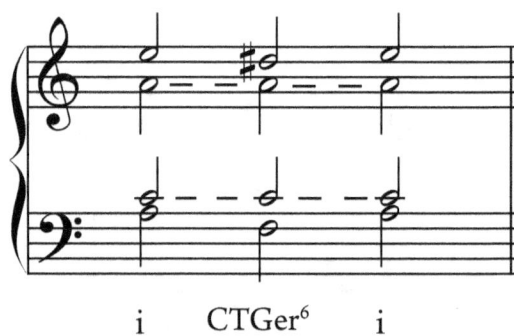

i   CTGer⁶   i

In major keys, there is only one common tone between the tonic chord and the CTGer⁶. In Figure 5.13a, the CTGer⁶ is in first inversion; in 5.13b, it is in root position. The enharmonic respelling of the fifth in the CTGer⁶ chord (D sharp instead of E flat) emphasizes the neighbor function of this chord.

Figure 5.13

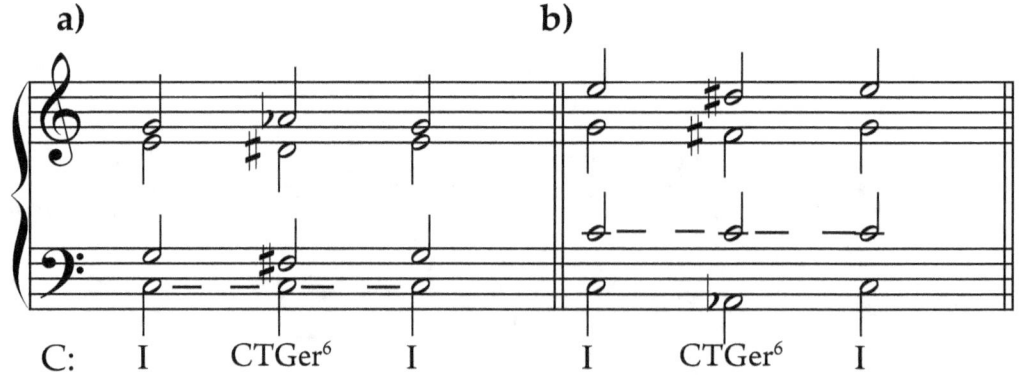

C: I CTGer⁶ I   I CTGer⁶ I

Chapter 5: Common-tone Chords

6. Provide a harmonic analysis of the following excerpts using functional chord symbols. Circle and identify all non-chord tones.

Franz Schubert
Moment musical
op. 94, D 780, no. 6

key:___

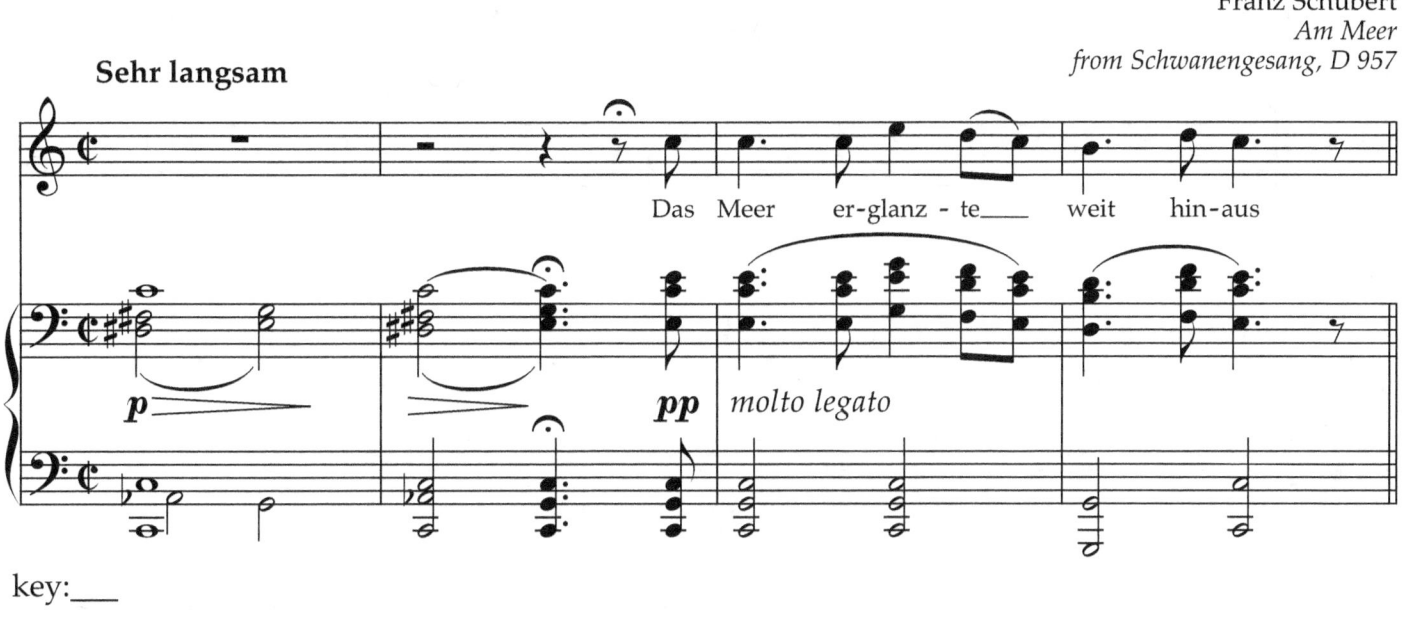

Franz Schubert
Am Meer
from Schwanengesang, D 957

key:___

key:___

Franz Schubert
Waltz
op. 9 D 365, no. 36

7. Complete the following in four parts.

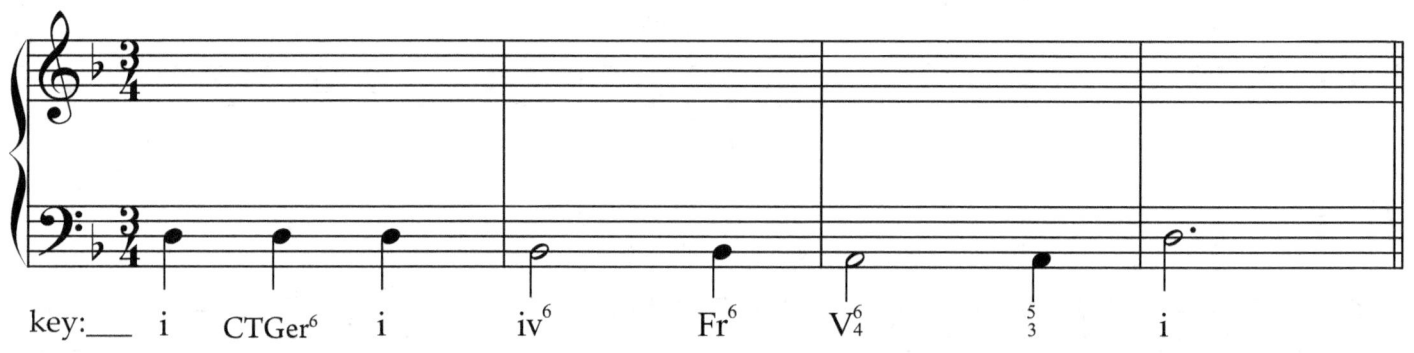

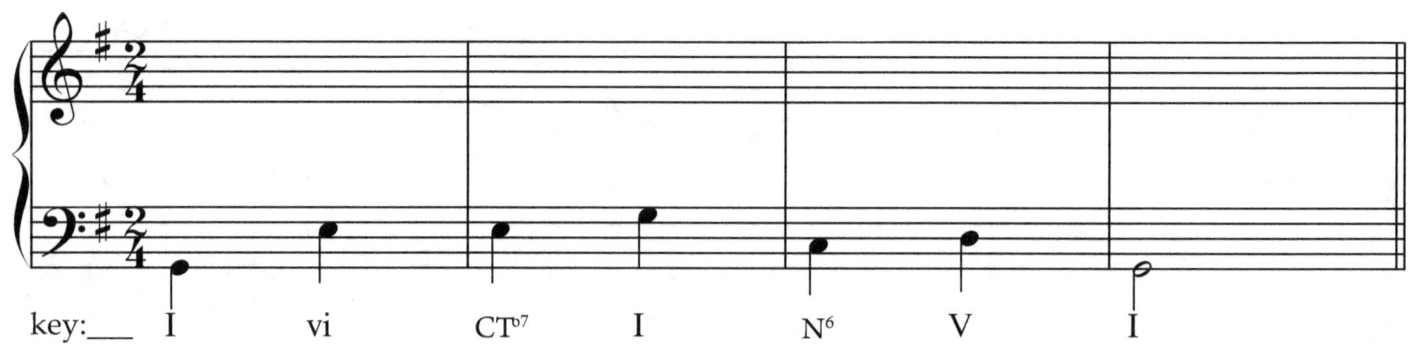

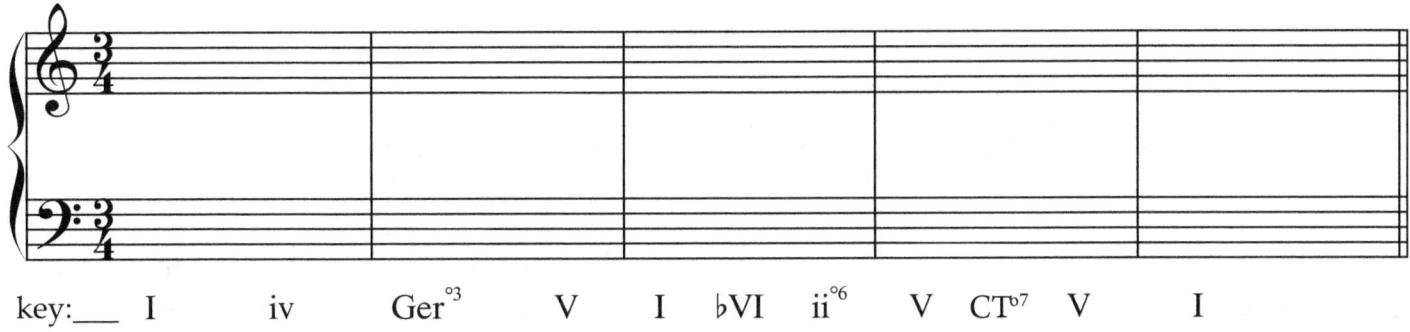

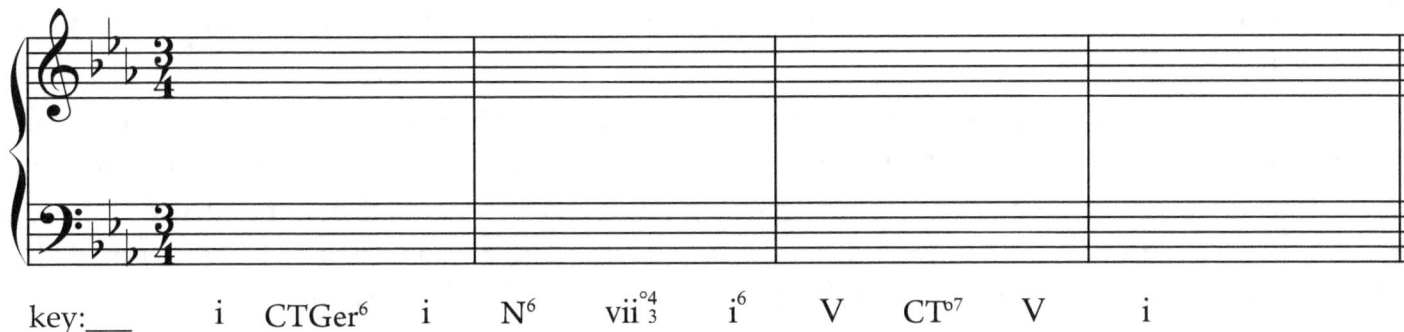

SUMMARY

1. The common-tone diminished 7th chord is an embellishing chord that is used to decorate other chords.

2. Most often – but not always – the seventh of the CT^{o7} becomes the root of the chord to which it resolves. Thus, a CT^{o7} can be built by using the root of the chord to which it will resolve as the seventh of the diminished 7th chord.

3. The CT^{o7} is usually used to embellish I (in major keys) or $V^{(7)}$ (in both major and minor keys).

4. The CT^{o7} has a weak harmonic function and commonly acts as a neighbor chord or a passing chord.

5. Because the CT^{o7} has no functional root, inversions are not indicated in the figuration.

6. Common-tone diminish 7ths are usually built on $\sharp\hat{2}$ or $\sharp\hat{6}$ but other degrees are also possible.

7. The common-tone German sixth chord is built on $\hat{6}$ in minor keys and $\flat\hat{6}$ and major keys. It is symbolized $CTGer^6$. This chord is usually used as an embellishing chord between two statements of the tonic chord.

6
Chromatic Mediants

In Western tonal music, harmonic relationships form the basis of progression, development, and expression. Among these, chords related by chromatic third also called **chromatic mediants** represent a particularly striking and colorful relationship. These chords are not diatonically related, but share certain structural and aural affinities, making them both unexpected and musically satisfying. This lesson will explore the definition, characteristics, and usage of chords related by chromatic third in Western classical music.

The chromatic, third relationship produces a rich and unexpected harmonic shift because the chords do not belong to the same key and often lack a strong, functional connection. However, due to their shared chord quality, and sometimes common tones, they create a sense of distant familiarity. In voice leading, these progressions often feature smooth stepwise motion in individual voices, despite the harmonic contrast. This enhances the dramatic or expressive quality of a passage.

The interval of a 3rd is a basic unit of chord construction: in root position triads, and 7th chords the notes are a 3rd apart. It follows that the movement of chord roots by 3rd also plays an important role in composition. Progressive harmonic movement occurs when roots move downward by diatonic 3rds, as shown below:

I - vi - IV - ii - vii° - V - iii - I

Composers of the 19th century, exploited root movement by 3rds, and more particularly by chromatic 3rds. In fact, root movement by chromatic 3rds greatly expands the tonal resources available to a composer. Chord movement by chromatic, rather than diatonic 3rds will produce altered chords that are not part of the diatonic harmony, and will allow for greater tonal expansion.

When the roots of two or more chords are a 3rd apart, those chords are in a **mediant** or **3rd relationship**. In Figure 6.1a, vi (the submediant) is a 3rd below I, and iii (the mediant) is a 3rd above I. In other words, vi and iii have a mediant relationship with I because their roots are a 3rd away from the root of the tonic chord.

Similarly, in 6.1b, ii is a 3rd below IV and vi is a 3rd above IV. Thus ii and vi have a mediant relationship with IV.

Figure 6.1

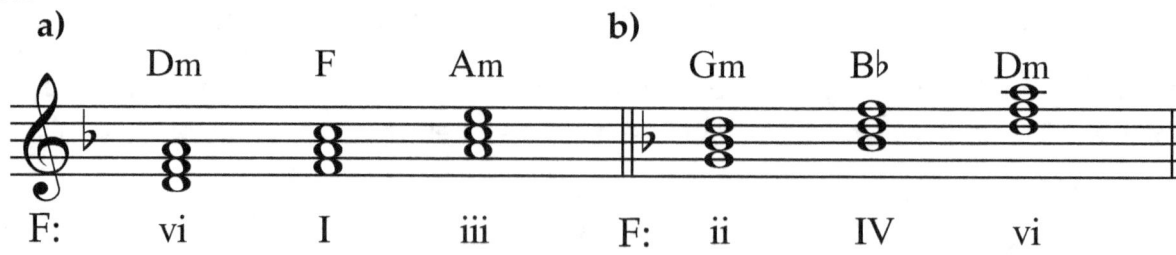

Chromatic Mediants

Figure 6.2 shows all the major and minor triads, both diatonic and altered, that are in a mediant relationship with the C major triad

Figure 6.2

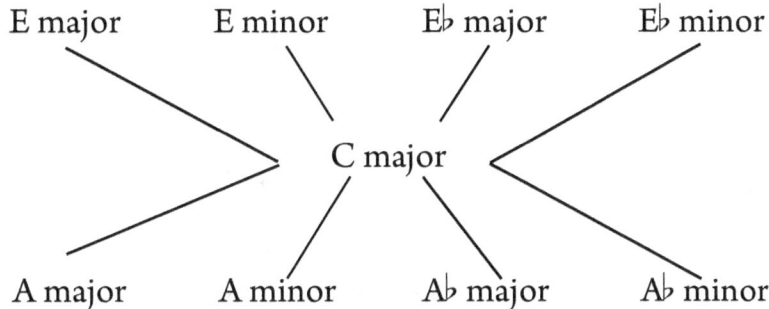

Note that only the A minor and E minor triads (A – C – E and E – G – B) are diatonic chords in C major. In the key of C major, the other six triads are altered chords because they belong to diatonic scales other than C major. These altered chords have a chromatic relationship to C major.

Chromatic 3rd-relation harmony makes use of major and minor triads, but augmented and diminished chords are usually analyzed as other types of altered chords. The six triads that are related to the major triad by a chromatic third (in Figure 6.2: E major, E flat major, E flat minor, A major, A flat major, and A flat minor) are called chromatic mediants. Note that four of the six chromatic mediants have a common tone with the C major triad.

The chart in Figure 6.3 shows all the chords that are in a mediant relationship with the C major triad. The common tones are shown in brackets.

Figure 6.3

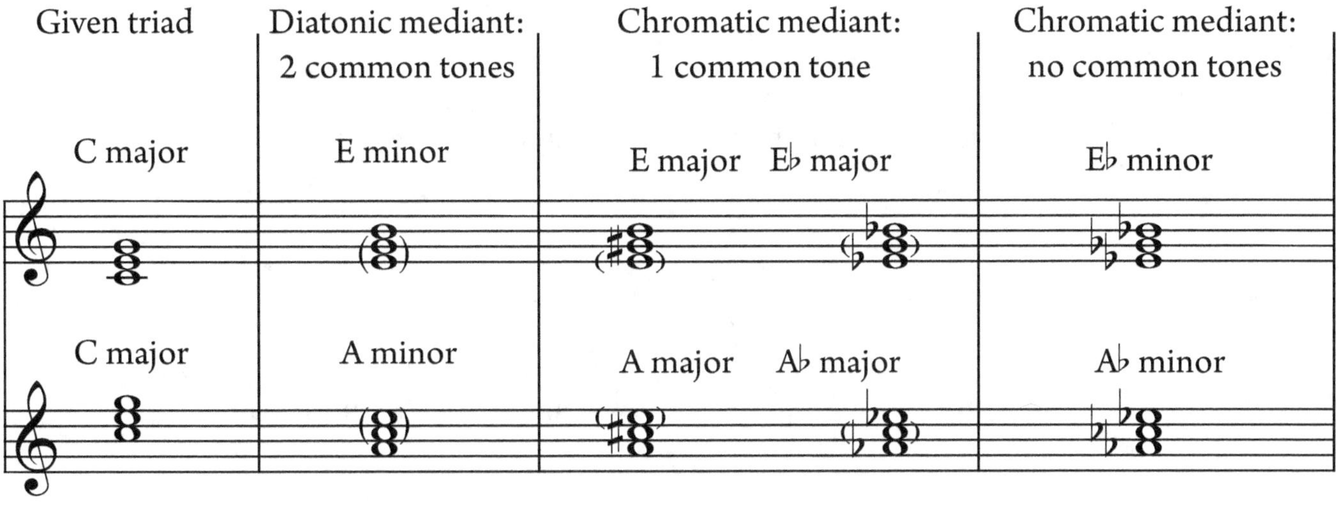

Given triad	Diatonic mediant: 2 common tones	Chromatic mediant: 1 common tone		Chromatic mediant: no common tones
C major	E minor	E major	E♭ major	E♭ minor
C major	A minor	A major	A♭ major	A♭ minor

1. Complete the following chart by adding all the major and minor triads that have a mediant relationship to G major. Write the common tones as whole notes.

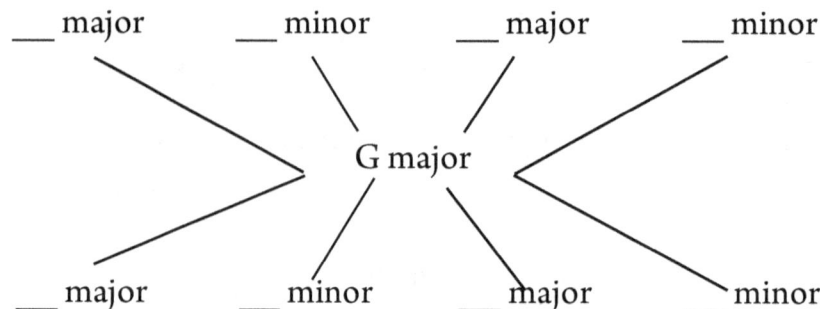

Given triad	Diatonic mediant: 2 common tones	Chromatic mediant: 1 common tone	Chromatic mediant: no common tones

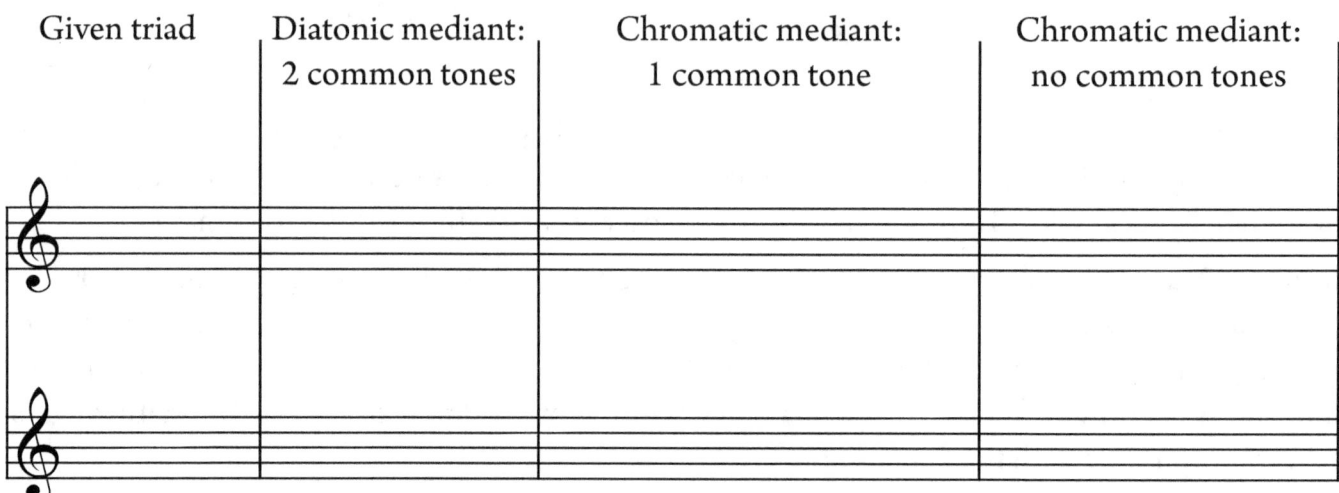

Figure 6.4 shows all the major and minor triads, both diatonic and altered that are in a mediant relationship with the C minor triad.

Figure 6.4

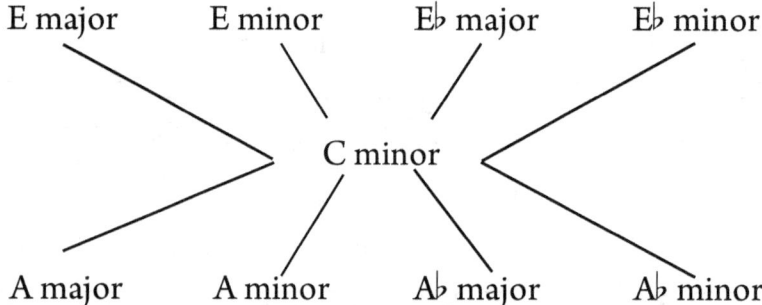

Chapter 6: Chromatic Mediants

Note that the A flat major and the E flat major triads (A flat – C – E flat and E flat – G – B flat) are diatonic chords in C minor. In the key of C minor, the other six triads are altered chords because they belong to diatonic scales other than C minor.

The chart in Figure 6.5 shows all the chords that are in a mediant relationship with the C minor triad. The common tones are shown in brackets.

Figure 6.5

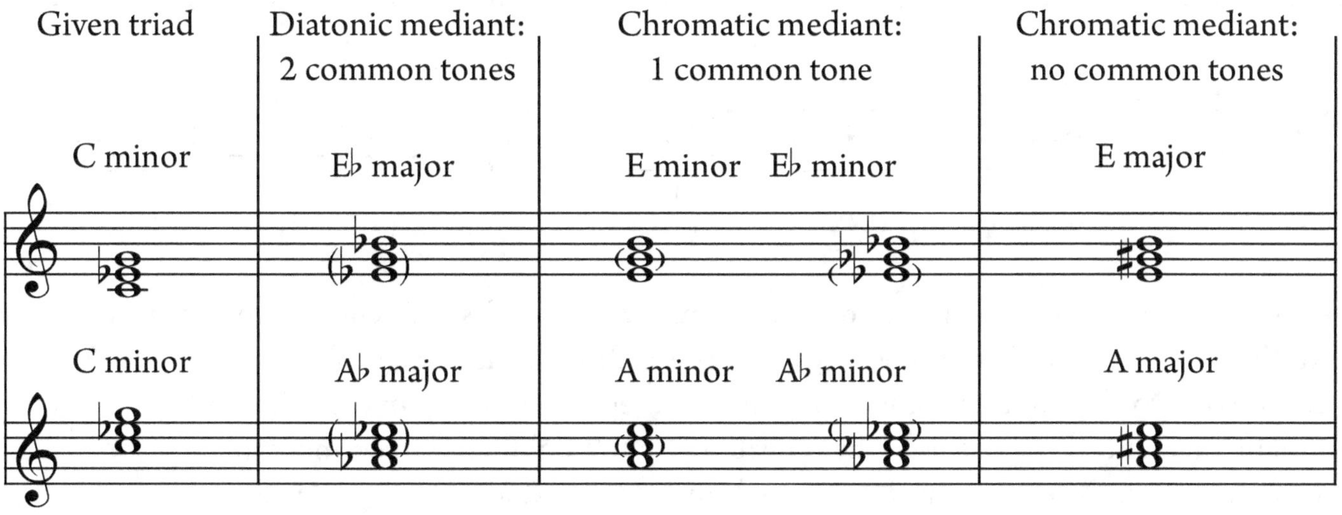

Given triad	Diatonic mediant: 2 common tones	Chromatic mediant: 1 common tone		Chromatic mediant: no common tones
C minor	E♭ major	E minor	E♭ minor	E major
C minor	A♭ major	A minor	A♭ minor	A major

The analysis of chromatic mediant chords is determined by the harmonic progression in which they occur. The four major triads in Figure 6.6 are chromatic mediants of C major.

Figure 6.6

C: VI   ♭VI   III   ♭III
     V/ii   V/♭II   V/vi   V/♭VI
              V/N

Some of these triads could be analyzed as borrowed chords or secondary dominants:

- The A major triad could be analyzed as V/ii (if it is followed by ii, it should be described as a secondary dominant).
- The A flat major triad could be analyzed as a borrowed chord from C minor.
- The E major triad could be analyzed as V/vi.
- The E flat major triad could be analyzed as a borrowed chord from C Minor.

Both progressions in Figure 6.7 use an E major triad (marked with an asterisk *) in the harmonic context of C major. Play each one, listen to the sound, and examine the analysis of the chords.

Figure 6.7

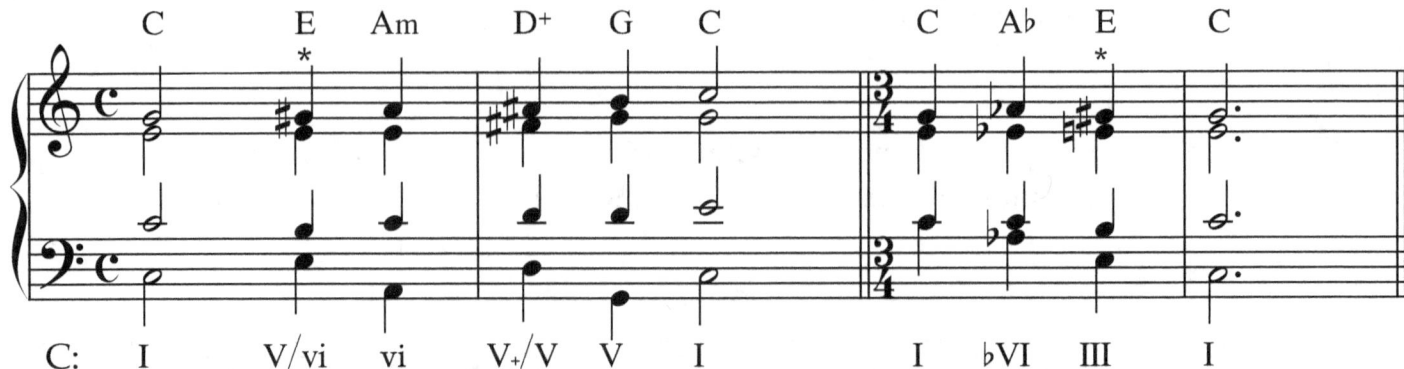

The excerpt in Figure 6.8 is in the key of C sharp minor, but the first two chords are not related according to the normal rules of harmonic function. These chords, i and vi (C sharp minor and A minor) do not belong to the same diatonic scale. They are related by a chromatic third and are considered chromatic mediants. Liszt has used the repeated E in the right hand to connect the first three chords by a common tone. The iv^{ø7} is an altered pre-dominant chord with a lowered fifth.

Figure 6.8

Franz Liszt
Il penseroso
from Annees de pelerinage

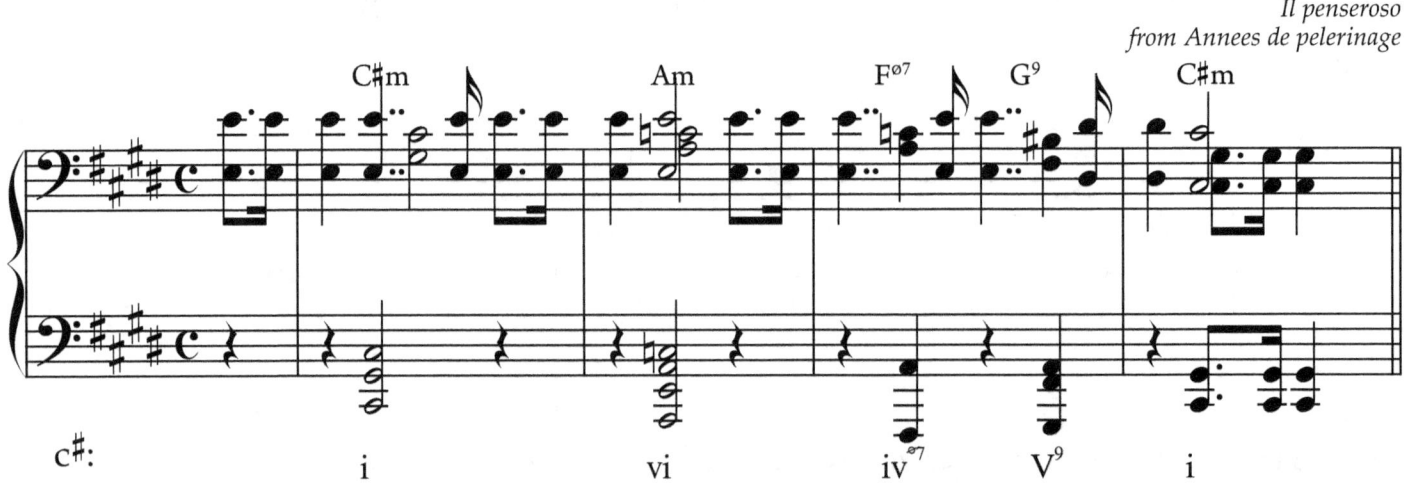

Chromatic mediants most often relate to the primary triads I, IV, and V, but they may also relate to more than one chord at a time. Sometimes it is difficult to determine the chord to which they relate.

For example, the VI chord in Figure 6.9 has a chromatic 3rd relationship to both the I chord that precedes it and the IV chord that follows: the root of VI is a 3rd below I and a 3rd above IV.

Figure 6.9

Robert Schumann
Fantasy in C major
op. 17 (3rd mvt.)

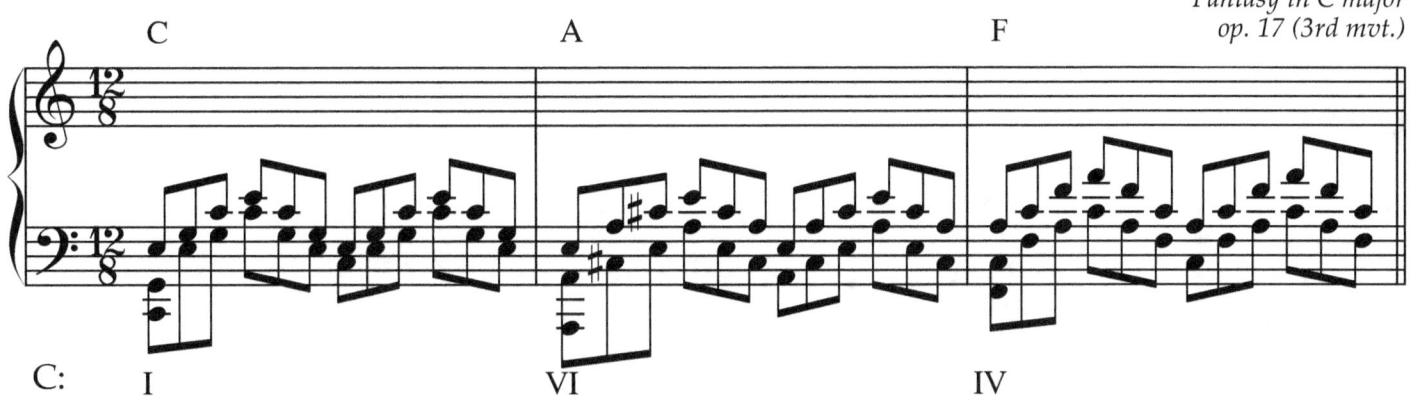

2. Analyze the following excerpts by providing functional and root/quality chord symbols.

Frederic Chopin
Prelude
op. 28, no. 9

key:___

Franz Liszt
Sonetto 47 del Petrarca
from annees de pelerinage

A:

3. Complete the following progressions for four voices.

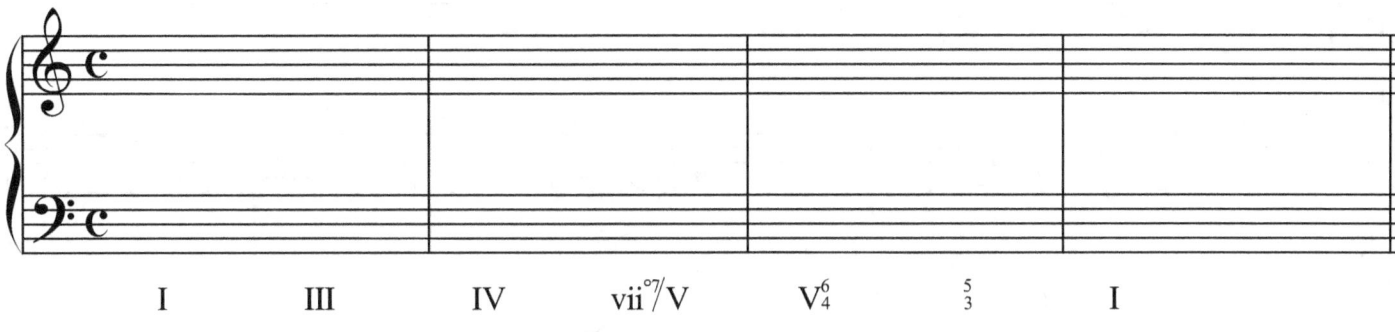

Chapter 6: Chromatic Mediants

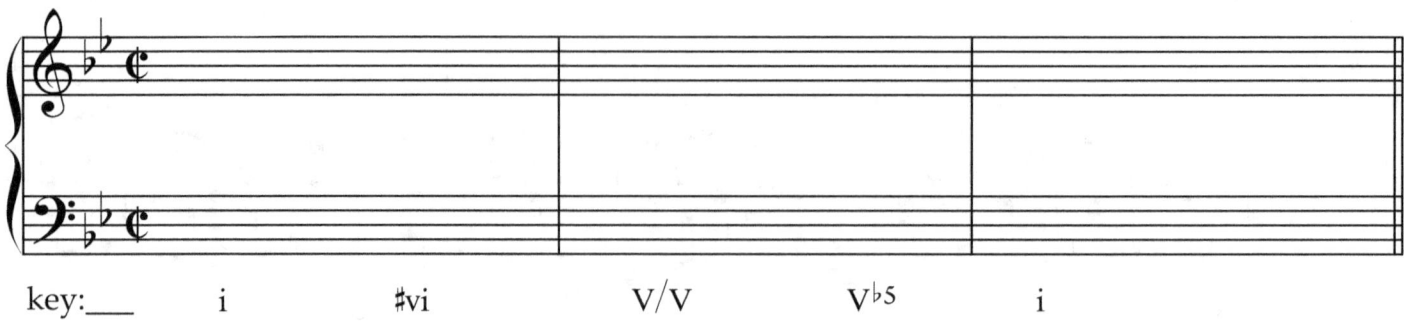
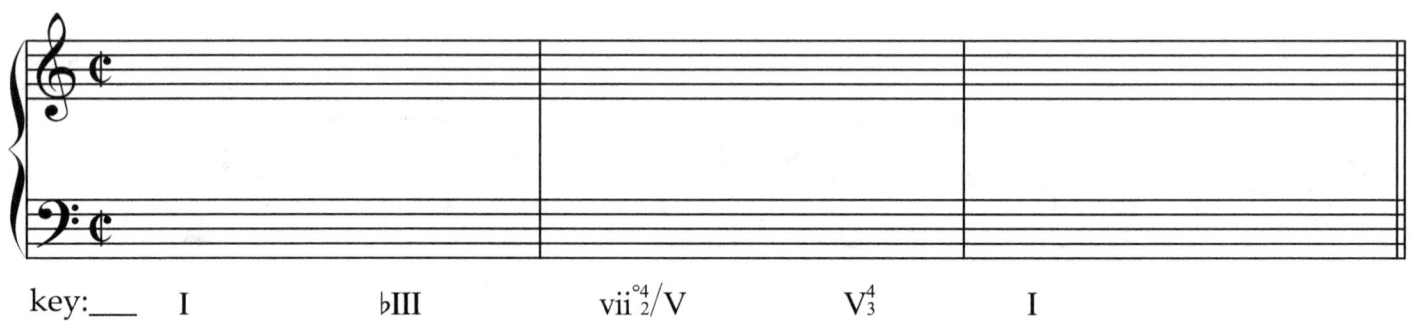
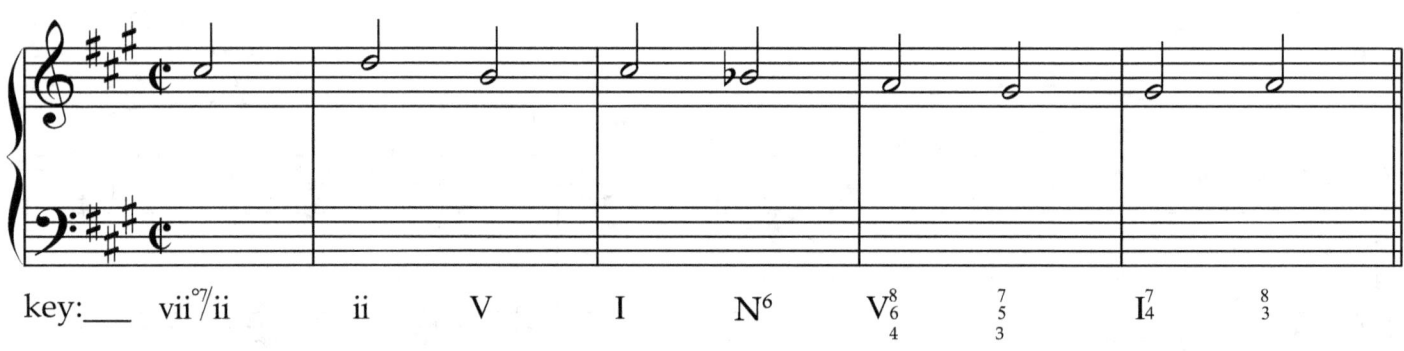
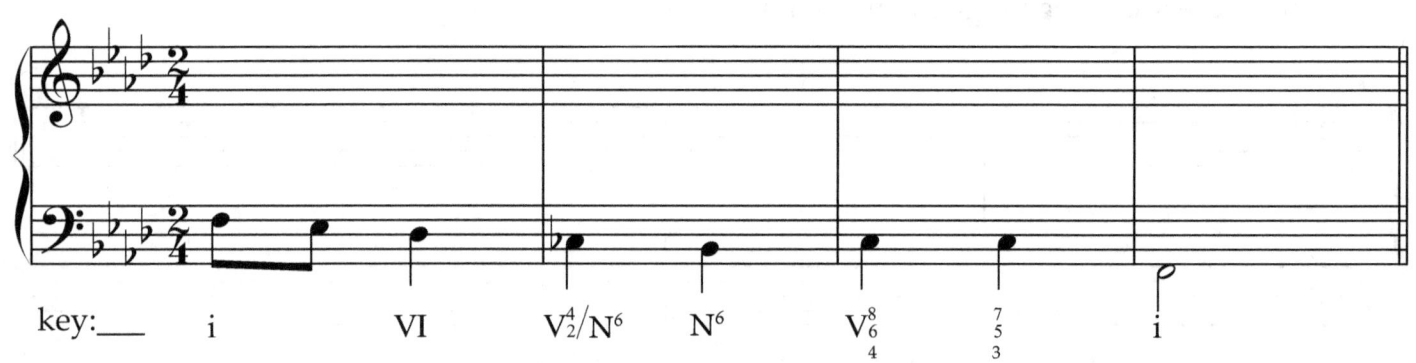

Chapter 6: Chromatic Mediants

4. Complete the following passages in four parts. Provide functional chord symbols.

key:___

key:___

SUMMARY

1. Two chords with roots a 3rd apart are in a mediant relationship.

2. If the notes of the two chords do not belong to the same diatonic scale, (for example, a C major triad, C – E – G, and an A major triad, A – C sharp – E), the chords are related chromatically.

3. The six triads related by chromatic 3rd to a major or minor triad are called chromatic mediants.

4. Chromatic mediants, most commonly relate to I, IV, or V, but they may relate to more than one chord at a time.

7
Modulation

Closely Related Keys

Modulation – a progression in which one tonal centre is replaced by another – adds tonal interest to a composition and often contributes to the formal design of the work. Sometimes a composer will choose to move to a **closely related key**. This type of modulation is discussed in *Essential Music Theory Level 10*. Two keys are closely related if their key signatures differ by only one sharp or flat: for example, A major (three sharps) and E major (four sharps) are closely related because there is a difference of only one sharp between the two key signatures. Because the key signatures of these two keys differ by only one sharp, they have a number of notes in common.

For any given key, there are five closely related keys: the relative minor (or major) of the key, the two keys that differ in key signature by only one sharp or flat, and the relative minors (or majors) of those keys. Thus, the closely related keys to F major are:

- D minor (vi): the relative minor
- B flat major (IV): the key signature with one more flat
- G minor (ii): the relative minor of B flat major
- C major (V): the key signature with one less flat
- A minor (iii): the relative minor of C major

Distantly Related Keys

Distantly related keys are key signatures that differ by more than one accidental. The distance in pitch between the two keys may be quite small: for example, the key signatures of F major and E flat major differ by two flats, but they are much closer together in pitch than F major and C flat major with the difference of six flats. Because the key signatures of distantly related keys are substantially different, they have few notes in common. Thus, modulation to a distantly related key can provide greater tonal variety, than modulation to a closely related key.

A Change of Mode

Tonic major and minor keys are distantly related because there is a difference of three flats or sharps between the two key signatures: for example, C major has no flats or sharps, but C minor has three flats. However, these two keys, share the same tonic, supertonic, subdominant, and dominant notes. They differ in mode rather than in key.

Since modulation involves a change of tonal center, a shift from a tonic major to its tonic minor is a change of mode rather than a modulation. The ear will accept a change of mode easily because parallel modes share the same three primary notes ($\hat{1}$, $\hat{4}$, and $\hat{5}$). Thus, a change of mode can be an effective way to introduced tonal contrast and chromatic variety into a composition. A change of mode can also lead to an expansion of closely related keys. For example, the five closely related keys to G major (E, minor, D major, B minor, C major, and A minor) and G minor (B-flat, major, E flat, major, C minor, F major, and D minor) provide a total of 10 possible keys to be used in modulation.

In the excerpt in Figure 7.1, Haydn shifts from D major to D minor at the beginning of the first episode. The D minor section then modulates to F major, which is closely related to D minor, but distantly related to the original key of D major.

Figure 7.1

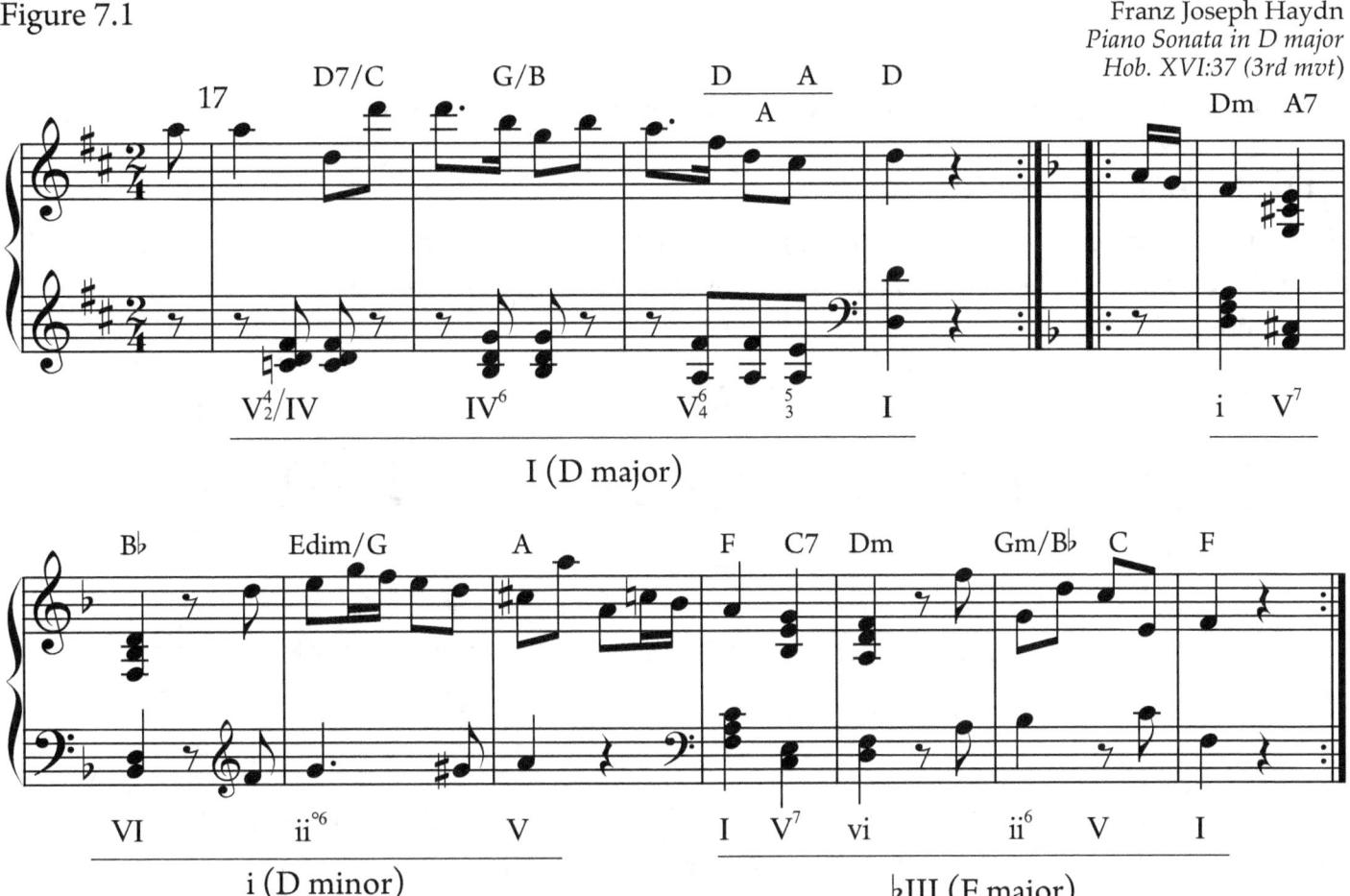

Franz Joseph Haydn
Piano Sonata in D major
Hob. XVI:37 (3rd mvt)

Altered Pivot Chords

One method of modulation is by means of pivot chords. In *Essential Music Theory Level 10*, we studied modulation using diatonic pivot chords – that is, chords that are common to both the original key and the new key. However, if the key signature of the new key differs by more than three accidentals, there are no diatonic pivot chords available. In this case, modulation can be achieved by means of a pivot chord that is an altered chord in one or both of the keys involved. The use of altered chords expands the repertoire of available pivot chords, even for closely related keys. The following chart lists a few of the altered pivot chords that could be used in a modulation from G major (one sharp) to the distantly related key of B-flat major (two flats).

Original key: G major	Pivot chord	New key: B♭ major
I (diatonic)	G (G-B-D)	V/ii (altered)
♭VI (altered)	E♭ (E♭-G-B♭)	IV (diatonic)
V⁷/IV	G⁷ (G-B-D-F)	V⁷/ii (altered)

107   Chapter 7: Modulation

There are four available pairings in pivot-chord relationships:

- diatonic/diatonic
- diatonic/altered
- altered/diatonic
- altered/altered

In the following pages, we will examine the last three of these relationships in detail.

Diatonic/Altered Pivot Chords

In a diatonic/altered pivot relationship, the pivot chord is diatonic in the first key and altered in the second. In Figure 7.2, the pivot chord F – A – C is a diatonic chord in F major (I^6) and an altered chord in E major (N^6).

Figure 7.2

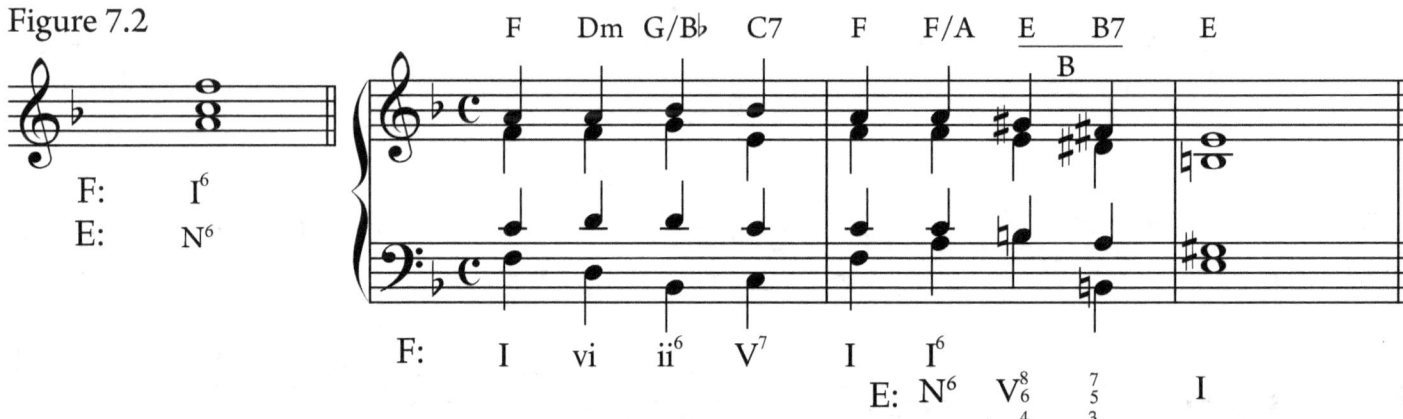

In Figure 7.3, Wagner's pivot chord (A flat – C – E flat) is diatonic in the original key (VI of C minor) and altered in the new key (N in G minor). Since the modulation is to a closely related key, Wagner could have used a pivot chord that was diatonic in both keys, but he chose to use a diatonic/altered-pivot chord, possibly for the addition of chromatic color.

Figure 7.3

Richard Wagner
Schmerzen
from Funf Gedichte (Wesendonck Lieder)

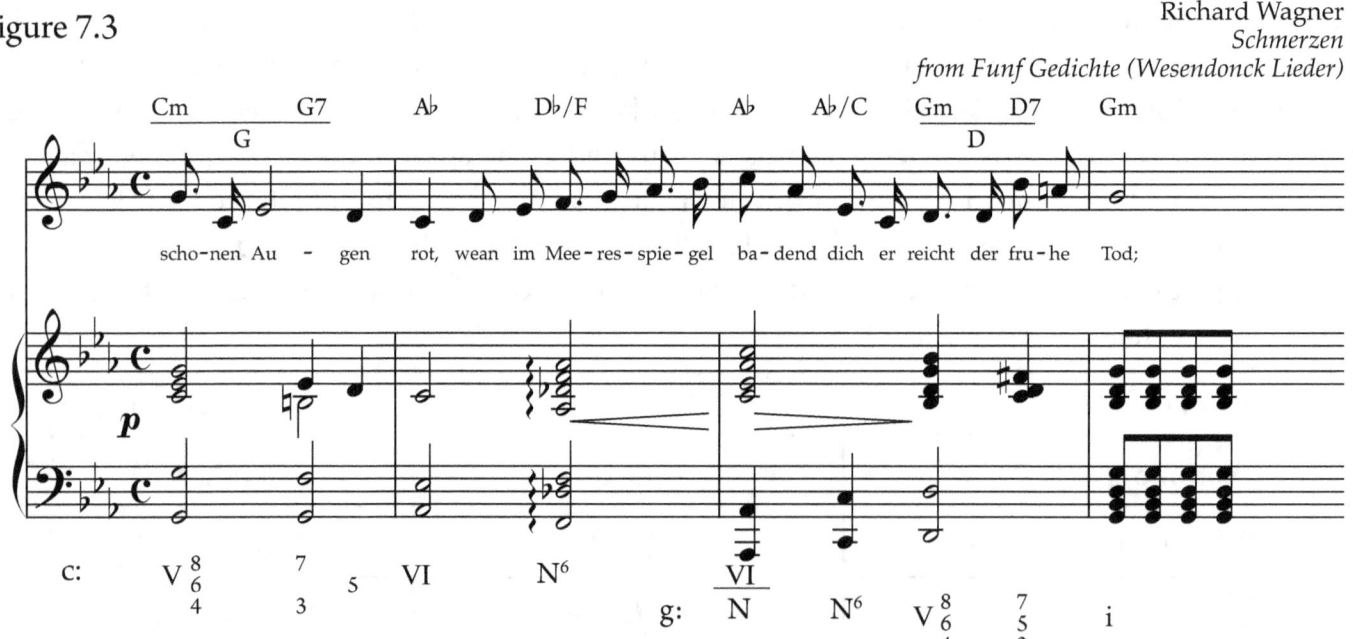

Altered/Diatonic Pivot Chords

In an altered/diatonic pivot relationship, the chord is altered in the first key and diatonic in the second. In the progression in Figure 7.4, the pivot chord C – E flat – A flat is an altered chord in G minor (N^6) and a diatonic chord in E flat major (IV^6).

Figure 7.4

In the example in Figure 7.5, the same pivot chord (C – E flat – A flat) is N^6 in G major and V^6 in D flat major. In a Neapolitan 6th chord, the third (here, C) is normally doubled. However, in a first inversion dominant chord, the third (again, C) is the leading tone, so it is not normally doubled. Because D-flat major is the new key in this progression, and because this chord functions not only as a pivot chord, but also as a dominant chord in an authentic cadence, the root, rather than the third, is doubled.

Figure 7.5

Occasionally, a pivot chord may be enharmonically respelled to reflect the key signature of the new key. In Figure 7.6, the N⁶ in B flat minor (E flat – G flat – C flat) may be respelled as IV⁶ in F sharp minor (B natural - D sharp – F sharp).

Figure 7.6

In Figure 7.7, Mozart uses a pivot chord that is altered (and respelled enharmonically) in the first key and diatonic (and spelled correctly in the second key).

Figure 7.7

Wolfgang Amadeus Mozart
Symphony No. 39 in E flat major
K 543 (4th mvt.)

Altered/Altered Pivot Chords

In an altered/altered, pivot relationship, the pivot chord is altered in both keys. The chord in Figure 7.8 is an altered chord (V⁷/IV) in both G major and (enharmonically respelled) in B major (Ger⁶): F natural and E sharp, are enharmonically equivalent.

Figure 7.8

Chapter 7: Modulation

The progression in Figure 7.9 illustrates an altered/altered pivot chord relationship in a modulation from G major to B major. Play this progression, and examine the resolution of the pivot chord: the 7th of V^7 normally resolves downward, but the augmented 6th of the Ger^6 usually resolves upward. In a pivot chord relationship, the resolution is determined by the chord that follows the pivot, whether the pivot is spelled in the new key or the old key. Here, the pivot is spelled as V^7/IV in G major. It resolves to V in B major, so this chord resolves as a German 6th chord: the F natural – acting as the augmented 6th, but spelled enharmonically - rises to F sharp.

Figure 7.9

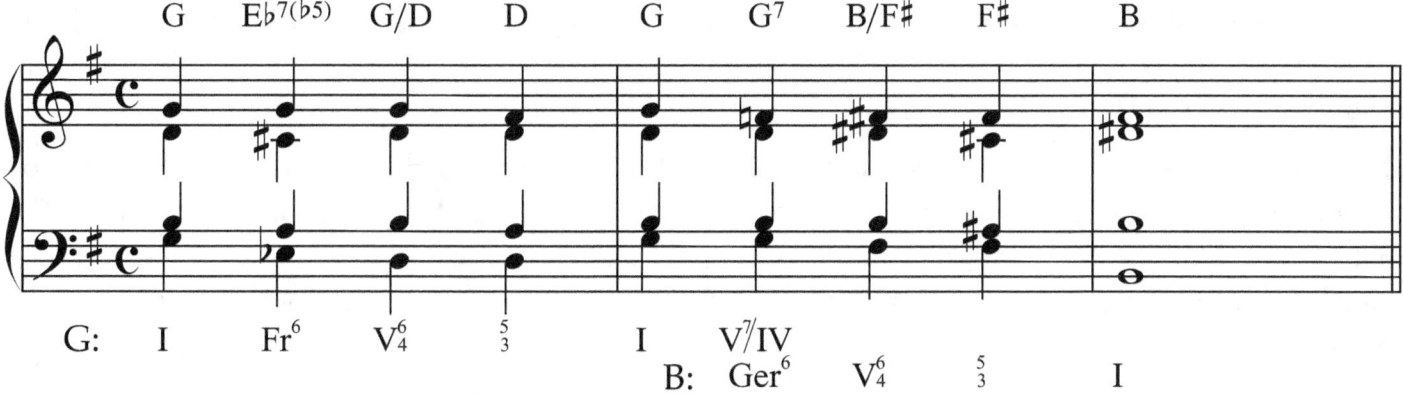

In Figure 7.10, the pivot chord is altered in both keys. In the first key (A flat minor), this chord is a Fr^6 built on $\flat\hat{2}$. In the second key (D flat major), it is a Fr^6 built on $\flat\hat{6}$.

Figure 7.10

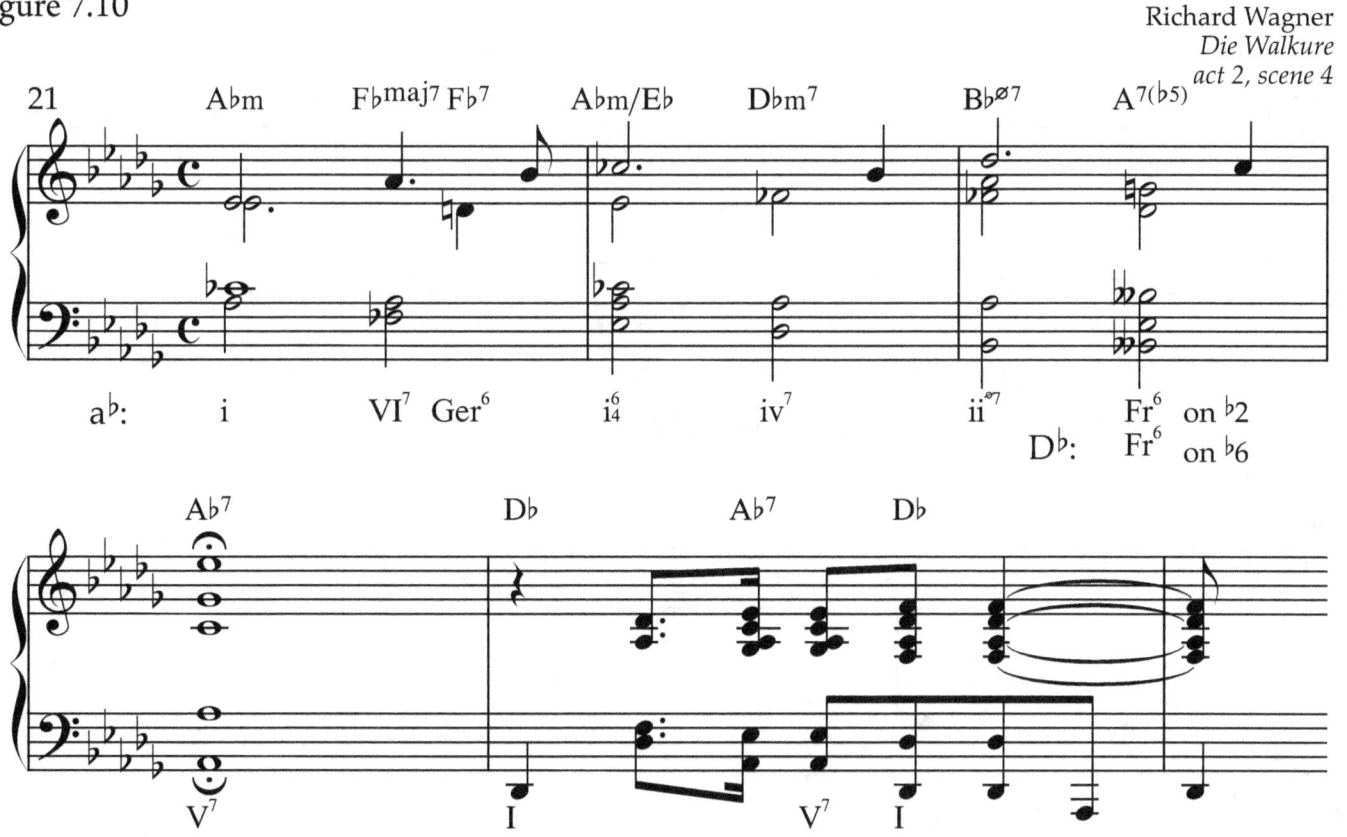

Richard Wagner
Die Walkure
act 2, scene 4

Chapter 7: Modulation

Using Altered Pivot Chords in a Modulation

The procedure for writing a modulation, using a diatonic pivot chord is discussed in *Essential Music Theory Level 10*:

1. Establish the original key.
2. Select a suitable pivot chord.
3. Follow this chord with a dominant chord in the new key and resolve it to a tonic function chord.

The procedure for writing a modulation using an altered, pivot chord is similar, but the choice of keys is much wider. First, you must establish which keys you will use in the modulation and explore the possible pivot chords available in these keys. For example, if you want to modulate from C major to E major, you might choose IV of C major (F – A – C), which is a Neapolitan chord in E major. This would be a diatonic/altered, pivot chord relationship.

If you decide to use a specific pivot relationship, such as a borrowed chord, in the modulation, you need to explore the possible keys to which you can modulate using that particular pivot chord. For instance, the borrowed chord iv in A major (D – F – A) can become ii in C major, vi in F major, or a chord in another key. There are several other choices, depending on the key to which you choose to modulate.

Here are the steps involved in writing a modulation using an altered chord. In Figure 7.11 We will create a progression that modulates from C major to B-flat major. Follow through this example by filling in the upper voices, according to the bass line and the chord symbols provided.

1. Write a progression that establishes the first key in C major.

Figure 7.11

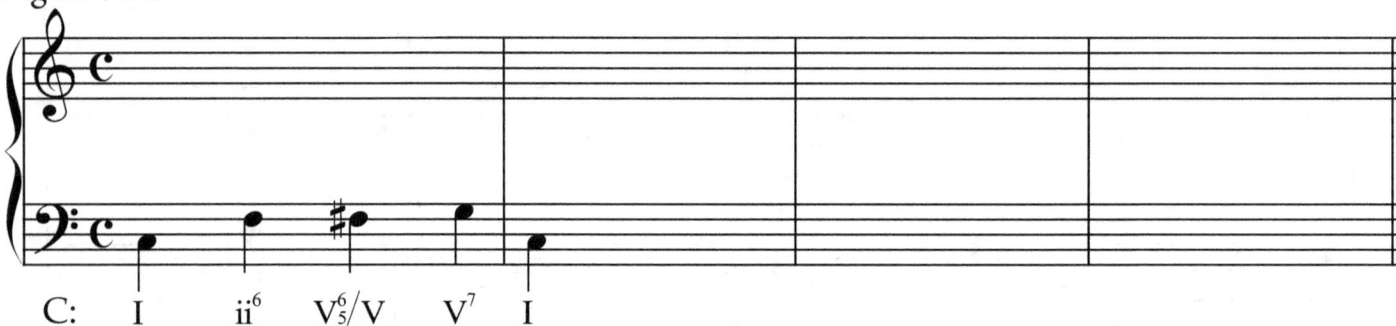

2. Select an appropriate pivot chord. Here we will use E - G – C, which is I^6 in C major and N^6 in B major.

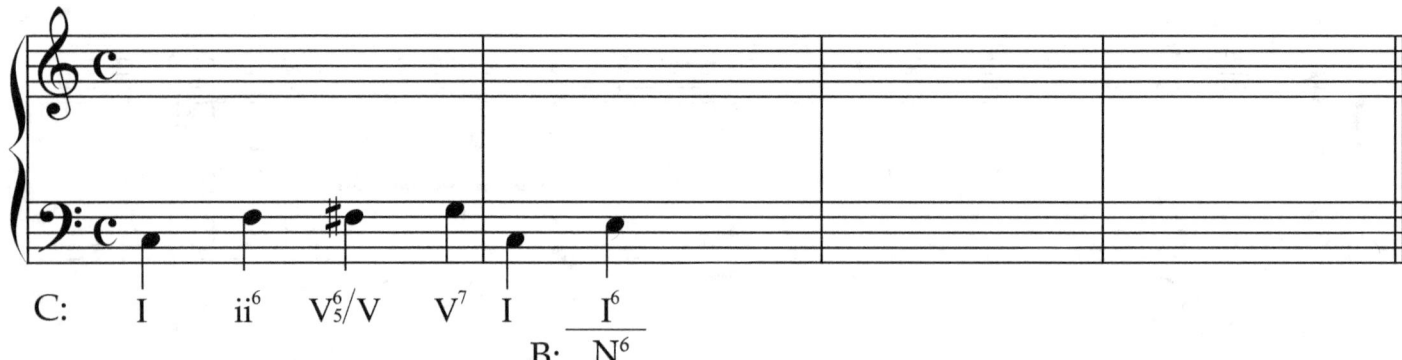

3. Write a cadence in the new key, and complete the exercise by writing a progression that will establish the tonality of the new key.

C: I   ii⁶   V⁶₅/V   V⁷   I   I⁶
B: N⁶   V⁸₆ ⁷₅₃   I   I⁶   ii⁶   V⁷   I

1. Using the given chord symbols, add soprano, alto, and tenor voices to the following bass line.

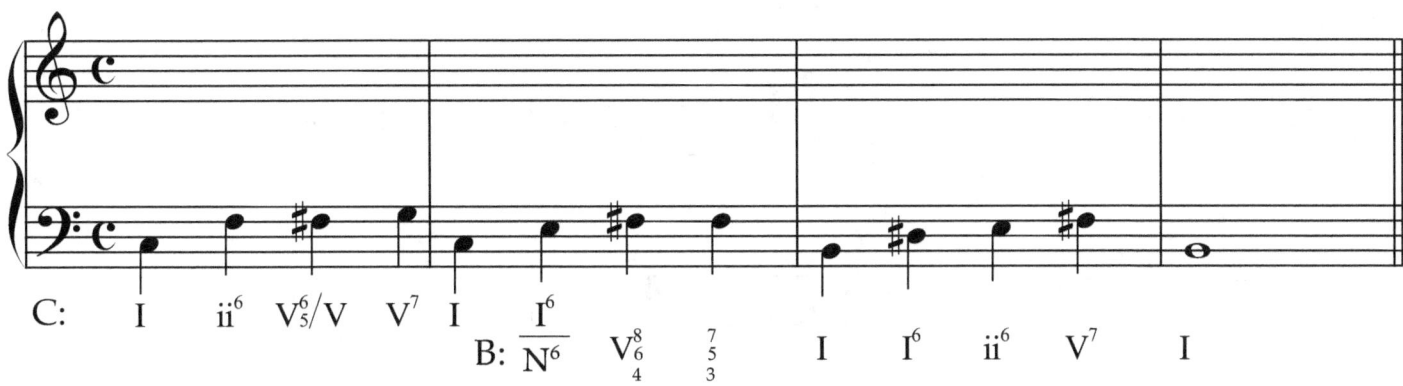

C: I   ii⁶   V⁶₅/V   V⁷   I   I⁶
B: N⁶   V⁸₆ ⁷₅₃   I   I⁶   ii⁶   V⁷   I

2. Complete the following chart by writing the root/quality chord symbols and adding the missing functional chord symbols.

Original Key: G major	Pivot Chord	Distantly Related Key: B flat major
_____ (diatonic)		V/ii or VI (altered)
_____ (altered)		V⁷/ii (altered)

Chapter 7: Modulation

Original Key: G major	Pivot Chord	Distantly Related Key: B flat major
i (altered)	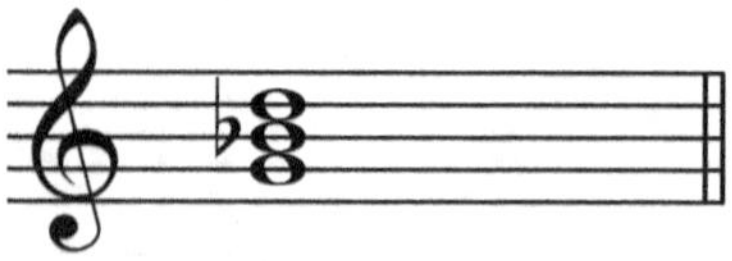	_____ (diatonic)
___ or ___ (altered)	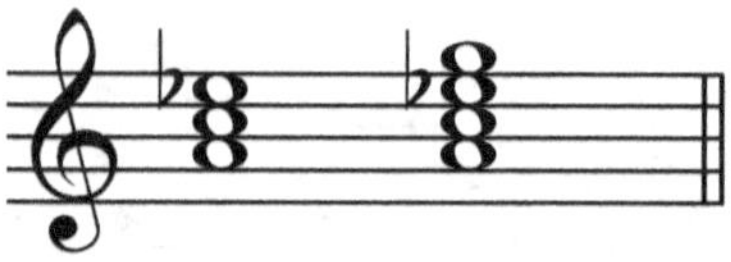	vii° or vii°7 (diatonic)
_____ (altered)	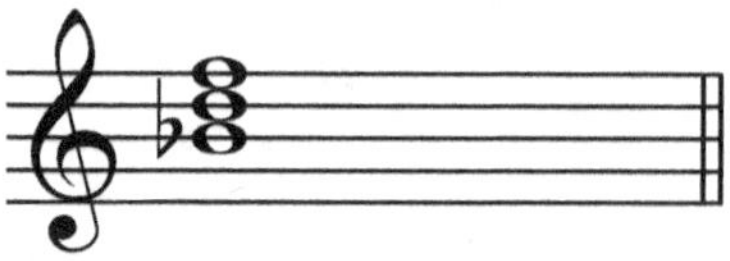	I (diatonic)
IV (diatonic)	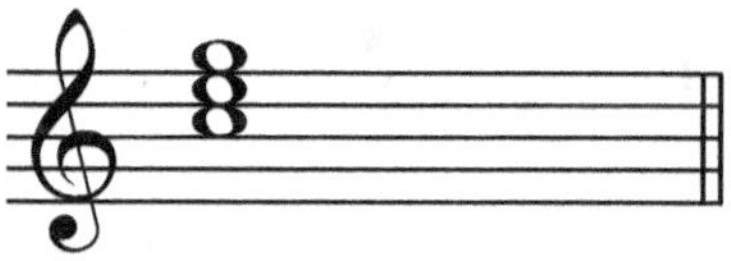	_____ (altered)
_____ (altered)	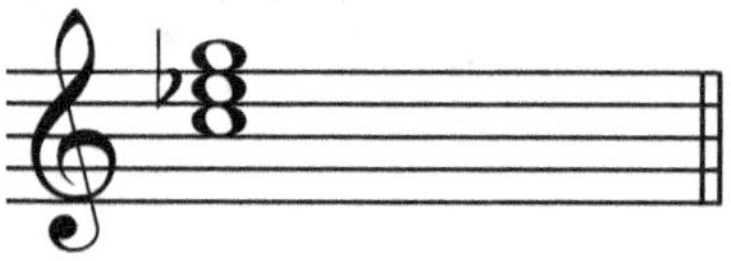	ii (diatonic)
___ or ___ (diatonic)	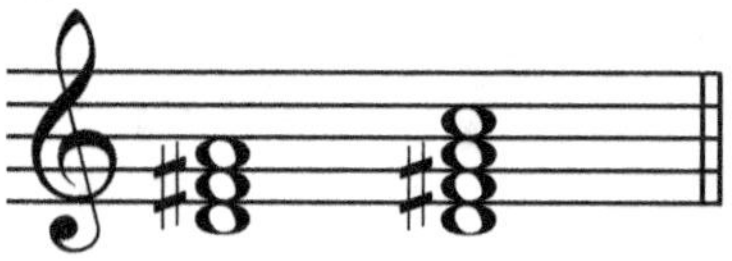	V/vi or III or V7/vi (altered)
_____ (altered)	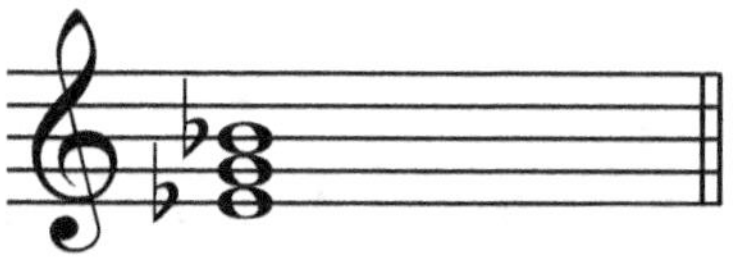	IV (diatonic)
_____ (altered)	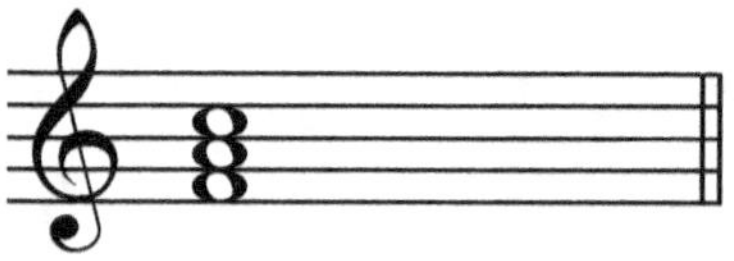	V (diatonic)

3. Write a progression containing a modulation from F major to E major using I⁶ in F major (N⁶ in E major) as the pivot chord. Choose your own time signature and length.

114

Chapter 7: Modulation

4. Write a progression containing a modulation from D major to F major using Gm as the pivot chord. Provide a functional harmonic analysis and give symbols for the pivot chord in both keys. Choose your own time signature and length.

5. Write a modulation with an altered/diatonic pivot relationship. Begin in G major and use N^6 of G major as the altered pivot chord. This chord will become V^6 (the diatonic equivalent) in the new key. Choose your own time signature and length.

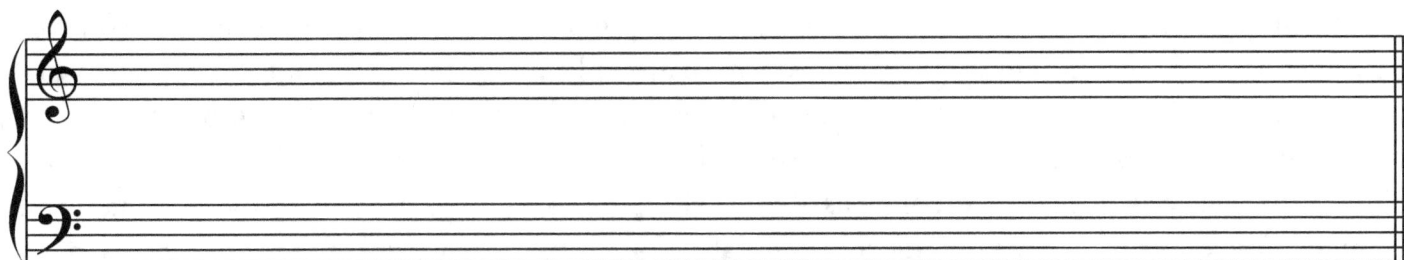

6. Write a modulation with a diatonic/altered pivot relationship. Begin in C major and use iii of C major as the diatonic pivot chord. This chord will become iv (a borrowed chord) in the new key. Choose your own time signature and length.

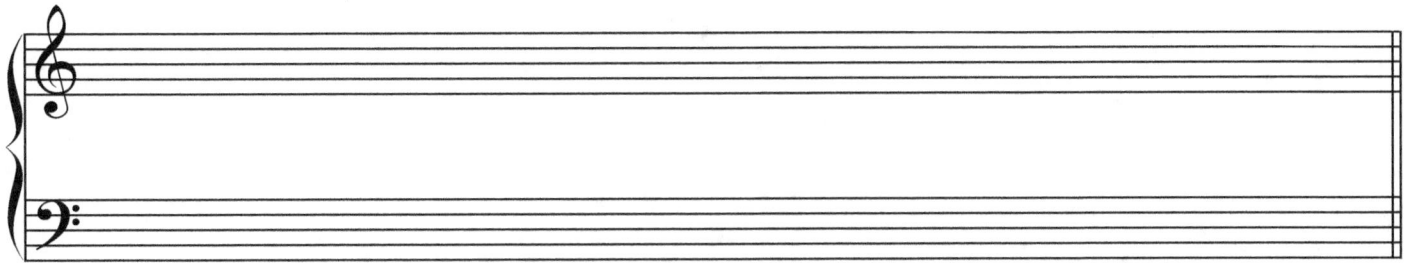

Reinterpretation of the German 6th Chord

As established earlier in this book, the German 6th chord has the same sonority as a major–minor 7th chord. Thus, a German 6th may be respelled as a dominant 7th in another key. Alternatively, a dominant 7th may be repelled as a German 6th. Both cases involve an enharmonic respelling of the chord. This combination is an effective pivot chord for modulations that shift up or down a half step. Notice the root/quality spelling of these chords. Root/quality chord symbols do not show the function of the chord, just what the chord is. This makes is easier to play from a lead sheet.

Figure 7.12

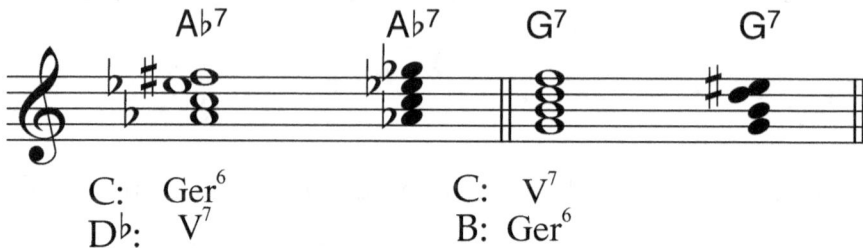

Although a half step is the closest distance between two pitches in a scale, tonally it can be the furthest possible distance away. For example, C and C-sharp are only a half step apart, but the key signatures of C major and C sharp major differ by seven sharps. A modulation between C minor and C sharp minor, the distance of one half step, can be easily achieved by using an enharmonic respelling of a Ger⁶ chord. The Ger⁶ of C Minor is respelled as V⁷ of C sharp minor: only one note (F sharp) remains unchanged. The other three notes of the chord, A flat – C – E flat are respelled as G sharp – B sharp – D sharp.

Figure 7.13

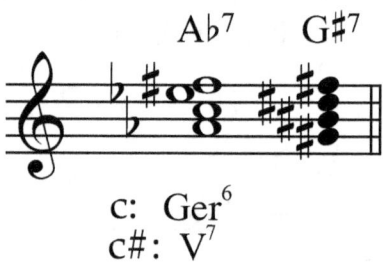

In Figure 7.14 the chord on the second beat of m.121 sounds like a Ger⁶ in C minor. The augmented 6th interval (A flat – F sharp) has been re-spelled enharmonically as a minor seventh (G sharp – F sharp). Beethoven has spelled this chord as V^7 in C-sharp, minor, and it resolves to i in C sharp minor, confirming the modulation that shifts the music up one half step.

Figure 7.14

Play this excerpt and pay special attention to the resolution of V^7. In keyboard textures, the seventh of a dominant 7th often resolves upward by step. Beethoven's choice of an upward resolution here is likely based on keyboard voice-leading for a dominant 7th, rather than the normal tendency of an augmented 6th to rise. In four voice (SATB) textures, the resolution of enharmonic pivot chords should be based on the new key, rather than the key that has just been left.

In Figure 7.15, Schubert uses the V^7/Ger^6 pivot chord relationship to modulate down one half step from G flat major to F minor. In m. 46, the dominant 7th of G flat major is spelled D flat – F – A flat – C flat, but on the last beat of m. 47, Schubert changes the spelling to D flat – F – A flat – B, which is the Ger^6 in F minor. The German 6th resolves to cadential six-four in F minor, confirming the new tonality.

Figure 7.15

Franz Schubert
Gefrorne Tranen from Winterreise
op. 89, D 911

7. Name the keys of the following German 6th chords built on ♭$\hat{6}$. Respell each one enharmonically as a dominant 7th chord and identify the new keys. Add root/quality chord symbols for each.

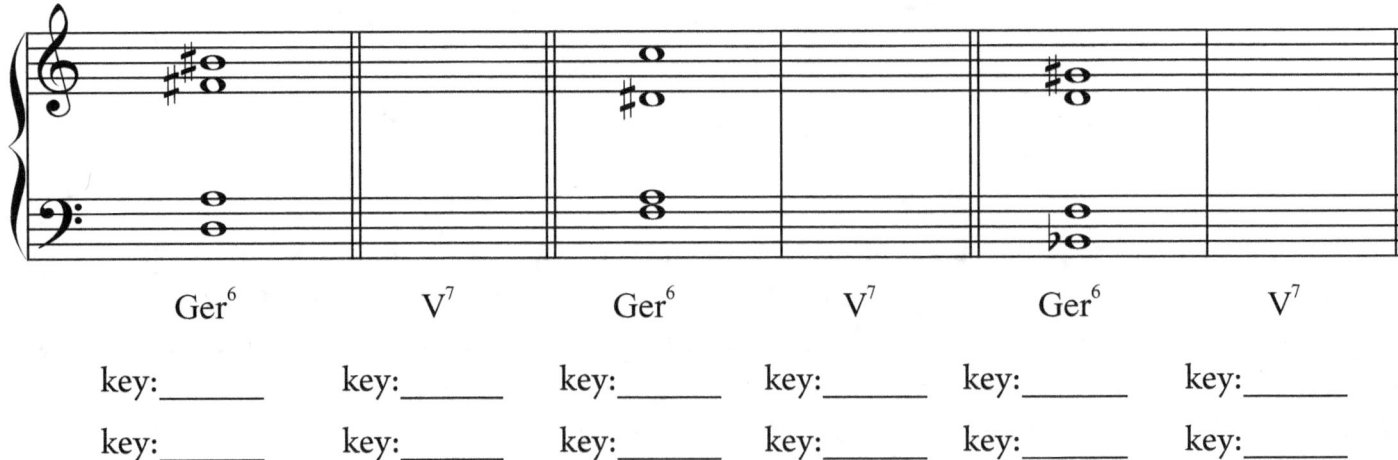

8. Name the major and minor keys of the following dominant 7th chords. Respell each one enharmonically as a German 6th chord built on ♭$\hat{6}$ and identify the new key. Add root/quality chord symbols for each.

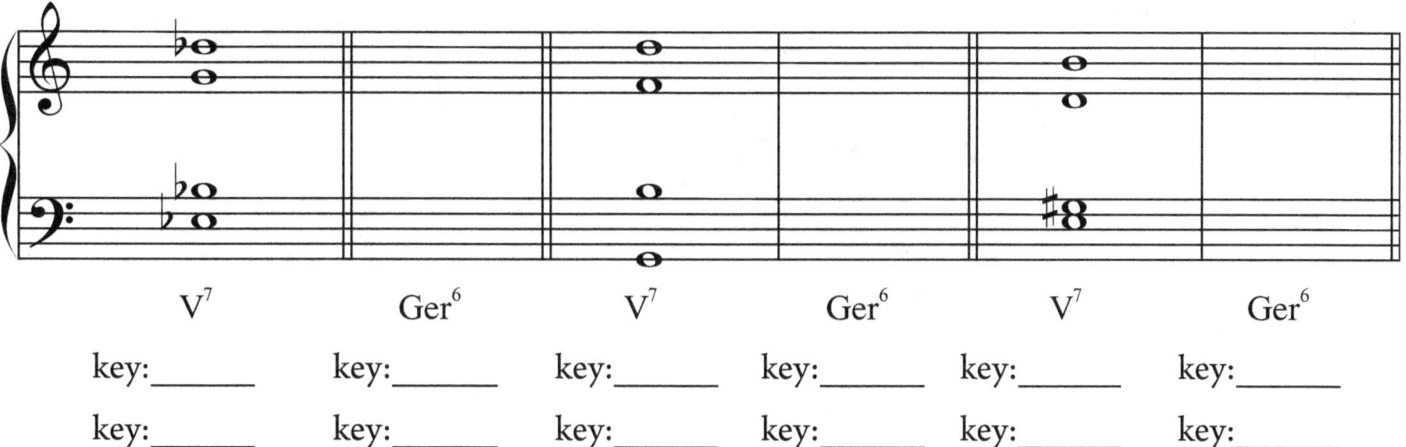

The German 6th chord can also be used in a modulation that moves up a major 3rd. As with modulations that shift a half step, this key change involves an enharmonic spelling of the dominant 7th chord. In this case, the chord is V^7/IV in the first key and Ger^6 in the second key.

In Figure 7.16, the chord in mm. 27–28 (A natural – C natural – E flat – G flat) functions as vii^{o7}/ii in A flat major, but it does not resolve as such. Instead, Beethoven moves to a chord that sounds like V^7/IV in A flat major. In the key of A flat major, V^7/IV would be spelled A flat – C – E flat – G flat, but this chord is spelled A flat – C – E flat – F sharp, which is the German 6th of C (major or minor). This chord resolves to a cadential six-four in C major, confirming the new tonality. In this case, Beethoven has chosen to modulate to the chromatic mediant – major III (C major) – rather than the diatonic mediant – minor iii (C minor), and he respelled V^7/IV in A flat major enharmonically as the Ger^6 in the new key of C major.

Figure 7.16

Ludwig van Beethoven
*Symphony no. 5 in C minor
op. 67 (2nd mvt.)*

9. Write the following V^7/IV chords in the first keys indicated. Respell each chord enharmonically as a German 6th on ♭$\hat{6}$ and name the new keys.

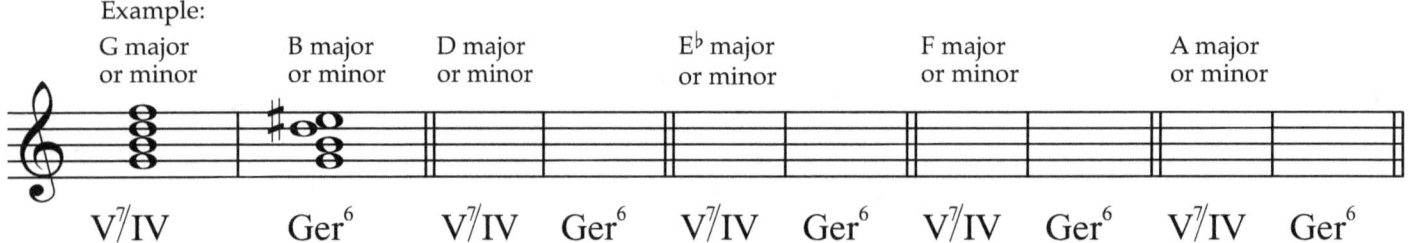

Three Modulations Using the German 6th Chord

1. To modulate from a major or minor key to a key that is one half step higher, write the Ger⁶ chord of the first key, but spell it as the V⁷ of the new key. Resolve this V⁷ chord to the tonic triad of the new key.

2. To modulate from a major or minor key to a key that is one half step lower, write the V⁷ in the first key, but spell it as the Ger⁶ of the new key. Resolve this Ger⁶ to a dominant – tonic progression in the new key.

3. To modulate from a major or minor key to a key that is a major 3rd higher, write V⁷/IV in the first key, but spell it as Ger⁶ of the new key. Resolve this Ger⁶ to a dominant - tonic progression in the new key.

10. Write progressions containing modulations using the Ger⁶ chord as a pivot. Begin with a progression establishing the first key, and complete each passage with progression in the new key.

(a) Modulate from C major to D♭ major

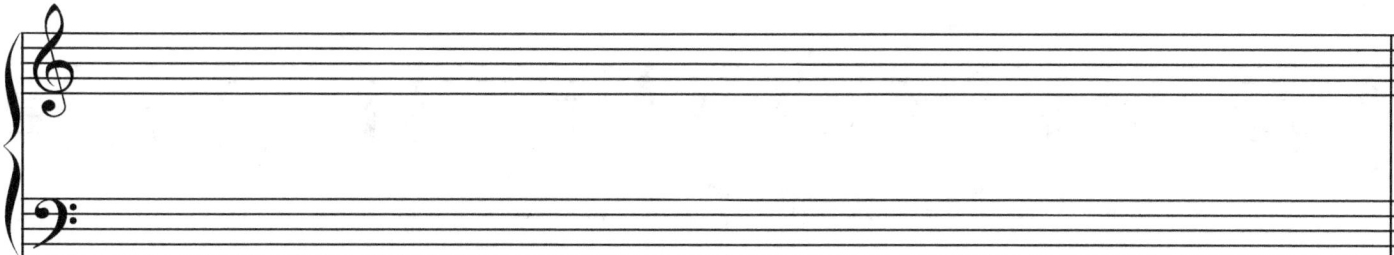

(b) Modulate from E♭ major to D minor

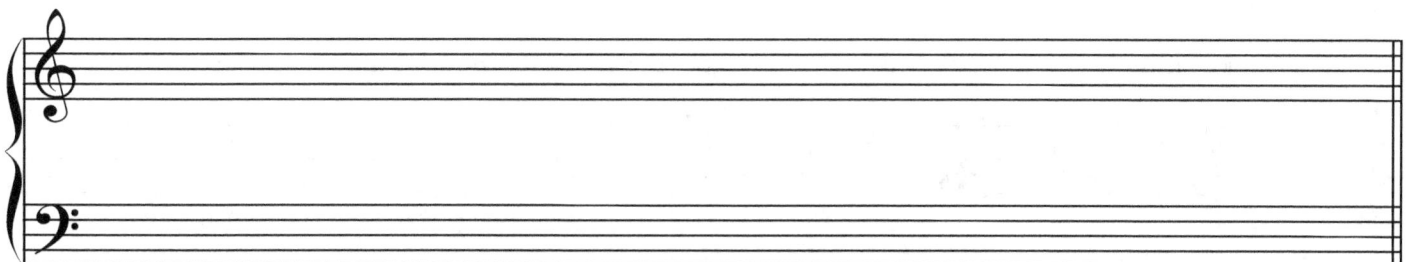

(c) Modulate from G major to B major

Reinterpretation of vii°7

The diminished 7th (vii°7) chord is a versatile chord in modulation. A single diminished 7th can be spelled in four different ways, allowing each tone to function as the root.

Figure 7.17

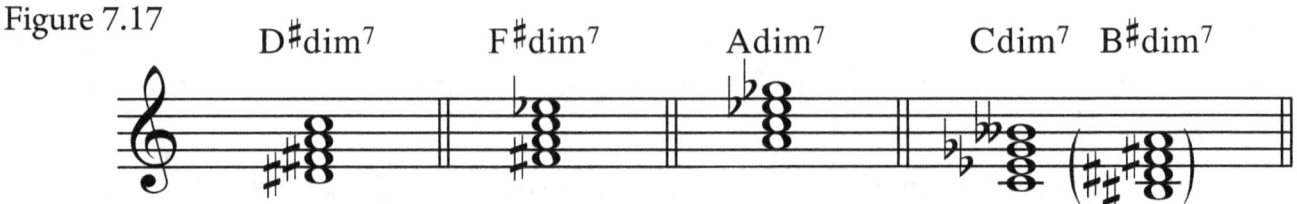

Since any of its four tones can function as a root, the vii°7 chord can be used as a pivot in a number of different keys. Figure 7.18 demonstrates this principle by starting with vii°7 of E Major, built on D sharp, the leading tone. The same sonority can be built on F sharp, A, and C, with each of these pitches acting as the leading tone. Each of these chords can be resolved to the tonic of a major key or it's parallel minor key.

Figure 7.18

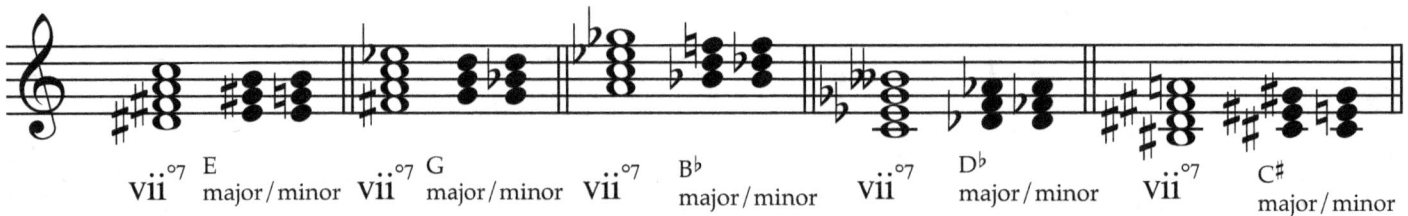

A vii°7 chord can have a variety of functions in a variety of keys. For example, it might be approached as vii°7/V in one key and left as a diminished 7th of another key, just by respelling the chord.

Figure 7.19

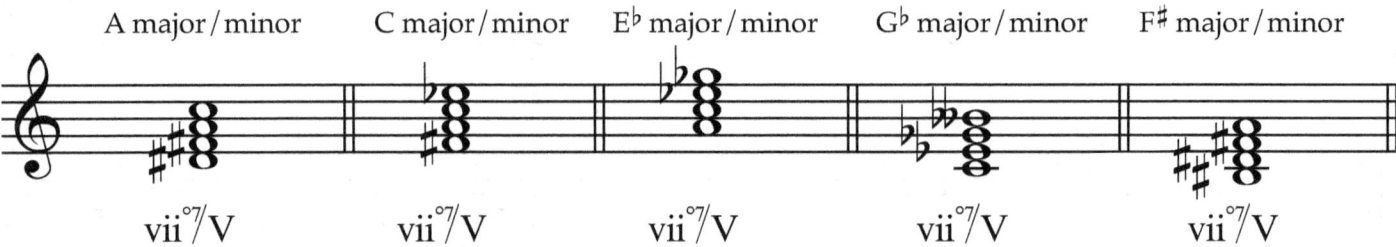

In addition, the position of vii°7 can be respelled to represent different inversions in different keys. All four chords in Figure 7.18 sound alike.

Figure 7.20

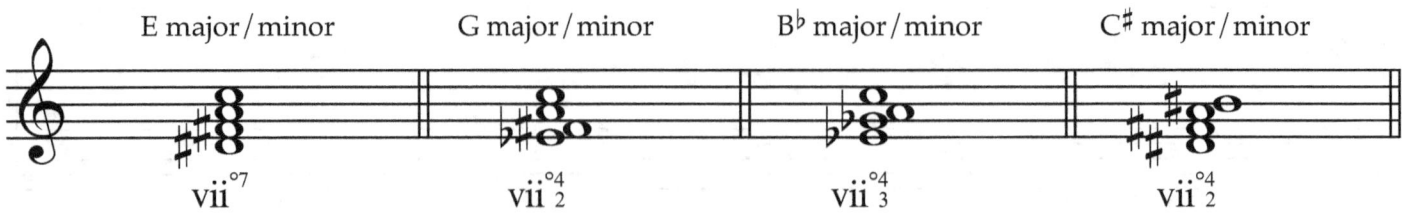

11. Write and resolve vii°7 chords in the following keys. Rewrite each chord in three other keys, keeping the bass note in the same place, but respelling it enharmonically as needed. Name each key, and resolve the vii°7 to the tonic triad. Provide functional chord symbols for each progression.

Figure 7.21 contains a modulation from C major to E flat major. The diminished 7th that is used as a pivot chord (F sharp – A – C – E flat) is spelled as vii°7 of V (G) in C major, but it also functions as vii°4/2 of V in E flat major. Its correct spelling in the key of E flat major would be A – C – E flat – G flat. Haydn resolves the diminished 7th to a cadential six-four in E flat major, confirming the new tonality.

Figure 7.21

Franz Joseph Haydn
String Quartet in G major
op. 54, no. 1, Hob.III: 58 (2nd mvt.)

Note that the seventh (F sharp/G flat) does not resolve down by step but instead skips to B flat, and the A flat and E flat also move by a skip rather than a step. This voice-leading is acceptable in a string quartet, texture, but in conventional four-voice writing you should follow normal resolution rules.

Using Diminshed 7ths in a Modulation

There are many options for modulation using a diminished 7th chord as a pivot. Figure 7.22 contains an example of a modulation from F major to B major and demonstrates a four step procedure for choosing the correct diminished 7th chord as a pivot.

1. Write a progression establishing the key (here, F major).
2. Examine the vii°7 chord of this key. (In F major, is E – G – B flat – D flat).
3. Determine whether this chord can be used as in the new key. The vii°7 chord in B major is A sharp – C sharp – E – G. This is an enharmonic spelling of E – G – B flat – D flat in second inversion. A second approach is to determine whether vii°7 of the first key can function as vii°7/V of the new key. You can also try vii°7/V in the original key as vii°7 or vii°7/V of the new key.
4. Write the modulation using the chosen, pivot chord, resolve the diminished 7th, and write a progression to establish the new tonality (here, B major).

Figure 7.22

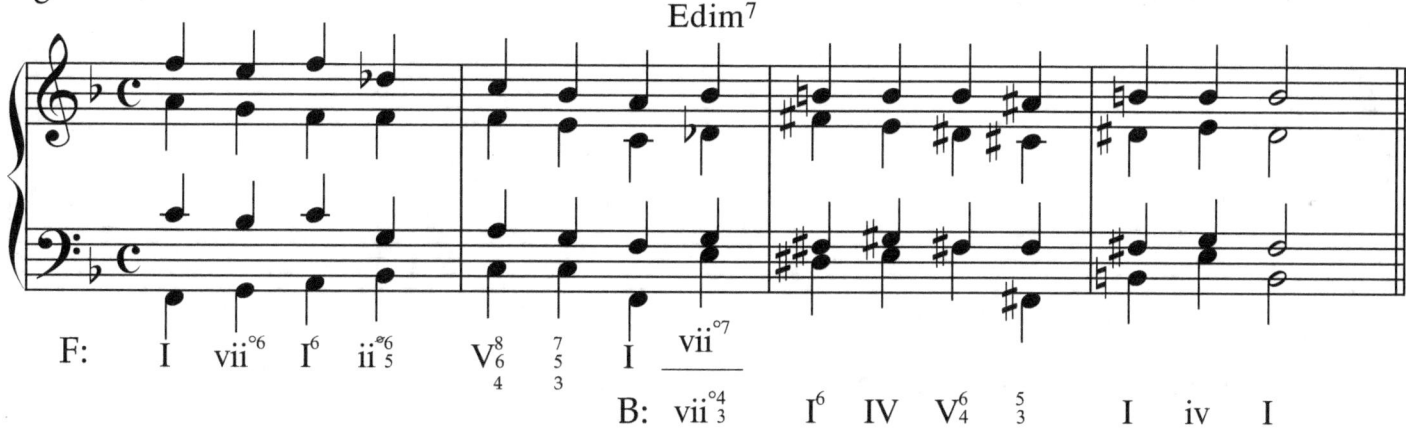

12. Write the following progression for four voices.

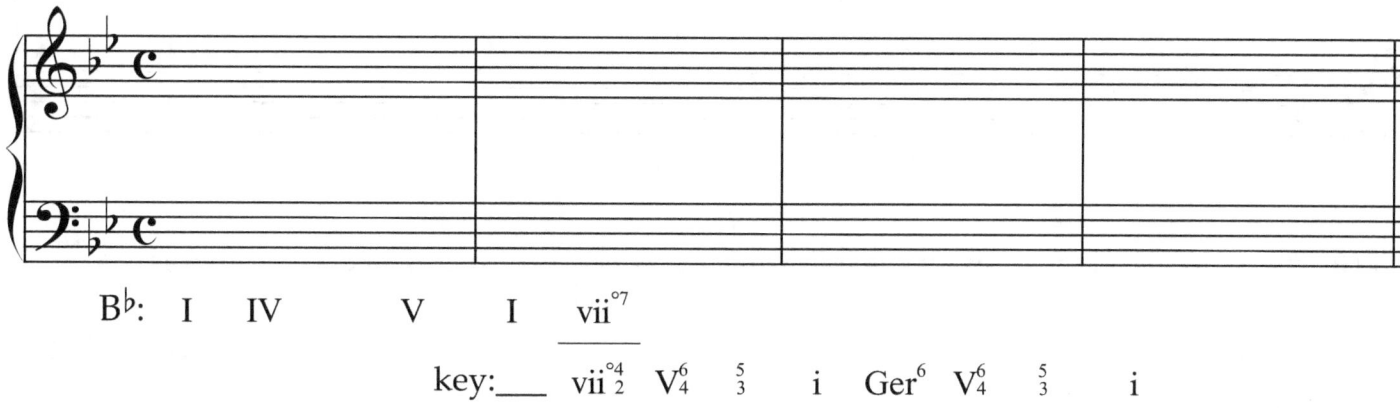

13. Write progressions containing the following modulations. Use an enharmonic reinterpretation of vii°7 as a pivot in each modulation.

(a) Modulate from C# minor to G major

(b) Modulate from G minor to E♭ major

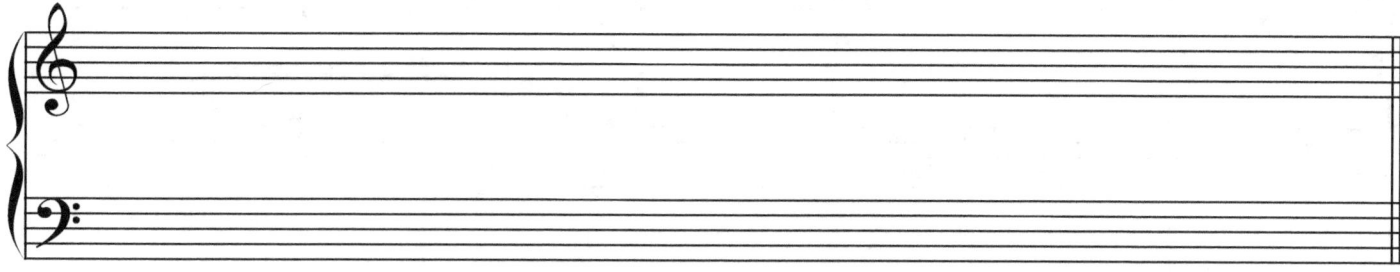

(a) Modulate from E♭ major to D major

(a) Modulate from A minor to D♭ major

14. Provide a harmonic analysis for the following excerpts using functional chord symbols.

Franz Joseph Haydn
String Quartet in C major
op. 74, no. 1, Hob.III: 72 (2nd mvt.)

Franz Joseph Haydn
String Quartet in Eb major
op. 76, no. 6, Hob.III: 80 (2nd mvt.)

15. Name the keys. Complete the following passages for four voices (SATB) according to the functional chord symbols.

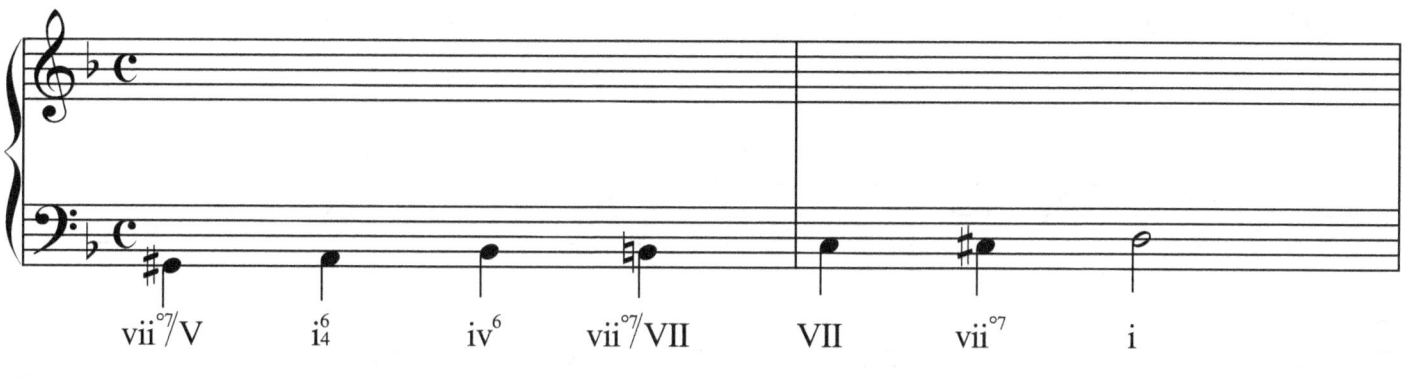

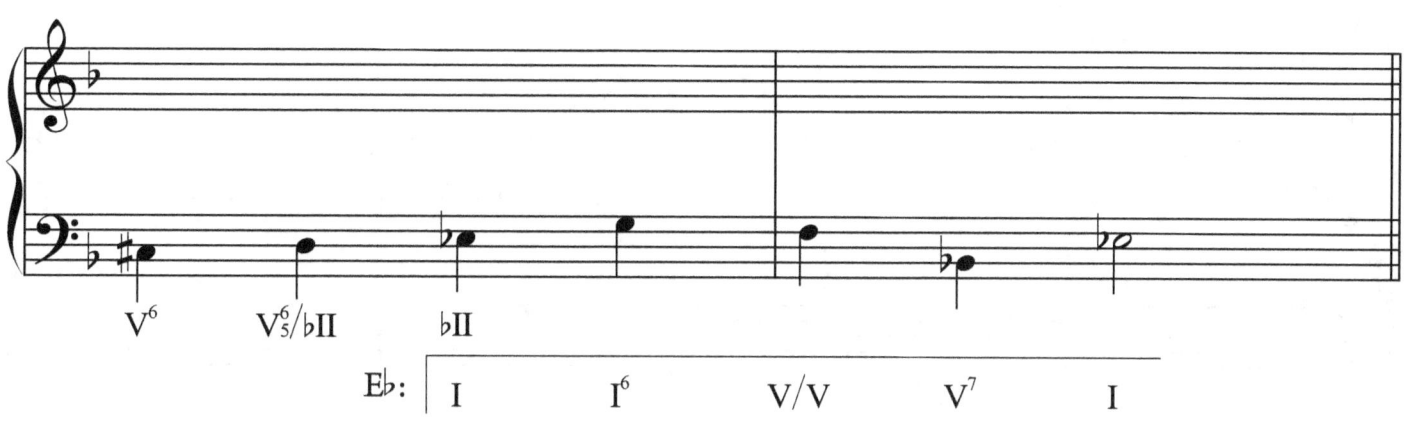

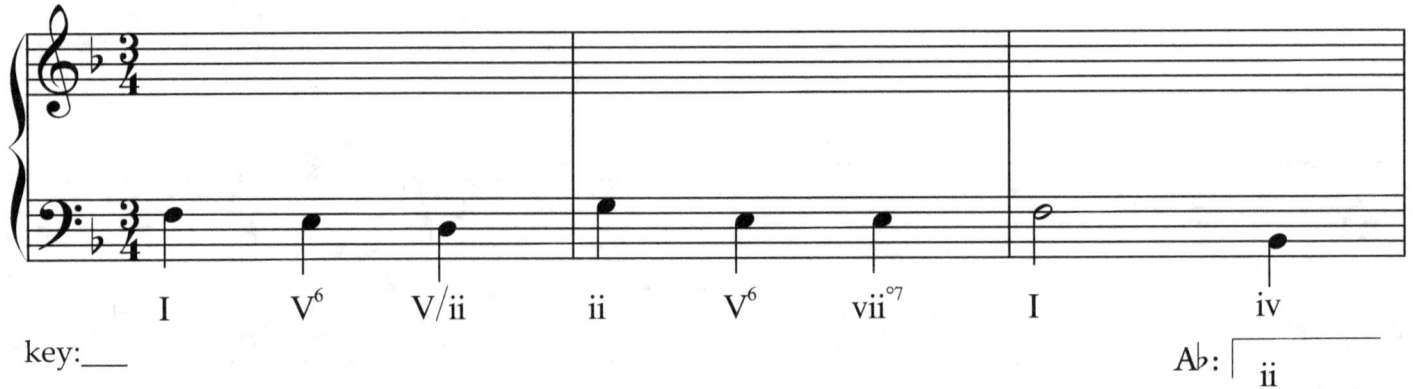

key:___

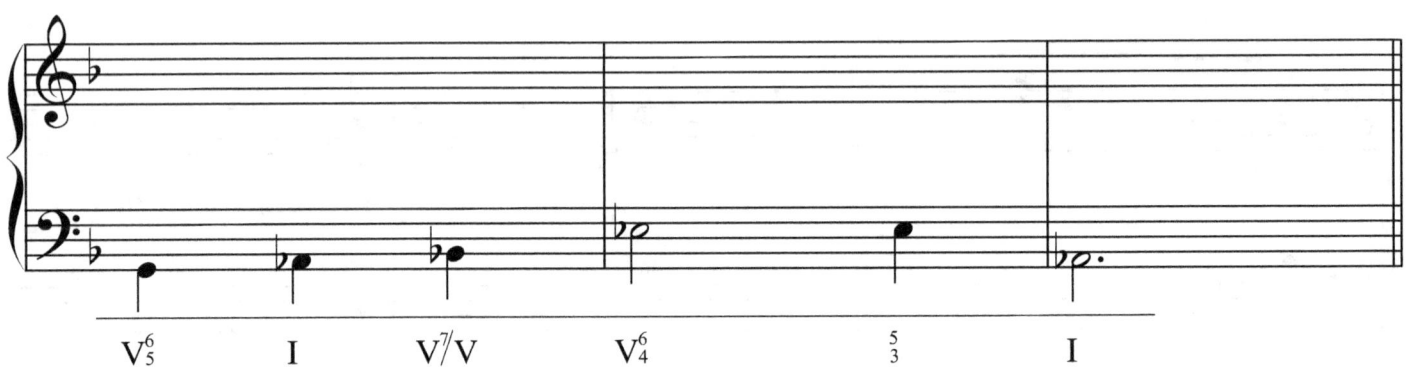

16. Name the key and complete the following progrression for four voices (SATB). Include a N⁶ chord, a Fr⁰³ chord and a V¹³ chord in the progression. Provide functional chord symbols.

key:___

17. Name the key and complete the following for four voices (SATB).

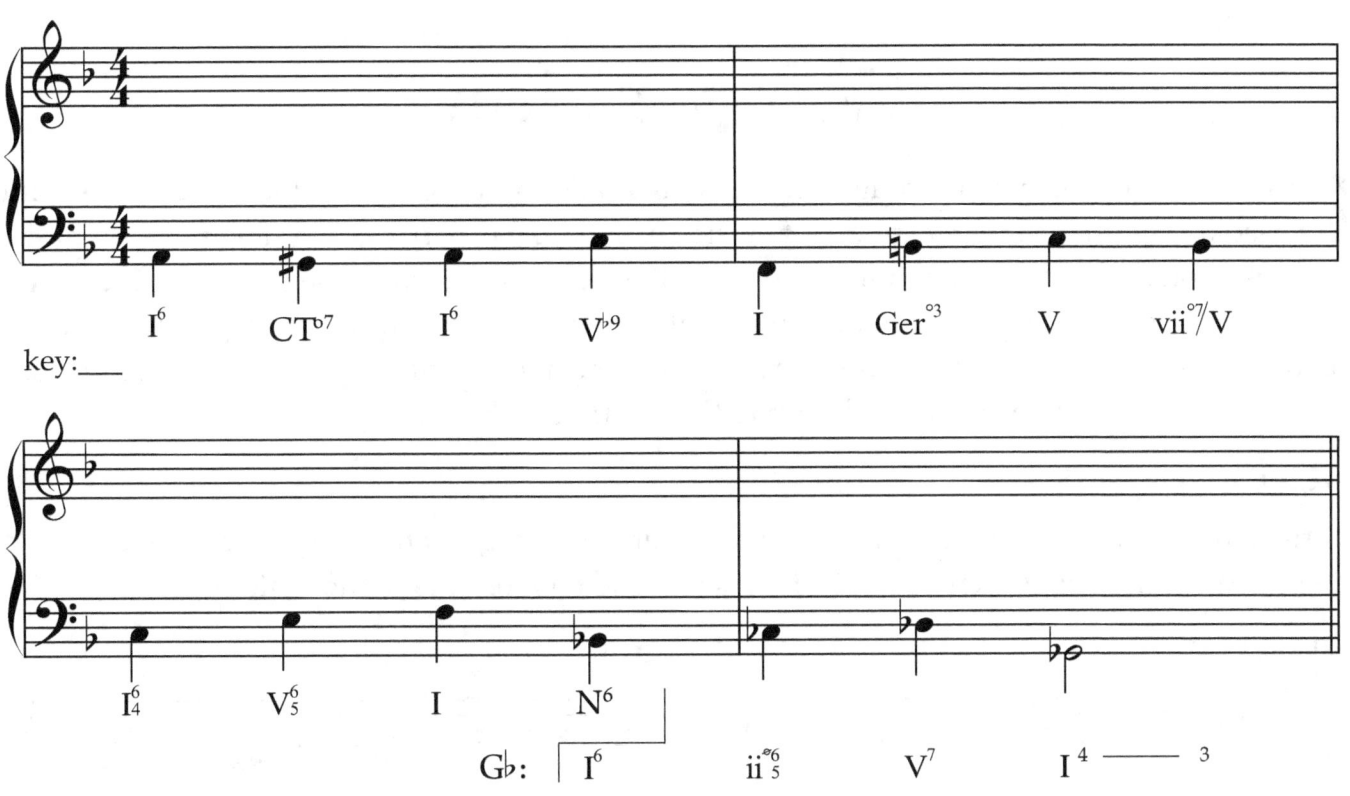

SUMMARY

1. Distantly related keys are keys with key signatures that differ by more than one accidental.

2. Modulation to a key that differs by more than three sharps or flats in the key signature requires an altered pivot chord in one or both of the keys involved in the modulation.

3. The four main pivot chord relationships are:

    diatonic/diatonic: The pivot is a diatonic chord in both the original key and the new key.

    diatonic/altered: The pivot is a diatonic chord in the original key and an altered chord in the new key.

    altered/diatonic: The pivot is an altered chord in the original key and a diatonic chord in the new key.

    altered/altered: The pivot is an altered chord in both the original key and the new key.

4. A German 6th chord has the same sonority as a major – minor 7th chord. This chord is an effective pivot chord and is often re-spelled enharmonically as V^7 of another key. This chord is useful for modulations that move up or down one half step.

5. Modulation to a key that is a major 3rd above the tonic of the old key can be achieved by using V^7/IV in the first key as a pivot chord, but respelling it enharmonically as a German 6th of the new key.

6. Because diminished 7th chords have many possible options for resolution, and because their roots are ambiguous, they are effective in modulations to distantly related keys. Their neutral quality makes them easy to approach and easy to leave.

8
Composition

This lesson will guide you through the steps involved in writing a short four voice composition based on a given opening fragment of music, maintaining the style of that fragment. In these assignments, you are expected to modulate to a specified key and return to the tonic key. The purpose of these exercises is to help you to develop a greater awareness and understanding of form, musical structure, and four part writing. These exercises give you an opportunity to apply all the knowledge you have acquired about harmony and form to the creation of short compositions.

Here is the typical assignment:

Continue the following opening fragment, maintaining the style, to create a composition that modulates to and cadences in the key of ♭VI (E flat major) and then returns to the tonic key.

Figure 8.1

Step 1: Analyze the Opening Fragment

It is important to make a complete harmonic analysis of the given fragment. Examine the harmonic rhythm and note the style. Is the tempo fast, slow, or moderate? What sort of non-chord tones are used? Are there any rhythmic motives?

The given opening in Figure 8.2 has a fairly straight forward harmonic structure. The harmony is mostly diatonic, with one borrowed chord in m. 2. The relatively fast harmonic rhythm – the harmonies change on each beat – suggests a slow to moderate tempo. The rhythm consists of quarter notes with a little eighth note motion for added movement and interest. The non-chord tones are passing tones or accented passing tones.

Figure 8.2

Step 2: Establish the Length and Form of the Composition

The next step is to establish an overall structure for the composition that will accommodate the required modulation and the return to the home key. Here is a 12 measure layout in rounded binary form. This structure will allow you to complete the opening phrase with a modulation to the new key, return to the home key at the end of the second phrase, and present a varied repetition of the opening fragment in the third phrase to unify the composition.

Figure 8.3

Chapter 8: Composition

Step 3: Write the Melody and Harmony

The final step is to create the melody and harmony, according to the structure you have established. Here is the finished composition. Note that the modulation to E flat major occurs at the end of the first phrase. The second phrase begins with a repetition of the opening phrase in the new key and then modulates back to G major, ending with a half cadence in G Major. Since the piece is in rounded binary form, the final phrase starts with a repeat of the opening fragment, but concludes with an authentic cadence in the tonic key of G major.

Figure 8.3

Guidelines for Modulations in a Four-Part Composition

The three step process will serve a basis for writing short compositions. Here are some important additional guidelines to keep in mind as you work on the modulations in short four-part compositions.

1. In short compositions, such as the one in Figure 8.3, you do not have to write a new key signature when you modulate to a different key. Note that in this example, the three flats for E flat major are written as accidentals.

2. The accidentals are very important. Make sure you include all the correct accidentals for the new key, and remember to cancel any unnecessary sharps or flats from the original key signature. In Figure 8.3, the F naturals in the second phrase are needed to cancel the F sharp in the key signature of G major.

3. Select pivot chords with care, and make sure they work correctly in both the original key and the new key. It helps to think of accidentals along with the letter names (E flat rather than just E) when choosing a pivot chord. For example, ii of C major and V of G major have the same letter names (D – F – A) but in G major the F is sharp. Take a second look at the pivot chords in Figure 8.3. In m. 3, the borrowed chord iv of G Major (C– E flat – G) is also the diatonic chord vi of E flat major. In m. 7, the diatonic chord IV^6 of E flat major (A flat – C – E flat) is also the N^6 of G major.

4. The harmony used to approach and follow pivot chords should be strong and logical. Do not surround a good pivot chord with weak harmonic progressions. If you use a dissonant chord as a pivot, take care to resolve it correctly.

5. Remember that aside from pivot chords, it is not necessary to use a lot of complex, chromatic harmony.

6. Melodic lines play an important role in defining a key, particularly in the soprano and the bass. Ending a phrase with a root position cadence, and the soprano on $\hat{1}$ will do more to clarify a key area than anything else. Take the time to mark the phrases, name the cadences, and plan both the melody and the bass line.

1. Continue the following opening fragment, maintaining the style, to create a composition that modulates to and cadences in the key of ♭II (D flat major) and then returns to the tonic key. Use a reinterpretation of the German 6th chord as a pivot from the principal key to the new key. Name the tonic key, write the functional chord symbols, and mark the phrasing. Label the pivot chord with root/quality chord symbols.

key:___

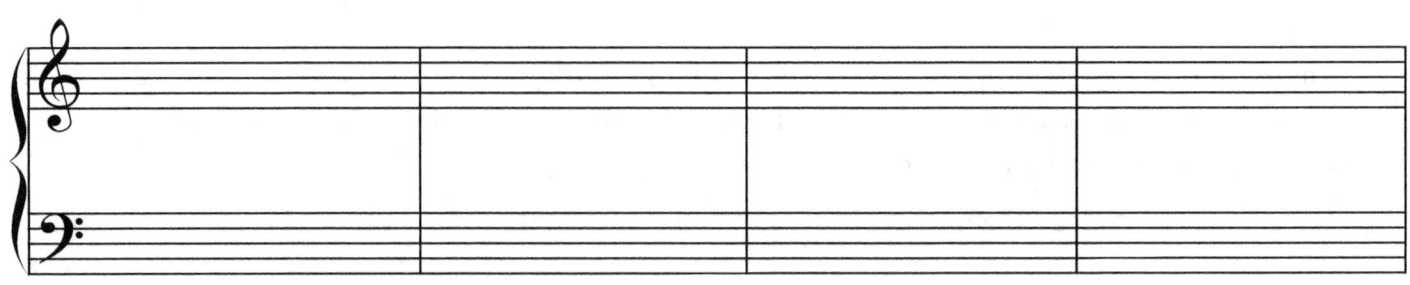

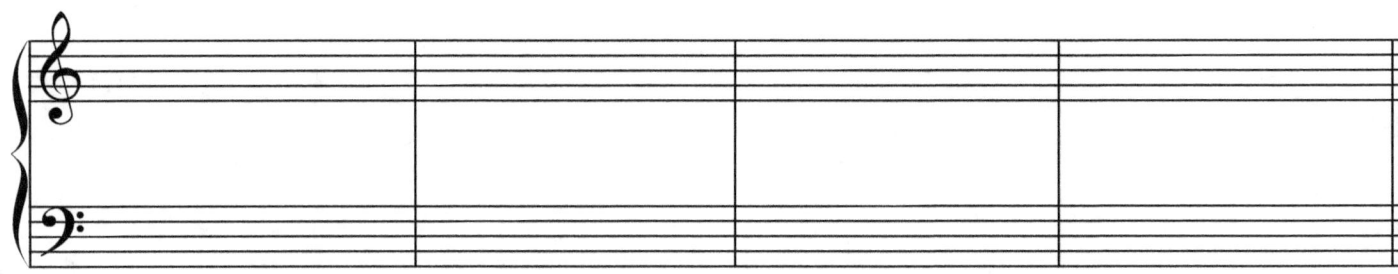

2. Continue the following opening fragment, maintaining the style, to create a composition that modulates to and cadences in the key of VI (E major) and then returns to the tonic key. Use a reinterpretation of the vii°7 as a pivot from the principal key to the new key. Name the tonic key, write the functional chord symbols, and mark the phrasing. Label the pivot chord with root/quality chord symbols.

key:___

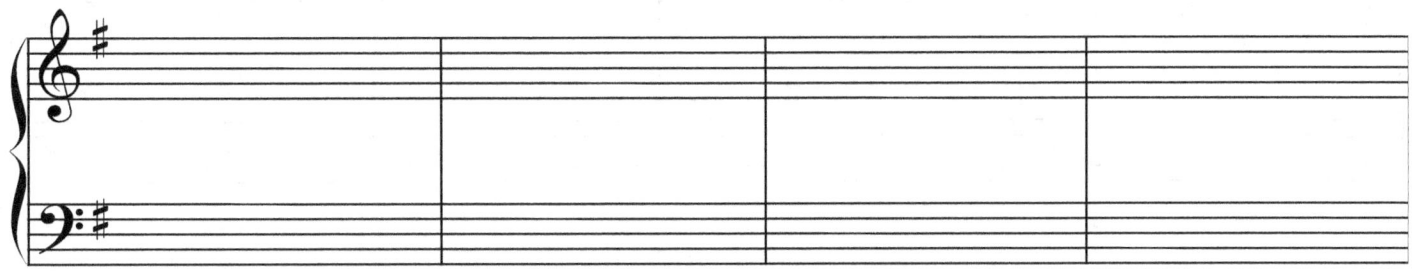

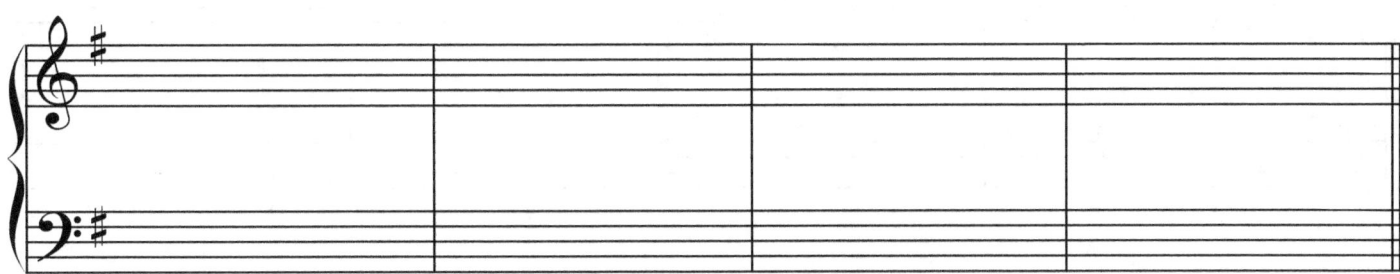

Chapter 8: Composition

3. Continue the following opening fragment, maintaining the style, to create a composition that modulates to and cadences in the key of ♯III (F sharp major) and then returns to the tonic key. Name the tonic key, write the functional chord symbols, and mark the phrasing. Label the pivot chord with root/quality chord symbols.

key:___

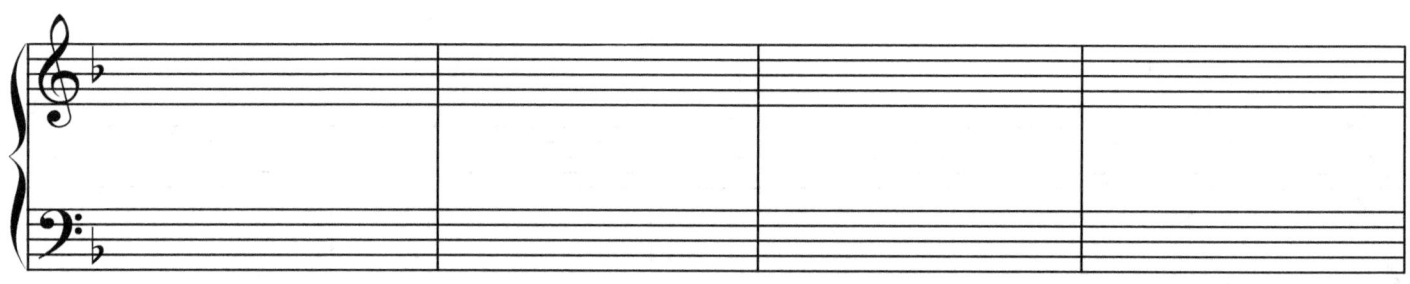

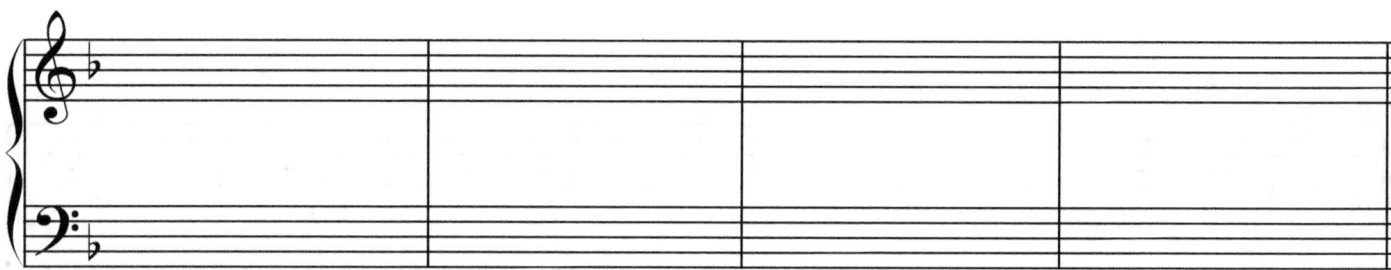

4. Continue the following opening fragment, maintaining the style, to create a composition that modulates to and cadences in the key of ♭VI (A flat major) and then returns to the tonic key. To modulate to the new key, use N^6 of the principal key. Use a different pivot chord to modulate back to the principal key. Name the tonic key, write the functional chord symbols, and mark the phrasing. Label the pivot chord with root/quality chord symbols.

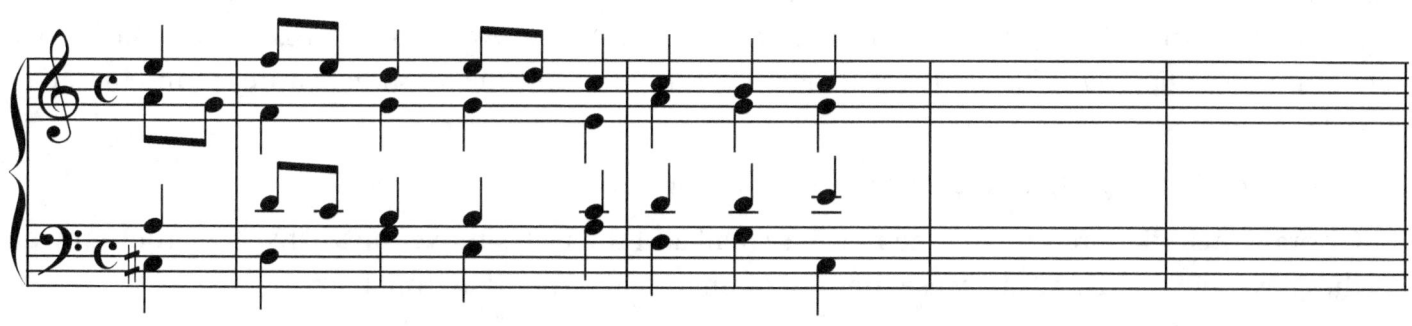

key:___

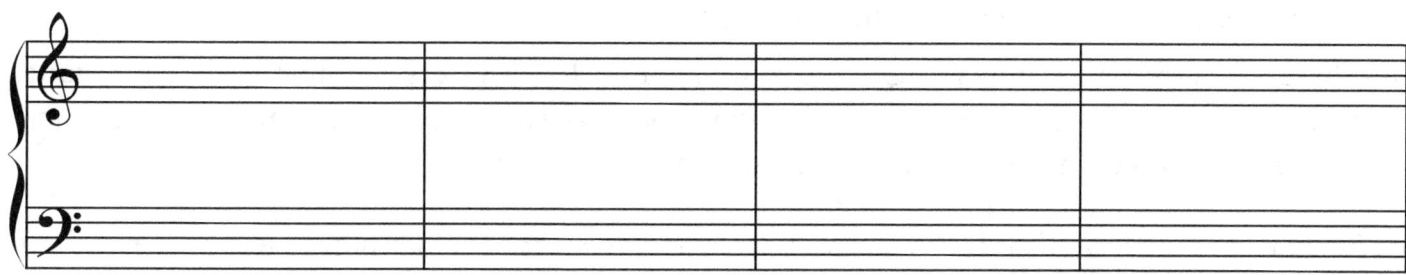

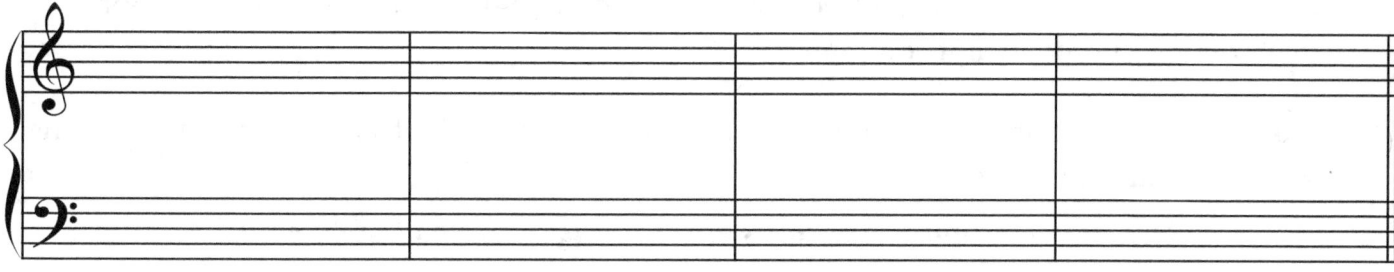

9
The Bach Chorales

The early hymn tunes of the German Protestant church are known as **chorales**. A number of composers wrote four-part harmonizations of the chorale tunes, and some of the finest examples are by Johann Sebastian Bach (1685–1750). Chorales are discussed extensively in *Essential Music Theory Level 9* and *Essential Music Theory Level 10*. Here is a short review of common features found in Bach's chorale settings.

1. Most chorales are in 4/4 time, but a few are in 3/4 time.
2. Chorale melodies are simple. The range is small and the notes move mostly by step. These melodies have few accidentals because they are often modal rather than tonal.
3. Each phrase ends with a *fermata* at the cadence.
4. The harmonizations are written for four voices (SATB) and each voice has an individual shape.
5. The texts are mainly set in syllabic style with one or perhaps two notes per syllable. Each voice sings the same word or syllable at the same time.
6. There is a fairly regular flow of eighth notes in the three lower voices. Common non-chord tones include passing tones, neighbouring tones, *appoggiaturas*, suspensions, and anticipations. *Échappées* and incomplete neighbours are used less frequently.

In *Essential Music Theory Level 11*, we have been studying chromatic harmony. Here are several important points about Bach's use of chromaticism in his chorale settings.

1. The chorale melodies contain very few accidentals, because they are often modal rather than tonal.
2. Bach uses chromaticism in the form of tonicicization or applied or secondary dominants.
3. Bach makes occasional use of borrowed chords, Neapolitan 6ths, and augmented 6th chords, but such chromatic chords are not common.

The following excerpts from Bach's chorale settings contain examples of some of the chromatic harmony we have studied in this text.

Note, however, that these chords are more the exception than the rule.

Borrowed Chords

Bach uses borrowed chords occasionally. The most common borrowed chord is the **picardy third** (or *tierce de picardie*) at the end of a chorale in a minor key. The borrowed chords in Figure 9.1 and 9.2 are indicated by asterisks (*).

Figure 9.1

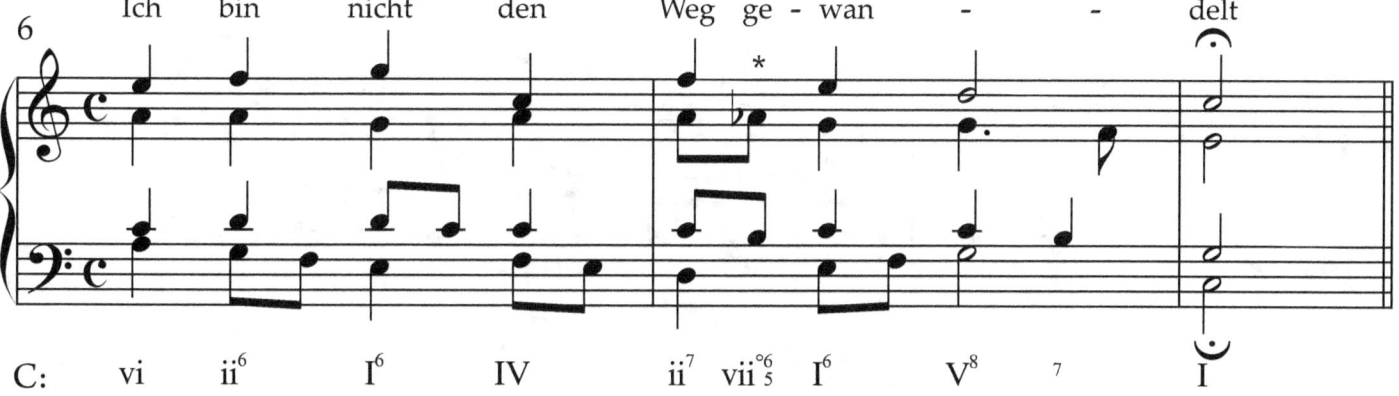

Johann Sebastian Bach
Chorale no. 6: Christus, der ist mein Leben
from 371 Four-Part Chorales

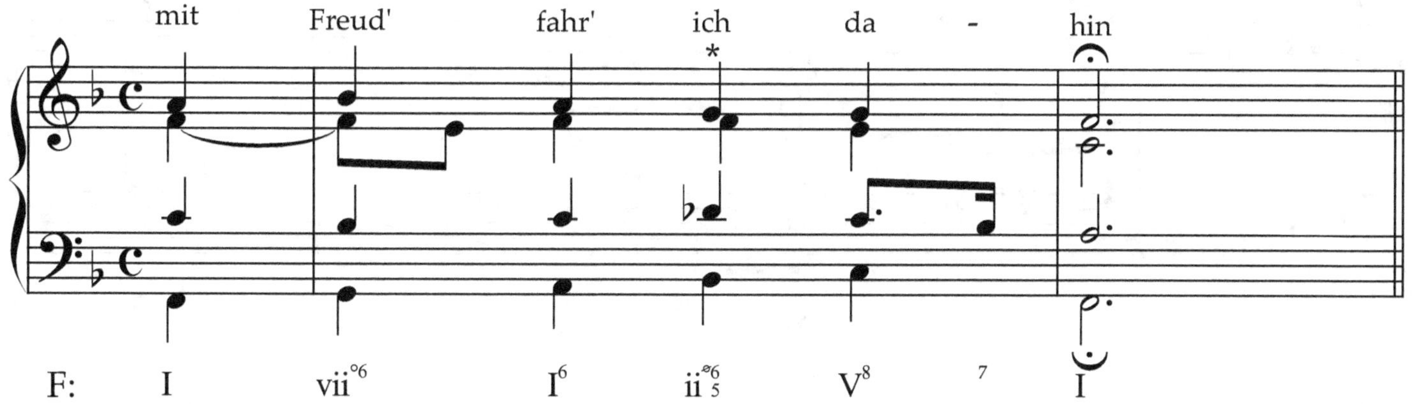

Figure 9.2

Johann Sebastian Bach
Chorale no. 287: Herr, ich habe missgehandelt
from 371 Four-Part Chorales

Augmented 6th Chords

The excerpts in Figure 9.3 and 9.4 illustrate Bach's use of augmented 6th chords (indicated by asterisks*), but these chords are rarely found in settings

Figure 9.3

Figure 9.4

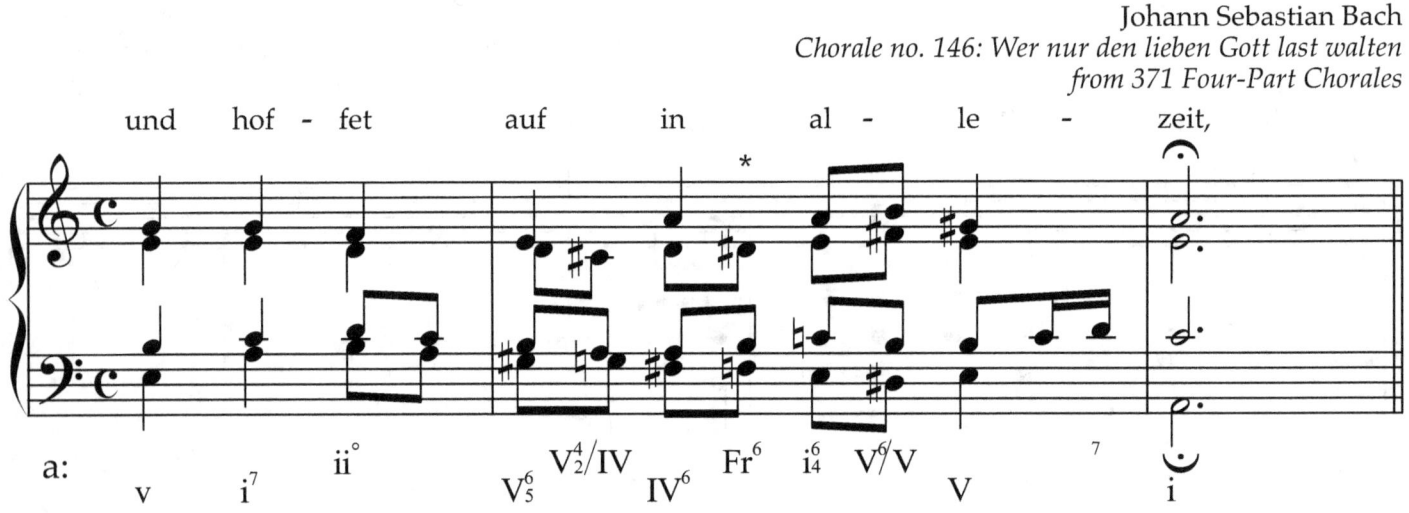

Neopolitan 6th Chords

Neapolitans 6th chords do not play a major role as a source of chromaticism in Bach's chorale harmonizations, and are found only rarely.

1. Complete the harmonic analysis for the following chorale excerpt.

Johann Sebastian Bach
Chorale no. 262: Ach Gott, vom Himmel sieh' darein
from 371 Four-Part Chorales

g: V N⁶

Secondary Dominants

Secondary dominants and diminished 7ths are common features in Bach's chorale settings. Much of the chromaticism in his harmonizations comes from his use of secondary dominants. Figure 9.5 is from one of Bach's six settings of this well-known chorale, and is a good example.

Figure 9.5

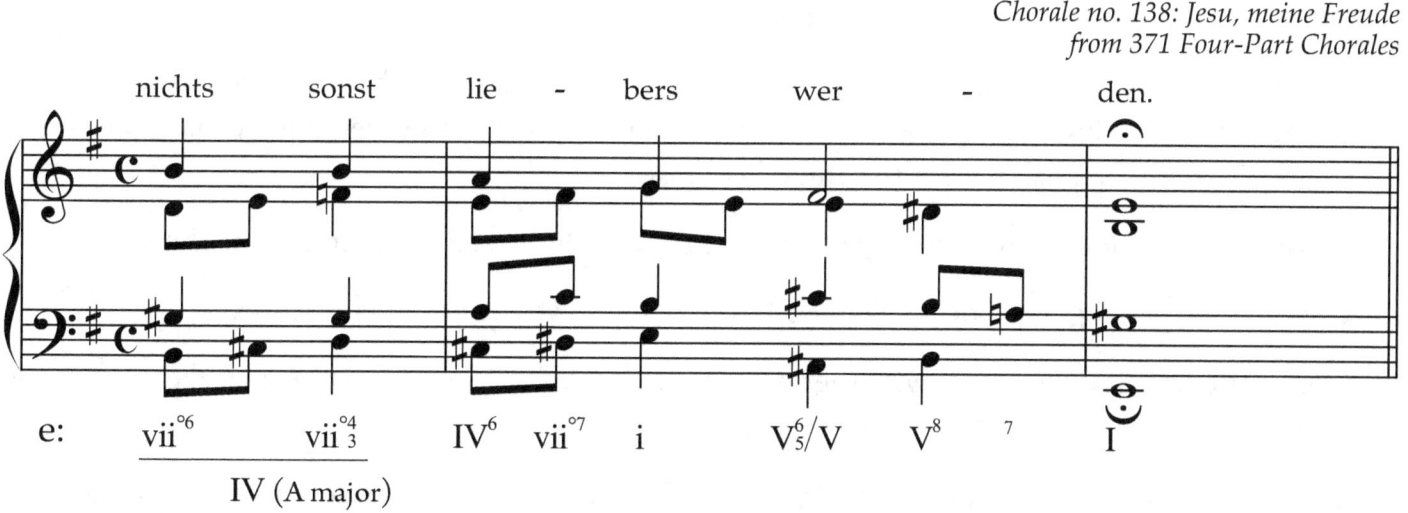

Johann Sebastian Bach
Chorale no. 138: Jesu, meine Freude
from 371 Four-Part Chorales

e: vii°⁶ vii°⁴₃ IV⁶ vii°⁷ i V⁶₅/V V⁸ ⁷ I
         IV (A major)

Stylistic Features of Bach's Chorale Harmonizations

So far, we have examined single phrases from Bach's chorale settings. Here is an opportunity to take a detailed look at one of his best known chorales. Play each pair of phrases, then find the features listed below in Figure 9.6.

Figure 9.6

Johann Sebastian Bach
Chorale no. 98: O Haupt, voll Blut und Wunden
from 371 Four-Part Chorales

a. Upbeats at the beginning are often harmonized with I or V.

b. The occasional changes of harmony on eighth note beats provide harmonic movement and variety.

c. Suspensions are common and are not always tied.

d. A half note in the melody occurring part way through a phrase is often harmonized either with two chords or with a single chord decorated with non-chord tones. However, Bach usually sustains a single chord under a half note at the end of a phrase.

e. Secondary 7th chords – particularly ii^7, vi^7, and IV^7 are often used as predominant chords.

f. Unaccented, passing notes occur frequently, often in two voices at the same time.

g. Dominant 7ths often follow V, with the seventh introduced on a weak beat, or a weaker part of the beat.

h. There are frequent modulations, usually to closely related keys. Bach often uses phrase modulation. The listeners ear accepts the immediate change of key at the beginning of a phrase because of the pause at the proceeding cadence. Modulation to distantly related keys is rarely found and is not characteristic of Bach's settings.

Figure 9.7

i. Double passing notes are used to create interest. These usually occur in 3rds or 6ths.

j. Bach maintains the movement through to the end of the phrase by decorating the cadence with a six-four progression.

k. The tonicization of ii adds chromatic interest to the end of the fourth phrase of the chorale.

Figure 9.8

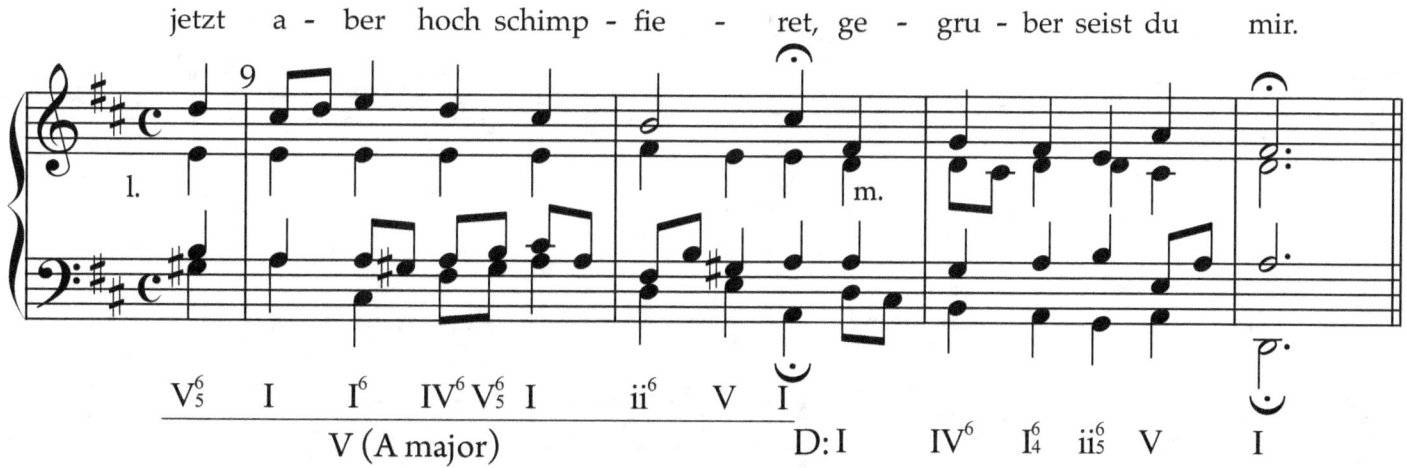

l. Bach uses phrase modulation again, setting the entire fifth phrase in the dominant key (A major), a closely related key to the home key of D major.

m. The music returns to the tonic key for the final phrase.

2. Provide a harmonic analysis of the following chorale. Use both functional and root/quality chord symbols. Circle and identify any non-chord tones.

Johann Sebastian Bach
Chorale no. 171: Shaut, ihr Sunder
from 371 Four-Part Chorales

We will continue with our examination of Bach's chorale harmonizations by comparing three different settings of the first two phrases of *O Haupt, voll Blut und Wunden*. Two of these excerpts have been transposed from other keys to facilitate a more direct comparison. Play each one through and examine the different approaches in each one. Take special note of the modulations to the relative major or minor key.

Figure 9.9

Figure 9.10

Figure 9.11

Johann Sebastian Bach
Chorale no. 345: O Haupt, voll Blut und Wunden
from 371 Four-Part Chorales

original key: a:

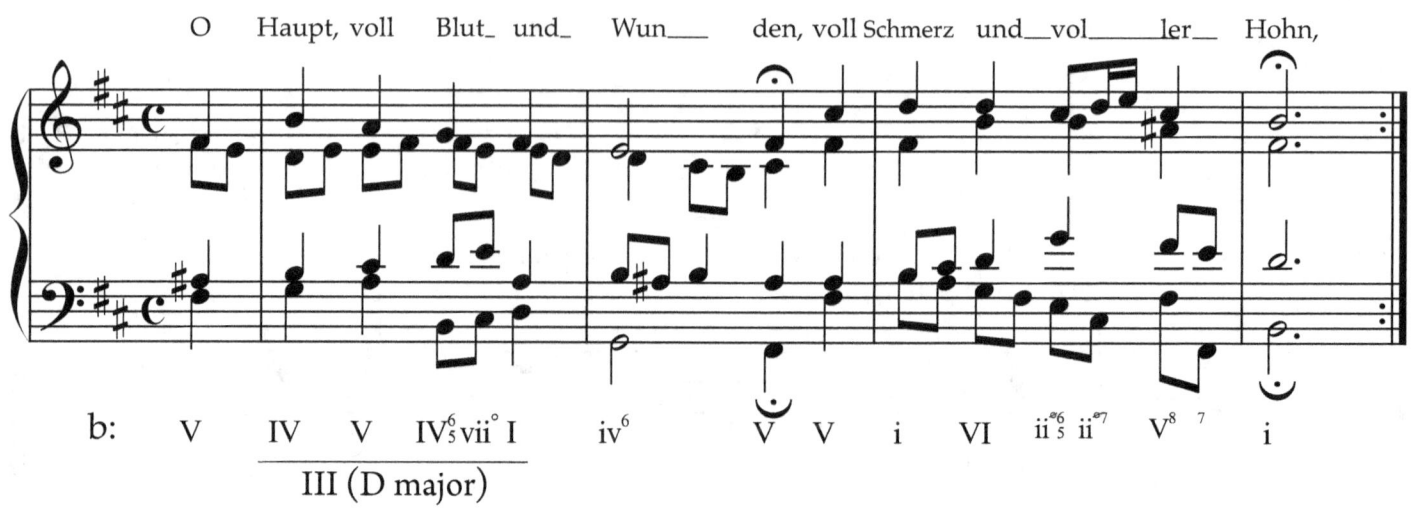

3. The following excerpts are from three different settings of the chorale melody *O Welt, sieh' hier dein Leben* by J.S. Bach. Play each one through and note the differences in harmonization. Provide a harmonic analysis of each excerpt using functional chord symbols. Circle and identify any non-chord tones.

Johann Sebastian Bach
Chorale no. 275: O Welt, sieh' hier dein Leben
from 371 Four-Part Chorales

key:___

Chapter 9: The Bach Chorales

Johann Sebastian Bach
Chorale no. 363: O Welt, sieh' hier dein Leben
from 371 Four-Part Chorales

Johann Sebastian Bach
Chorale no. 366: O Welt, sieh' hier dein Leben
from 371 Four-Part Chorales

4. Provide a harmonic analysis of the following chorale setting using functional chord symbols. Circle and identify any non-chord tones.

Johann Sebastian Bach
Chorale no. 278: Wie schon leuchtet der Morgenstern
from 371 Four-Part Chorales

5. Add alto and tenor parts to complete the following chorale fragments. Write all functional chord symbols.

Johann Sebastian Bach
Chorale no. 233: Werde munter, mein Gemute
from 371 Four-Part Chorales

Johann Sebastian Bach
Chorale no. 169: Jesu, der du selbsten wohl
from 371 Four-Part Chorales

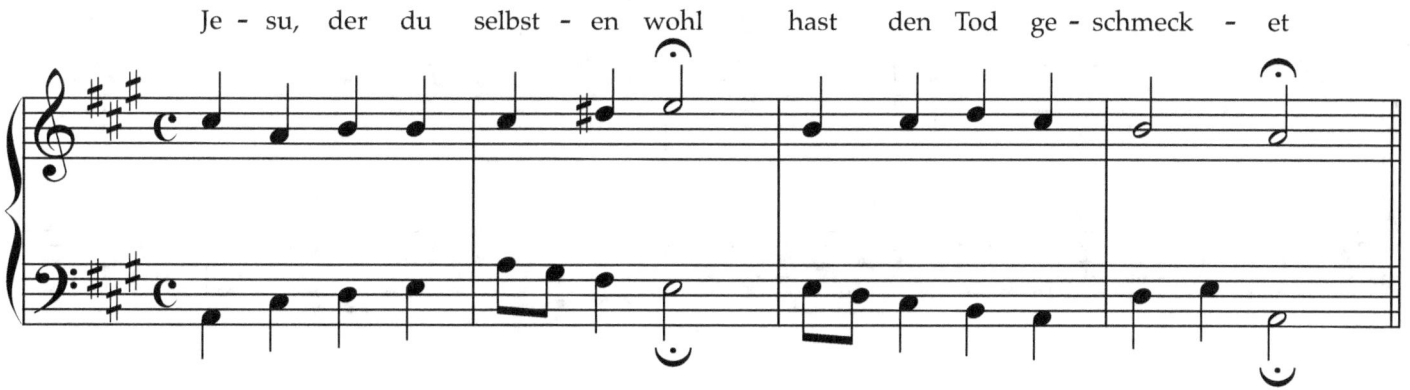

Johann Sebastian Bach
Chorale no. 94: Warum betrubst du dich, mein Herz
from 371 Four-Part Chorales

Johann Sebastian Bach
Chorale no. 246: Singt dem Herrn ein neues Lied
from 371 Four-Part Chorales

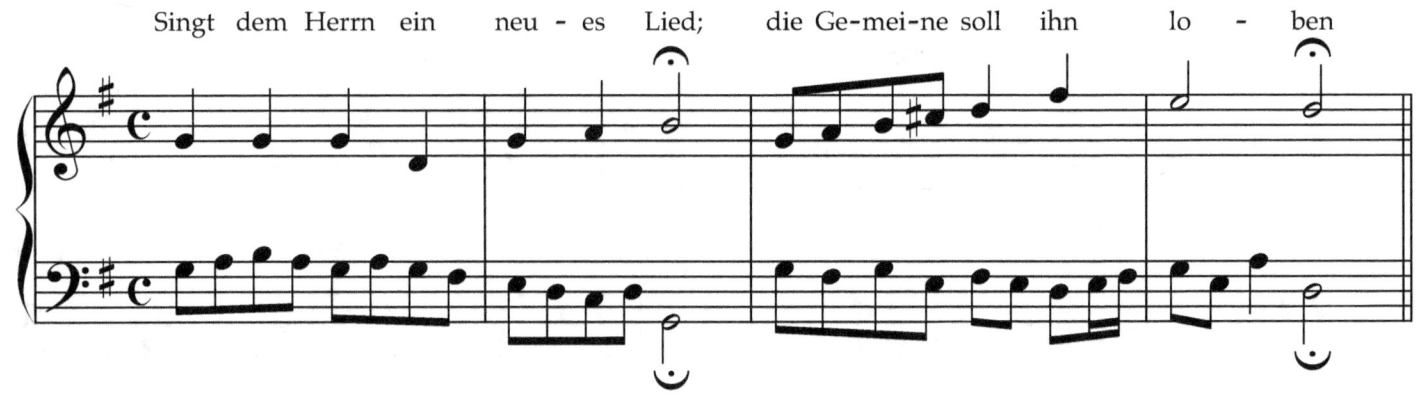

6. Complete the following chorale for four voices. Write out all functional chord symbols.

Johann Sebastian Bach
Chorale no. 115: Was mein Gott will
from 371 Four-Part Chorales

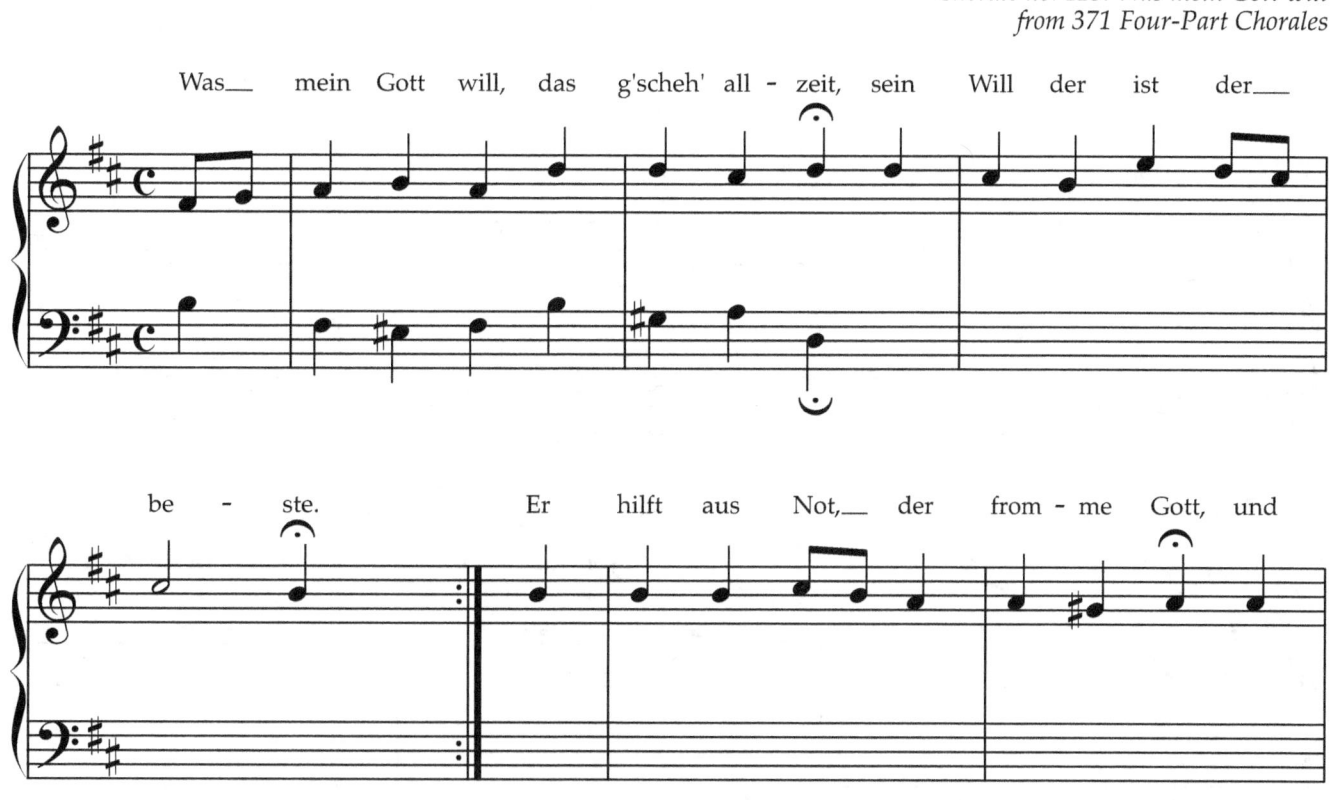

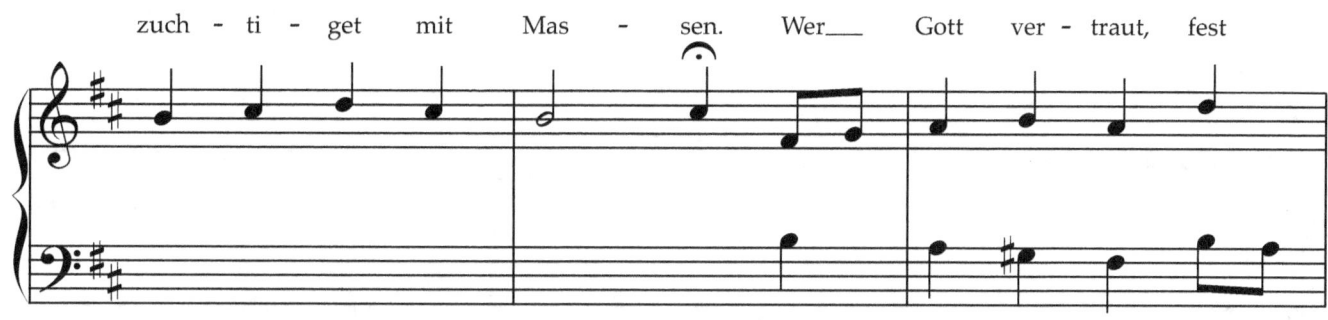

Chorale text by Albert von Brandenburg (1490-1545)
The bass line has been adapted

7. Complete the following chorale for four voices using diminished 7th chords at the places marked with asterisks (*). Write out all functional chord symbols.

Johann Sebastian Bach
Chorale no. 78: Herzliebster Jesu, was hast du verbrochen
from 371 Four-Part Chorales

8. Complete the following chorale for four voices. Write out all functional chord symbols.

Johann Sebastian Bach
Chorale no. 303: Herr Christ, der ein'ge Gott'ssohn
from 371 Four-Part Chorales

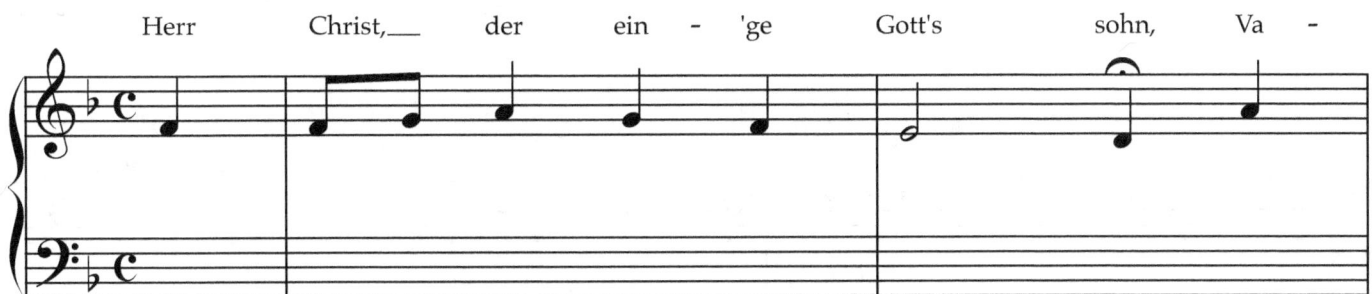

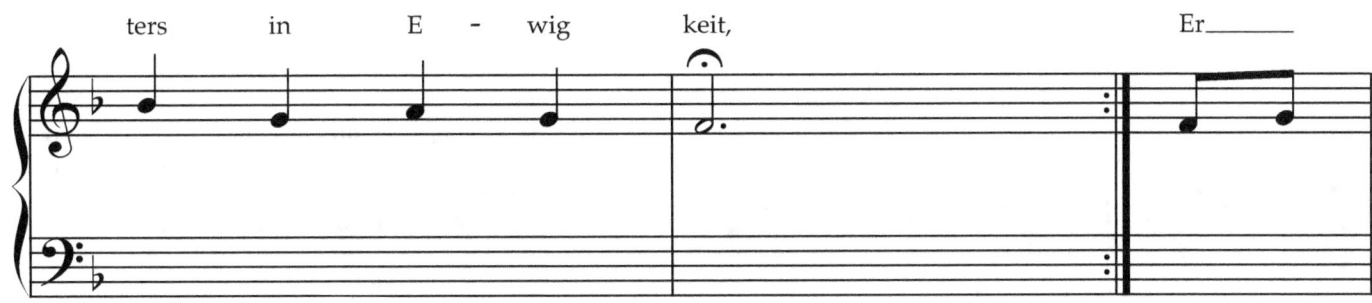

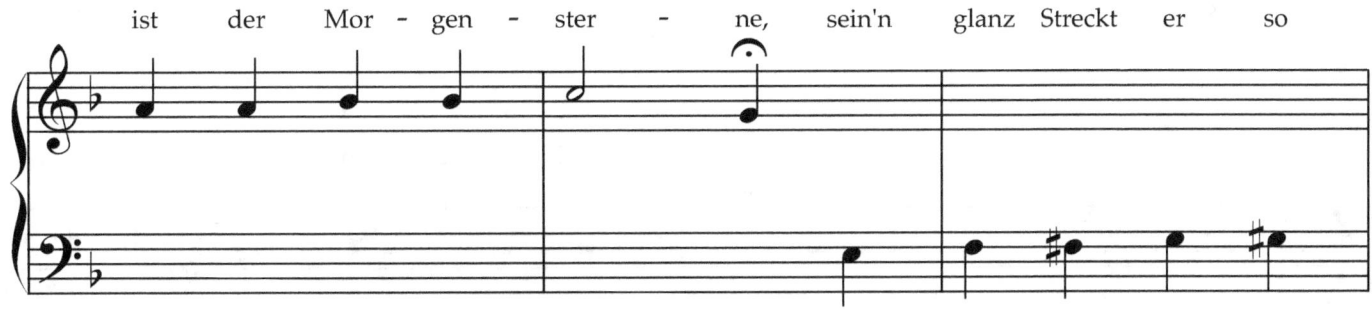

Chapter 9: The Bach Chorales

9. Complete the following chorale for four voices. Write out all functional chord symbols.

Johann Sebastian Bach
Chorale no. 249: Allein Gott in der Hoh' sei Ehr'
from 371 Four-Part Chorales

10
Figured Bass Realization

Music written in the baroque era often included a part called the **basso continuo** or **thorough bass**. This consisted of a single bass clef melody with various numbers and accidentals printed beneath the notes.

The part of the basso continuo was played by two instruments: a bass clef instrument like a cello, double bass, or bassoon, and a keyboard instrument like a harpsichord. During performances, the bass clef instrument would play the given melodic line and the keyboard player would improvise a part based on the melodic line and the symbols written below the line.

Figure 10.1 is an example of a this type of melodic line called a **figured bass**.

Figure 10.1

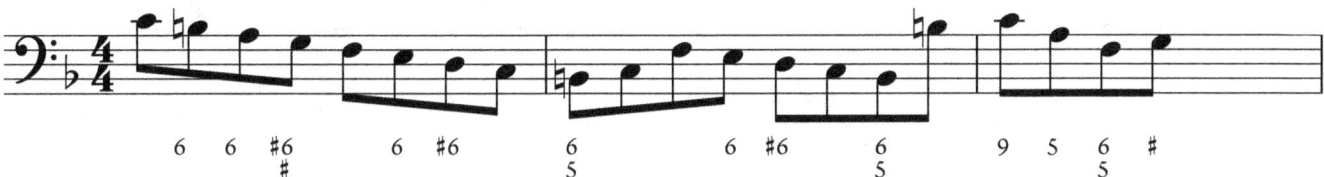

This figured bass line could be played like Figure 10.2. This is called **realizing the bass**.

Figure 10.2

The note given in the bass clef is always the lowest note played. It is the lowest note of the chord but not necessarily the root.

The numbers represent the intervals above the bass, even though some numbers are usually left out. The intervals created by these numbers are always diatonic. Always use notes from the key signature.

Figure 10.3

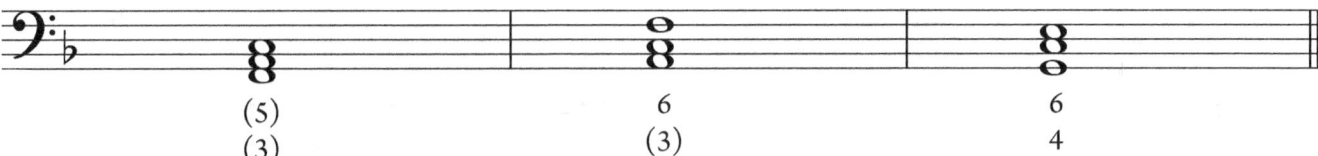

If there are no numbers, add a 3rd and a 5th above the bass to get a *root position triad*

A "6" by itself indicates a 6th and a 3rd above the bass note which creates a *first inversion triad*

A "6" and a "4" indicates a 6th and a 4th above the bass creating a *second inversion triad.*

Figure 10.4

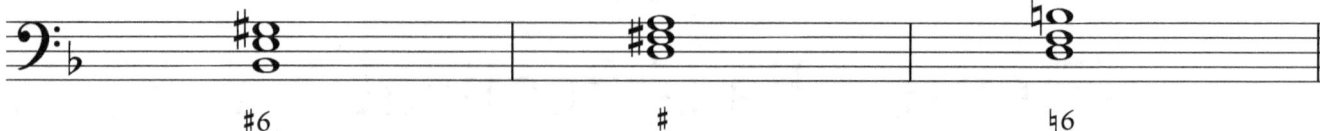

♯6	♯	♮6
In this chord the sharp applies to the 6th above the bass. We add a sharp to the G	If there is no number next to the sharp it always means to apply the accidental to the 3rd above the bass	This example uses a natural not a sharp. B is flat and a natural is used to raise it.

Accidentals are applied to the interval number that they appear with. An accidental by itself always applies to the third above the bass. If a composer wants a natural note raised by a half step, a sharp will be used. If the note is flat, a natural will be used in the figuration.

Study the following chart indicating figures used for triads and 7th chords and their inversions.

Chord		Complete Figure	Figures Used
Triad in root position		5 3	No figures used
Triad in first inversion		6 3	6
Triad in second inversion		6 4	6 4
Seventh chord in root position		7 5 3	7
Seventh chord in first inversion		6 5 3	6 5
Seventh chord in second inversion		6 4 3	4 3
Seventh chord in third inversion		6 4 2	4 2

Chapter 10: Figured Bass Realization

To **realize** a figured bass we play or write out the figured bass keyboard part. For written out figured bass parts in keyboard style, the bass note is placed in the bass clef and played by the left hand. The upper notes (soprano, alto, and tenor) are placed in the treble clef and are played by the right hand. The notes are written in close position with the distance between the three upper parts not more than one octave.

The voice leading rules are the same as those for chorale settings. No inappropriate doubling, voice crossing, or parallel motion is allowed.

In Figure 10.5 (a), all chords are in root position so no figuration is needed. Figure 10.5(b) illustrates the acceptable ranges is for the notes in each clef.

Figure 10.5

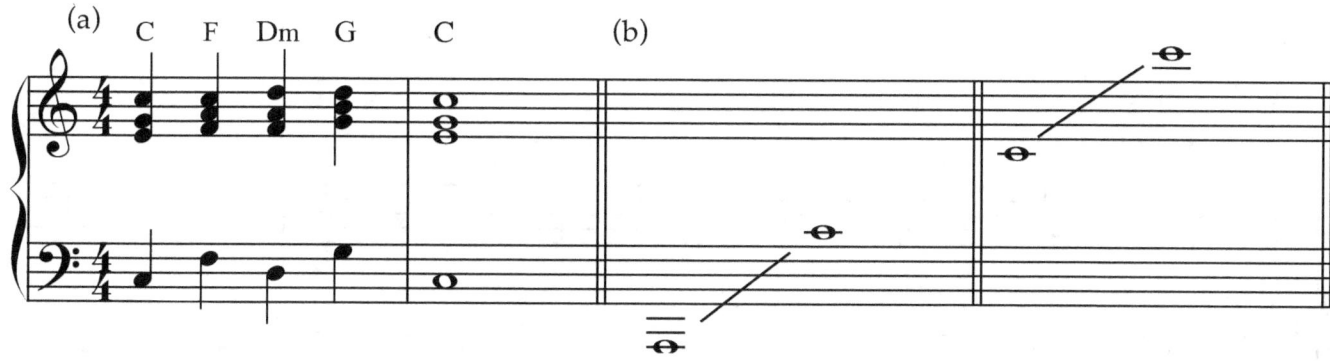

When notes are doubled, care must be taken with the placement of stems and doubled whole notes. Review the notation in Figure 10.6 (a).

A slash across the number, or a + after a number, means that the note is raised a half step. All three symbols in Figure 10.6 (b) have the same meaning.

Figure 10.6

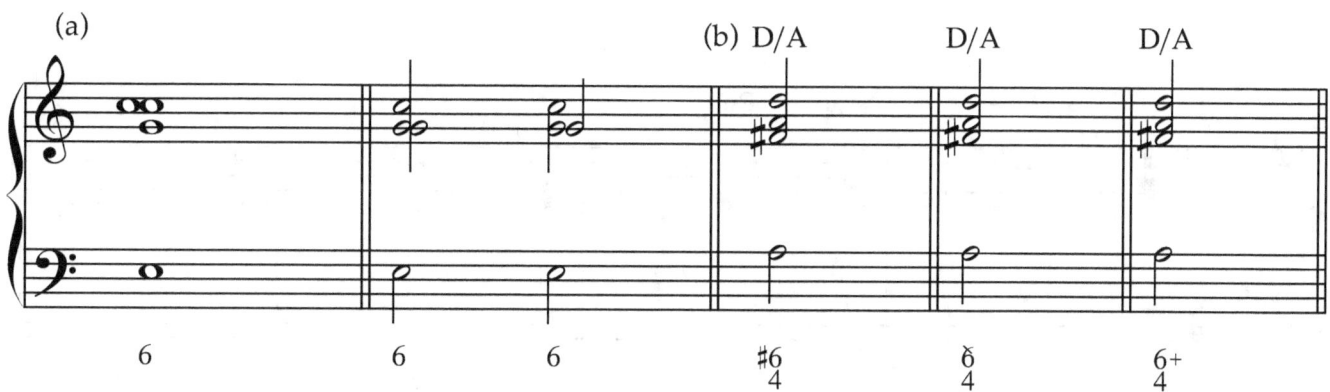

157   Chapter 10: Figured Bass Realization

Octave doubling may occur if the composer wants a certain note to be doubled, but they are not usually indicated in the figures. In Figure 10.7 (a), the line after the 8 means that the note an octave above the bass(G) must be repeated or sustained in the same voice.

Dashes between figures indicate movement in the upper parts. The 6th and the 5th above G must be placed in the same voice (6-5 = E-D) and the same applies to the 4th and 3rd above G (4-3 = C-B). In Figure 10.7 (b), with a dash over a stationary bass, the actual chord occurs with the figure at the end; here, a C major chord in first inversion.

Dashes placed below a moving bass indicate that the notes in the upper voices remain stationary (Figure 10.7(c)). The bass line here has a G and then a C with a 3 below it. This means that we keep the G and C chord while we play the remaining notes that follow in the bass.

Figure 10.7

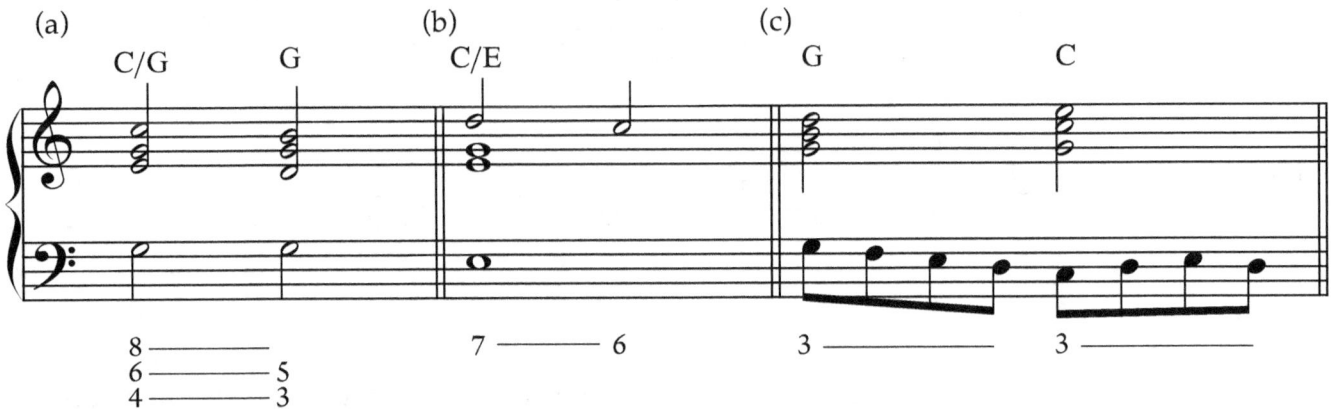

Occasionally, some segments of a figured bass may be realized in three part texture. In this case, two voices are placed in the treble clef above a single note in the bass. This voicing may be used when a series of first inversion chords occur in scale-wise succession (Figure 10.9).

Figure 10.9

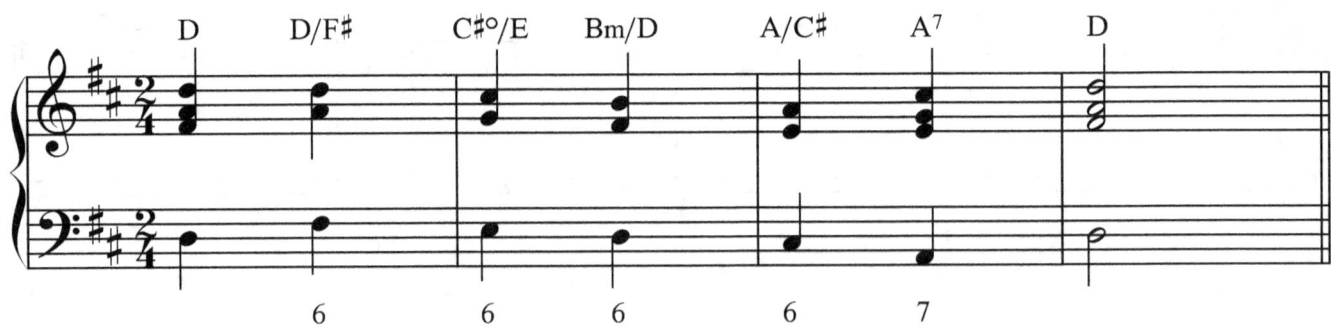

Chapter 10: Figured Bass Realization

1. Give the root/quality chord symbols implied by the following figured bass symbols.

2. Provide the figured bass and root/quality chord symbols for the following chords.

3. Complete the following chords in keyboard style according to the given figures. Add root/quality chord symbols.

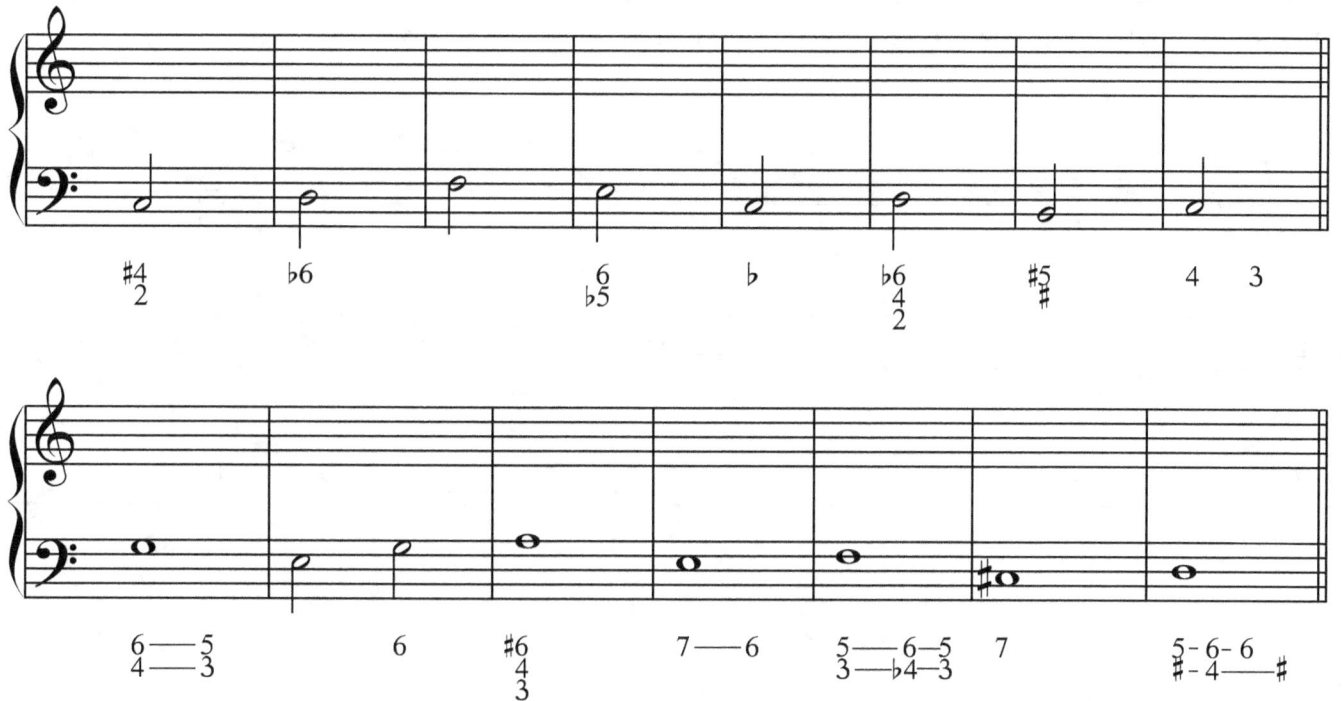

Chapter 10: Figured Bass Realization

If you were a keyboard player in the 17th or 18th century, your part may have looked like the bass clef line below. Two instrumentalists usually played this part. One played the bass line as written on a cello, double bass, or bassoon and the other realized the bass by filling in the harmonies from the given figures on a keyboard instrument. Together they formed a group called the *continuo* or *basso continuo*.

Figure 10.10

4. Here is a simple realization of the figured bass in Figure 10.10 in keyboard style. Play the keyboard part and provide a harmonic analysis of the continuo using root/quality chord symbols.

How to Realize a Figured Bass in Keyboard Style

1. Understand the components. The given (notated) lower voice must be played as written. Decide on the key of the example and do an examination of the figures written below the bass line.

Figure 10.11

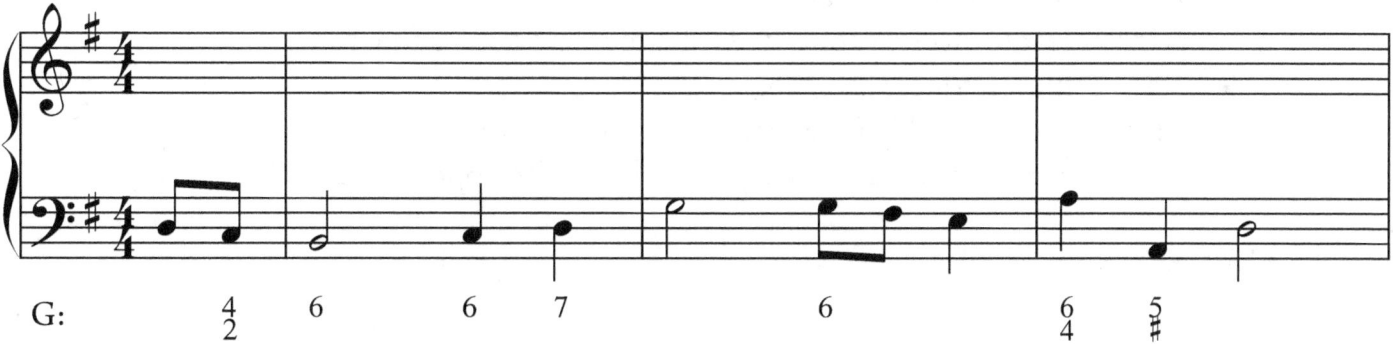

2. Interpret the figures. It might help to sketch in the functional chord symbols so you can see and understand the progression even better. Always assume the chord is built from the bass note, not from the key's tonic.
3. Determine the harmonic context. Analyze the harmonic function of the bass notes. This helps with voice leading, doubling and choosing chord tones.

Figure 10.12

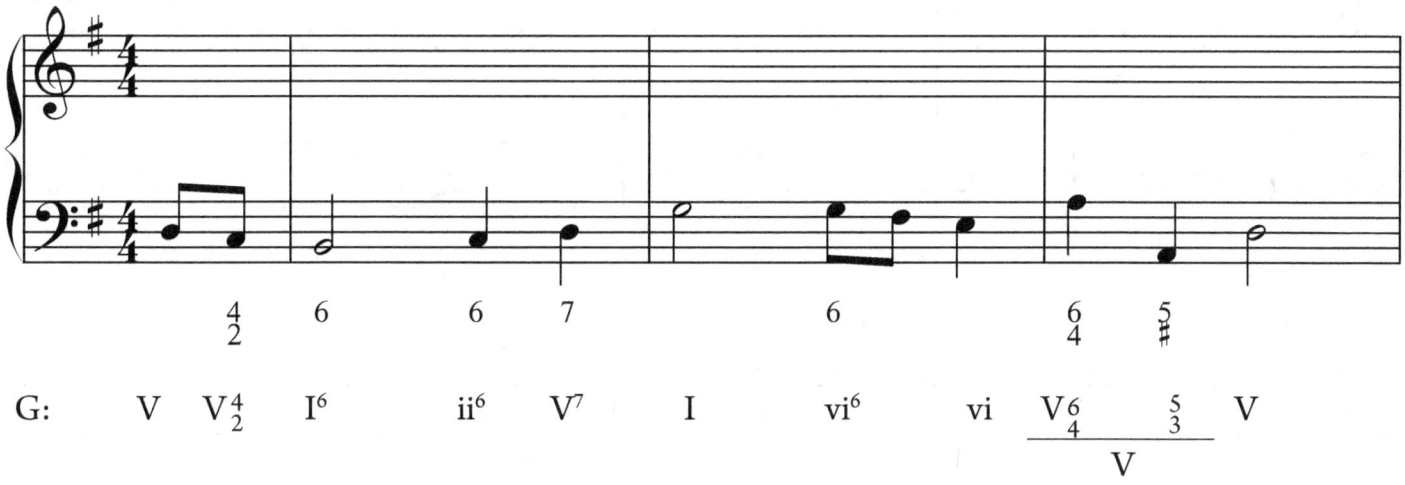

Chapter 10: Figured Bass Realization

4. Realize the chords. Use modern notation. Two staves (treble and bass clef). Write out all voices. The left hand (bass clef) remains as written. Build the chord indicated by the figures above the bass in the right hand (treble clef). Keep a clear rhythmic struture. Chords should match the rhythm of the bass line unless there is a reason to embellish.

   Use standard voice leading rules:
   - Avoid faulty parallel 5ths and octaves.
   - Resolve leading tones properly. Avoid doubling the leading tone.
   - Keep common tones when possible.
   - Move voices smoothly (preferably stepwise motion).
   - Try to maintain compact or closed voicing in the upper voices.

Figure 10.13

5. Realize the given figured basses in keyboard style.

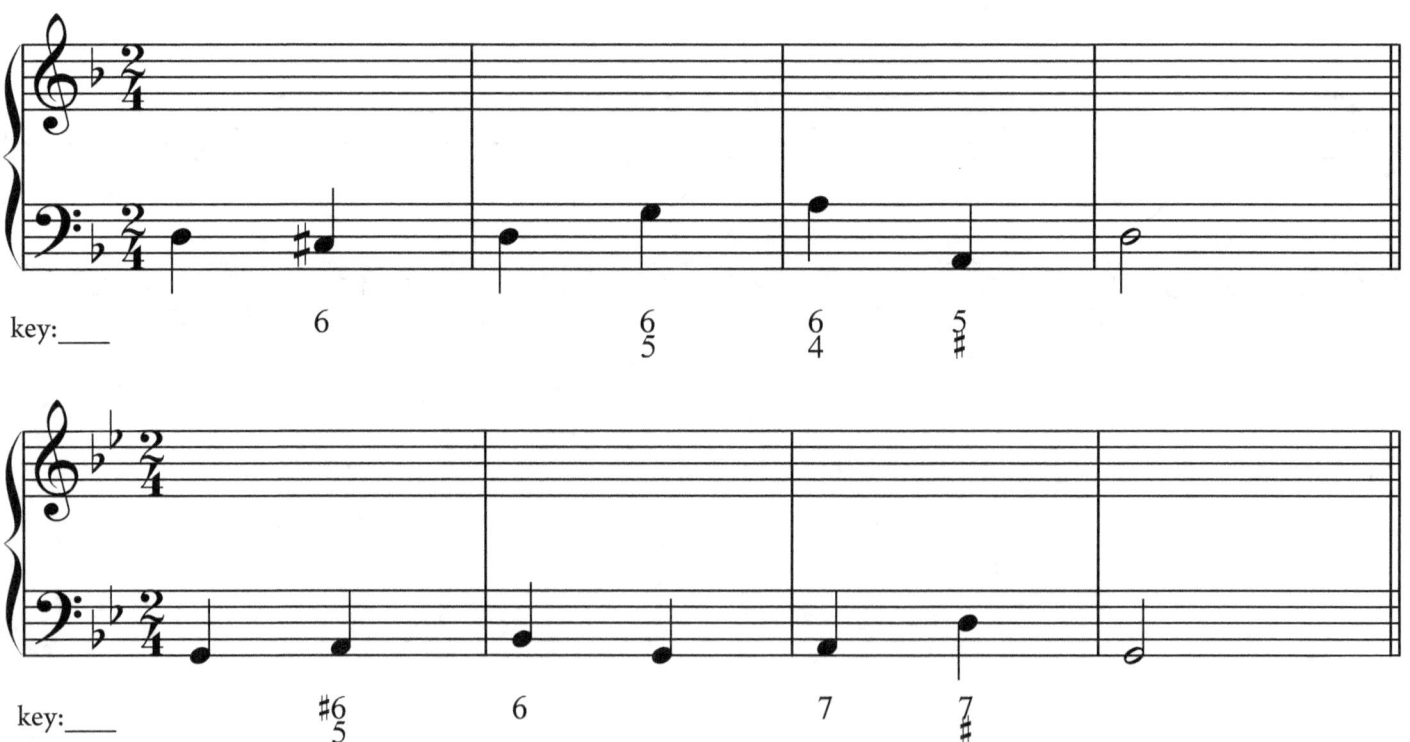

162 Chapter 10: Figured Bass Realization

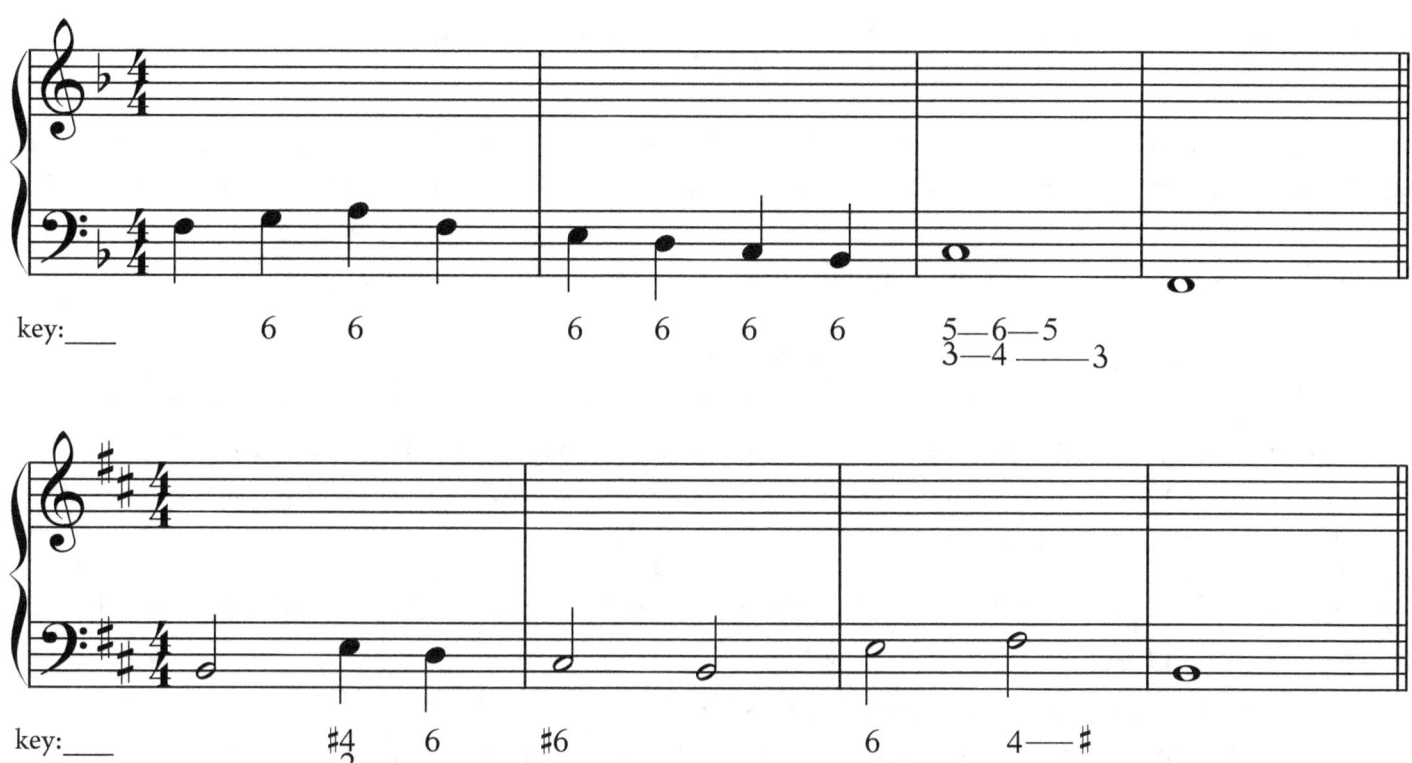

6. Realize the following figured bass in keyboard style. Label the continuo with root/quality chord symbols.

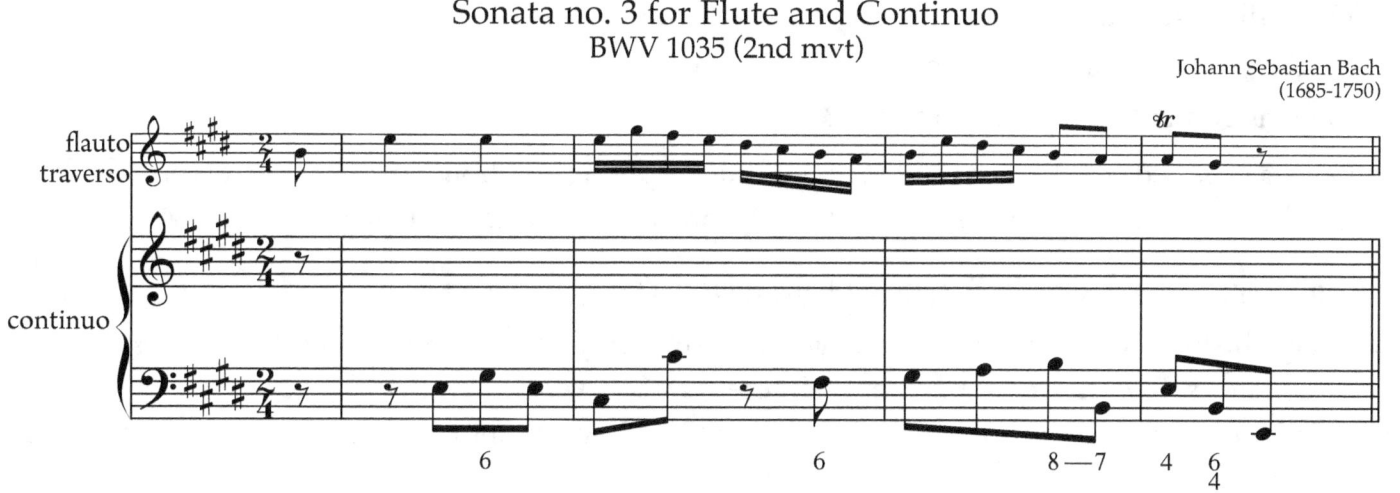

163   Chapter 10: Figured Bass Realization

Principles for Writing a Melody Above a Figured Bass

Learning to write a melody above a figured bass helps to create stylistically appropriate, harmonically solid melodies above a given bass line. This technique was central to music education during the 17th and 18th centuries and is important today for understanding the structure of tonal music, voice leading, and the musical style. Here are some ideas for writing a melody above a figured bass.

1. **Understand the harmonies.** The figures indicate the vertical harmonies. Before writing the melody, you must interpret the harmony implied by the figures. For example, a blank figure (or 5/3) implies a root position triad, a 6 implies a first inversion chord, a 7 may indicate a dominant 7th or a chord with a seventh in general. By realizing the chords, you understand the harmonies within which the melody must operate.

2. **Consider the voice leading.** Melodies derived from a figured bass must adhere to good voice leading principles:
   - Conjunct motion (stepwise movement) is best.
   - Avoid too many large leaps unless they are part of a melodic sequence or expressive gesture.
   - Approach and leave leaps correctly.
   - Resolve tendency tones correctly, for example, the leading tone rises to the tonic or the 7th of a seventh chord falls by step.
   - Correct voice leading must be used between the melody and bass line including avoiding faulty parallel motion. Avoid parallel 5ths and octaves.
   - The goal is an expressive melody that compliments and enhances the figured bass.

3. **Determine the role of the melody.** Ask whether the melody is:
   - A vocal line like an aria?
   - An instrumental line in a trio sonata?

Different factors require different style choices. In a more homophonic or solo like texture, the line has greater freedom, but must still follow the harmony and the style of the work.

4. **Apply stylistic features.** In Baroque music, melodies may include:
   - Embellishments. For example, passing tones, suspensions, neighbour tones.
   - Sequences. Repetitions of motives at different pitch levels.
   - Cadences. Particularly the authentic cadence (V - I), which should be approached and resolved with care.

5. **Melodic shape and phrasing.** A good melody has shape. It rises, reaches a high point, and falls, often in a predictable phrase structure. Phrase direction and climax help avoid monotony and give the melody musical meaning.

You may be given an example like the passage in Figure 10.14 and asked to complete the realization of the figured bass in keyboard style and to complete the melody, maintaining the style.

Figure 10.14

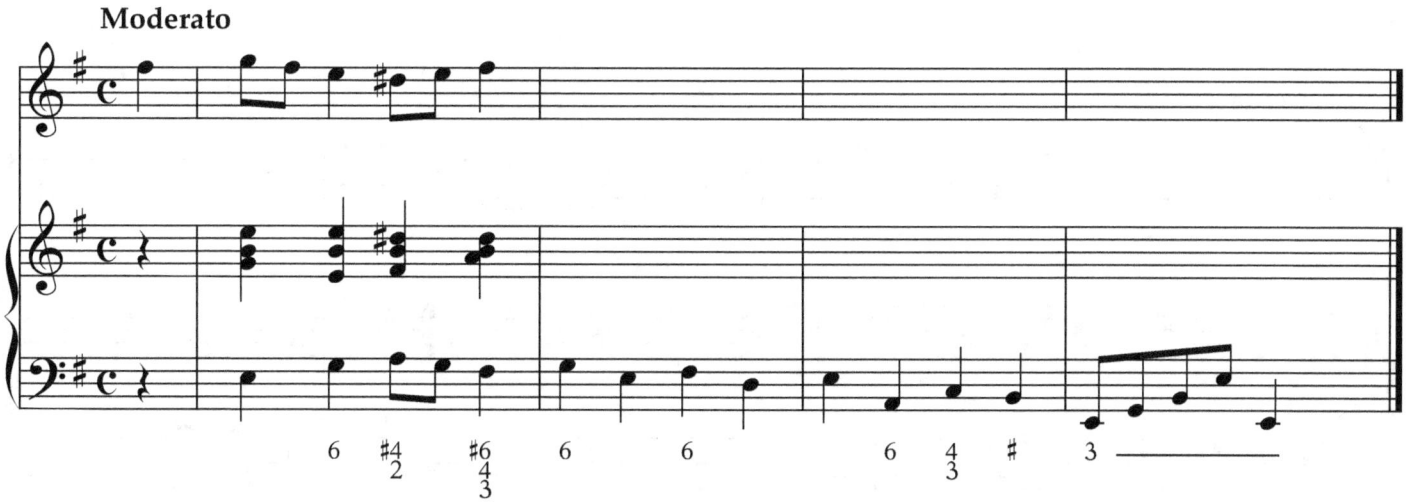

The first step is to complete the keyboard part of the figured bass by adding the chords in the right hand according to the steps we have discussed earlier in this chapter.

Figure 10.15

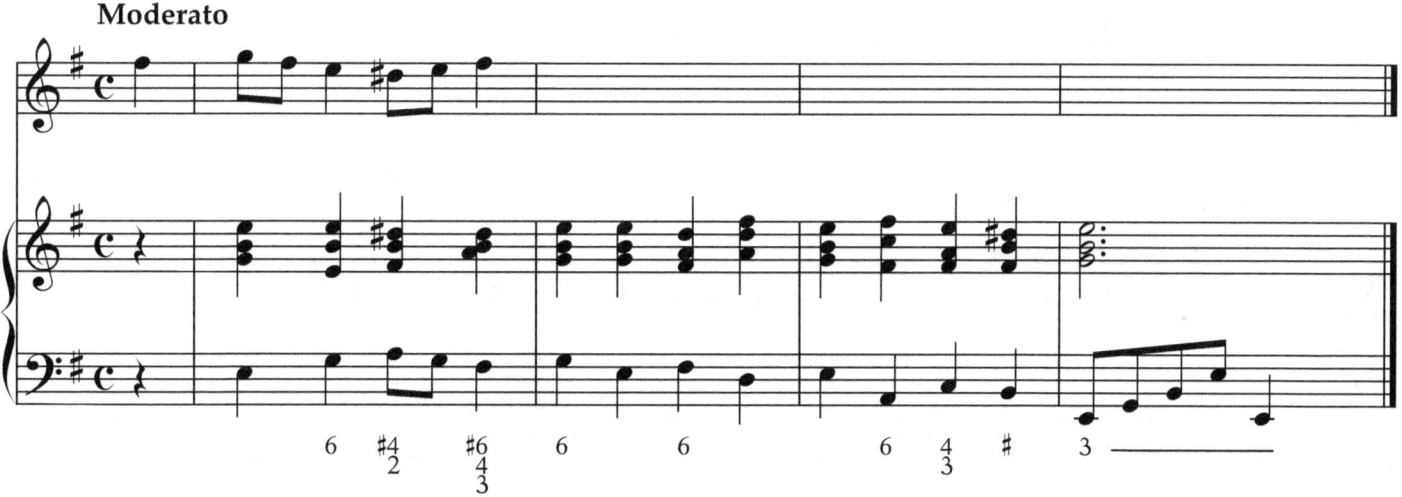

Chapter 10: Figured Bass Realization

After realizing the bass in keyboard style, complete the melody using the information discussed on Page 164. Try to adhere to the style given in the opening measures of the example. It does not have to be elaborate, and it is best to keep it simple. Follow the harmony outlined in the keyboard part when choosing notes for the melody.

Figure 10.16

7. For the following examples:

   a) Name the key.

   b) Complete the realization of the figured bass in keyboard style.

   c) Complete the melody, maintaining the style.

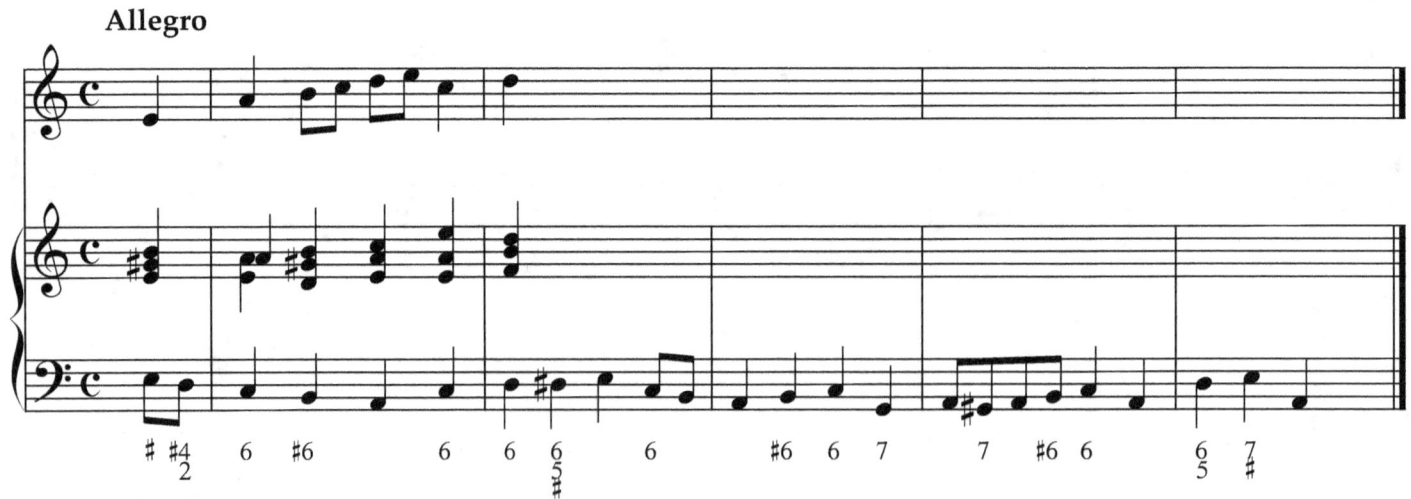

key:____

Chapter 10: Figured Bass Realization

168 Chapter 10: Figured Bass Realization

11
Counterpoint

In this lesson, you will learn to create a two-voice contrapuntal composition, using the harmonic vocabulary of an 18th century dance.

First of all, here are three important stylistic features of the 18th century two-part dance forms.

1. The harmony is fairly simple. Modulations move to the dominant in major keys and the relative major or the dominant minor in minor keys. The chromatic harmony you have studied throughout this text is not characteristic of this genre.

2. Each melodic line should be a strong, independent part with its own musical direction. The two melodies should maintain a good balance between stepwise motion and skips, with leaps used for added interest.

3. The music should have a strong rhythmic flow that keeps both lines moving.

Melodic Lines

In two-part writing, each voice is an independent part. As with voice leading in harmony, certain types of parallel motion between the two parts is forbidden. When voices move in parallel, octaves or unisons, it sounds as if one of the two voices has dropped out. Parallel perfect 5ths must also be avoided, but a perfect 5th followed by a diminished 5th is acceptable as long as the diminished 5th resolves correctly.

Figure 11.1

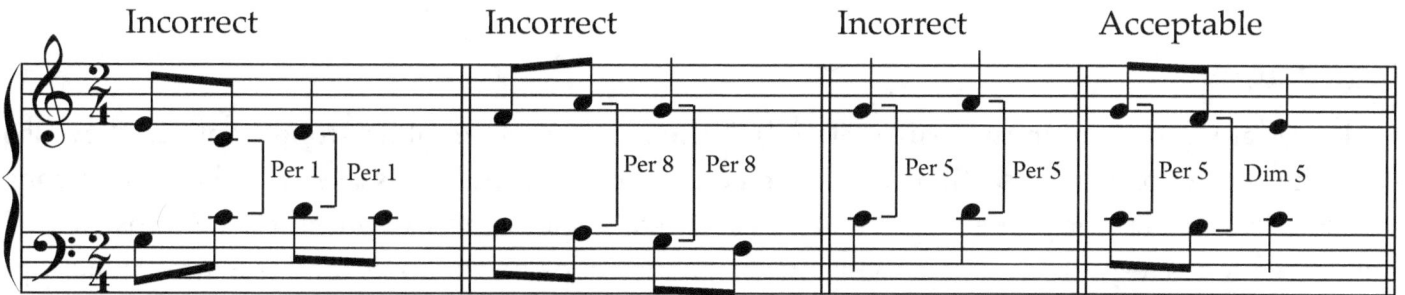

Rhythm and Harmony

In two part writing, rhythm should act as a unifying element. The two voices should have similar rhythmic structures, with the same types of note values used throughout. A steady pulse is also a characteristic feature of music of this period. Play the excerpt in Figure 11.2 and listen for both the rhythm and Harmony.

Figure 11.2

Johann Krieger
Bourree in A minor

Although there are only two voices, the implied harmony of the music is clear. The chords implied in a two-part composition must make harmonic sense and present a good harmonic progression. In two-part writing, just as in four-part writing, the basic harmonic structure of **tonic - pre-dominant - dominant - tonic** should be followed. Use your understanding of harmony to choose logical chord progressions.

As can be seen from the Krieger excerpt in Figure 11.2, the harmonic rhythm of these dances is generally slower than that of four--part compositions, often with only one or two chord changes per measure.

Cadences

Cadences are important in two-part writing because they help to establish tonal centers. They also mark the ends of phrases in sections within a piece. The cadence that ends a section should be strong and convincing. Play the four excerpts that follow and take special note of how these composers used non-chord tones, especially anticipations. Each cadence ends on the tonic, and the upper voice approaches the tonic note by step either from above or from below.

Figure 11.3

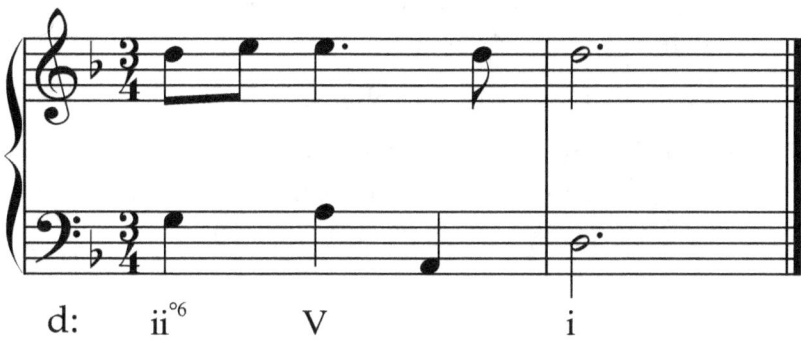

Archangelo Corelli
Violin Sonata in D minor
op. 5, no. 7 (Sarabande)

Figure 11.4

Jeremiah Clarke
March T 433

Figure 11.5

Johann Christoph Friedrich Bach
Allegro in G major
from Musical Leisure Hours

Figure 11.6

John Alcock
Minuet in A major
from Suite no. 1

Chapter 11: Counterpoint

Cadences that occur in the middle of a section can be challenging. It is important to create clear ending for each phrase, but the music should not seem to stop every four measures. The best way to maintain musical momentum through a phrase ending is to give one voice, a long note to slow the rhythm, well continuing to move the other voice in shorter notes to maintain the rhythmic momentum.

In Figure 11.7 a, the soprano establishes the end of the phrase by landing on the tonic on the strong beat and holding a note through the measure, while the bass continues to move, forming the link to the next phrase. In 11.7 b, the soprano holds on $\hat{3}$ (rather than $\hat{1}$) while the bass arppegiates the tonic chord. Note that the dominant chord is in first inversion.

Figure 11.7

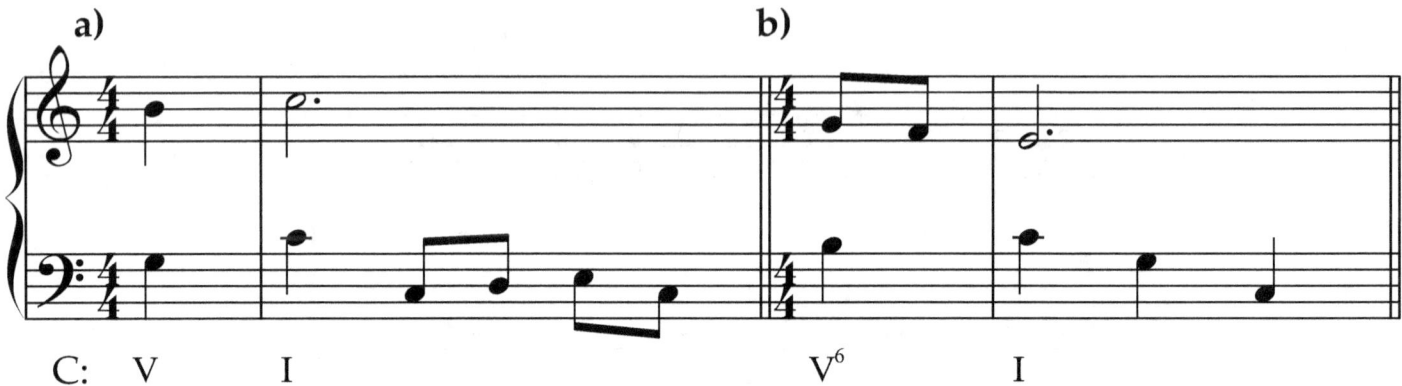

In Figure 11.8, the soprano continues to move through the last measure of the phrase while the bass arppegiates the tonic chord. When both voices are in motion right up to the end of the phrase, it is particularly important that the harmony remain clear.

Figure 11.8

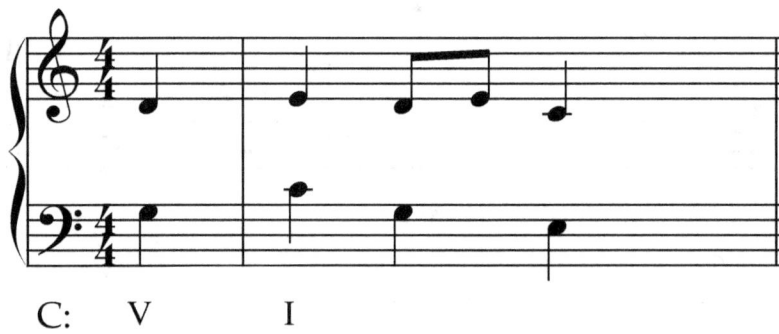

A half cadence in the middle of a composition can serve as a resting point to signal the end of a section. If you end a section with a half cadence, allow enough time on the dominant harmony to establish the cadence clearly, but make sure that the rhythm does not become too static. The following four cadences are all from the *Minuet in G major*, BWV Anh. 114, by Christian Petzold (1677-1733), from the *Notebook for Anna Magdalena Bach* (1725). Play each one and note the different techniques Petzold uses to keep the music moving.

Half cadence in the tonic key: the bass stays on the root of V while the melody keeps moving.

Figure 11.9

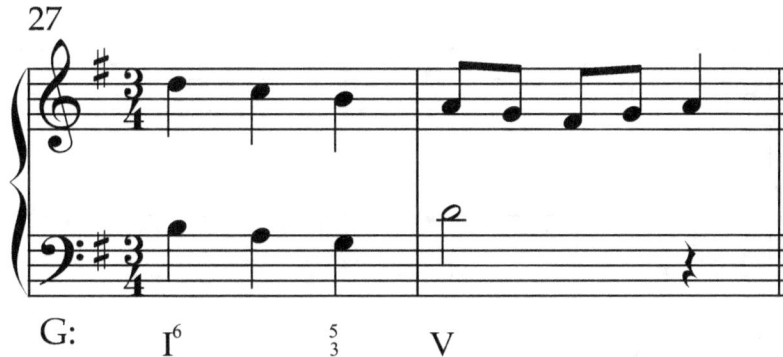

Half cadence in the dominant key: the bass stays on the root of V while the melody keeps moving.

Figure 11.10

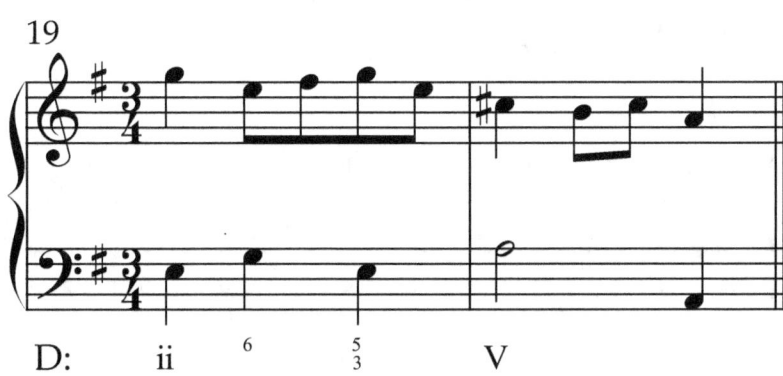

Half cadence in the tonic key: the soprano holds $\hat{2}$, (which is ornamented) while the bass keeps moving, but there is no change of harmony.

Figure 11.11

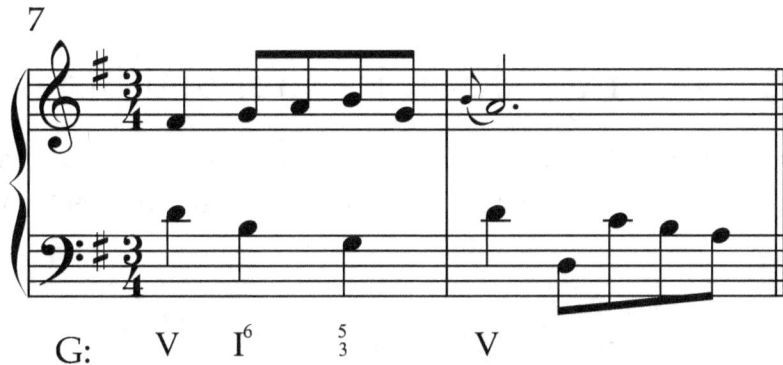

Authentic cadence in the dominant key (D major): the soprano holds $\hat{1}$ of the dominant key while the bass moves, transforming I of D major into V^7 of G major.

Figure 11.12

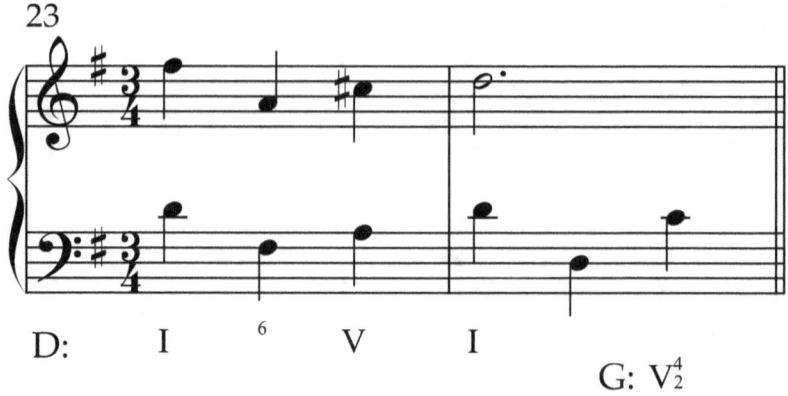

D: I ^{6} V I

G: V^4_2

Non-harmonic Tones

Non-harmonic tones have the same function in a two-part contrapuntal texture as they do in four-part (SATB) writing. Notes such as passing tones, neighbor tones, *echappées*, and *appoggiaturas* can be used to decorate a melodic line and provide rhythmic interest and motion. Use the following list to review non-harmonic tones and their usage.

Figure 11.13

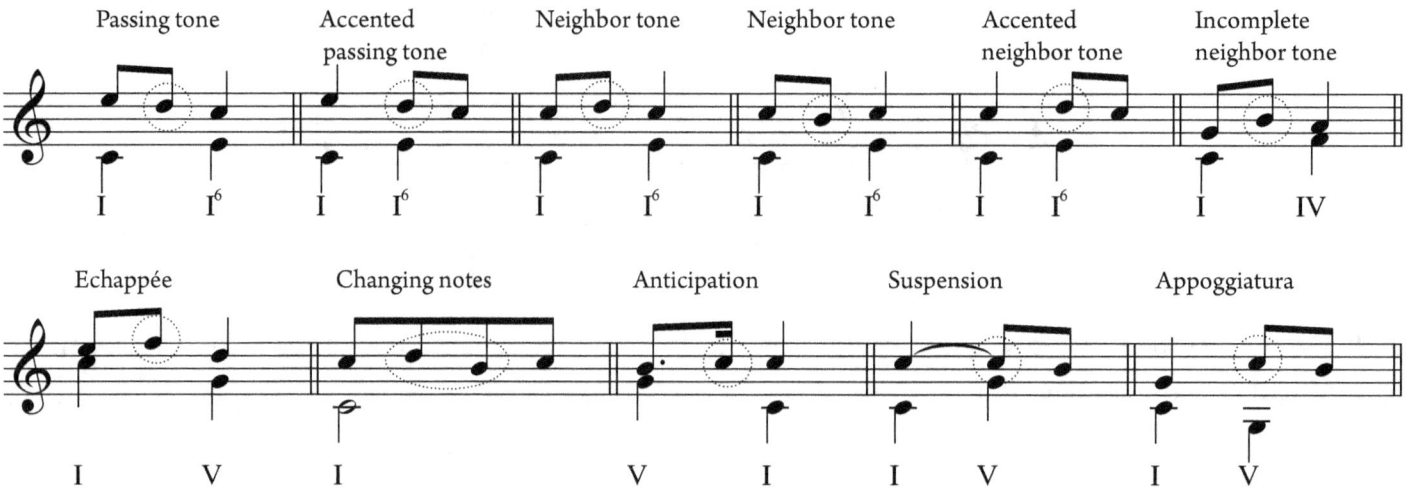

Writing a Two-Part Composition in Rounded Binary Form

Rounded binary form consists of two parts. The first part presents the A section. The second part presents the B section followed by a partial repeat of the A section. Both sections are usually repeated.

$$A^1 \; :||: \; B+A^2 \; :||$$

18th-Century Dances

This is a review of the characteristics of 18th century dances studied in other levels of *Essential Music Theory*. These dances were usually found in binary, rounded binary, balanced binary, and ternary form. They often used antecedent and consequent phrase structure with parallel and contrasting phrase periods. They modulated to closely related keys, usually standard goal keys. For major keys this is the dominant and for minor keys this is the relative major.

Menuet
Meter: 3/4 or 3/8
Tempo: *Andante, Moderato grazioso*
Characteristics: Graceful French dance; unhurried tempo; balanced phrases usually four measures long. May have an upbeat.

Gigue
Meter: Compound time, often 6/8 or simple time in triplets
Tempo: *Allegro, Vivace, Presto*
Characteristics: Derived from the English word jig, but evolved differently in Italy and France: French *Gigue* is in compound time (often 6/8); Italian *Giga* is faster and has running notes.

Sarabande
Meter: 3/2 or 3/4
Tempo: *Adagio, Lento*
Characteristics: Emphasis on second beat with long or accented notes. Can be chordal in texture.

Bourrée
Meter: 2/4, 3/4, or 2/2
Tempo: *Vivace, Allegro vivace*
Characteristics: Usually begins with an upbeat (quarter note or 2 eighth notes). Quick duple time; rhythmic and bright steady quarter notes.

Gavotte
Meter: 4/4 or 2/2
Tempo: *Allegro, Allegro moderato*
Characteristics: French dance; usually two quarter note upbeats, so the phrase begins and ends in the middle of the measure.

Here is a typical assignment:

1. For the following two-part work:

    a. Name the key.
    b. Name the type of baroque dance implied by the opening.
    c. Continue to create a two-part composition in the style of an 18-century dance.
    d. Use one of the binary forms with repeat signs. Name the form you use.
    e. Mark the phrasing.

There are many options for completing this assignment. The next few pages will guide you through the basic steps involved in writing a sixteen-measure contrapuntal piece in rounded binary form. We will start with a very simple example titled *Schwäbisch* (that is a tune from Swabia in Germany) by Johann Christoph Friederich Bach (1732 -1795) taken from a collection entitled *Musical Leisure Hours* (1787-1788).

Figure 11.14

Type of dance:_____
Form: _____

Step 1: Plan Your Composition

Decide on the type of dance. Set up the page, layout the measures, and add the repeat signs. If the given opening begins with an upbeat, pay special attention to the placement of the repeat signs.

Figure 11.15

Type of dance: Minuet
Form: Rounded binary form

Step 2: Complete the First Part - A¹

Before you begin, analyze the harmonic implications of the given fragment and take a close look at the melodic style. Write functional chord symbols for the implied harmony under the music.

In Bach's *Schwäbisch*, the first phrase begins in D major and ends in a half cadence (vi - V) in the tonic (D major). For the second phrase, mm. 5–6 are a repeat of mm. 1-2 in the tonic key. The last two measures of the second phrase remain in the tonic key, and A¹ concludes with an authentic cadence in D major (followed by repeat sign). Another option for mm. 7–8 would be a modulation to the dominant (for major keys), or the relative major or dominant minor (for minor keys).

Figure 11.16

Type of dance: Minuet
Form: Rounded binary form

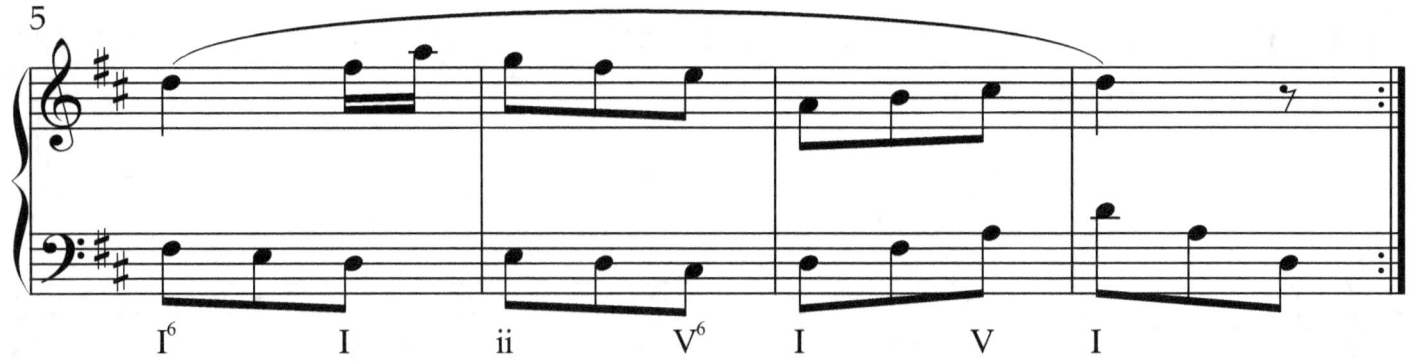

Step 3: The Second Part - B + A²

This section is also eight measures long. It will consist of two four-measure phrases and will begin with a repeat sign. In Bach's *Schwäbisch*, mm. 9–10 are in the tonic key and continue the style of the opening. Bach follows this with a tonicization of the dominant in mm. 11-12. Another option - if you chose to end the first part with a modulation – would be to begin this section in the new key and end the phrase with a half cadence in either the new key or the tonic key.

Figure 11.17

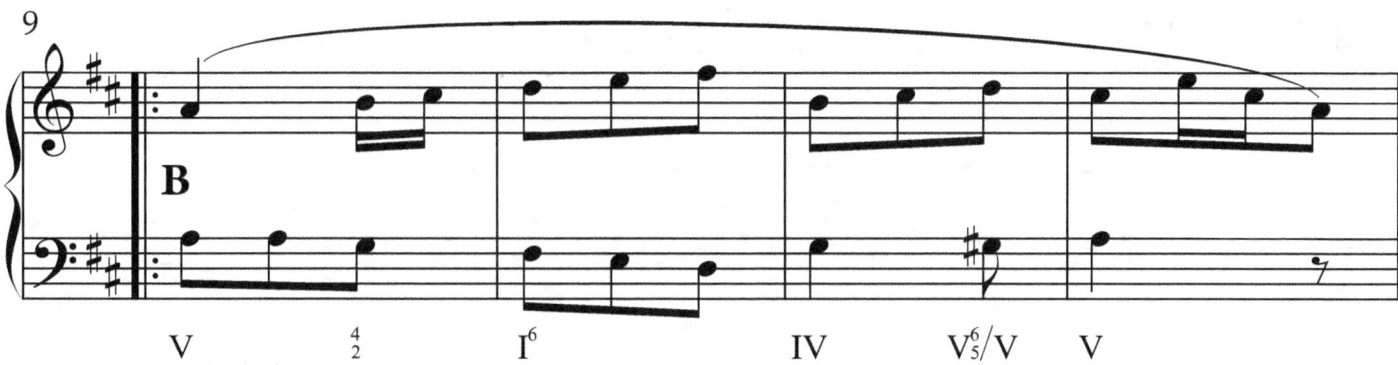

The last phrase mm. 13–16 begins with a restatement of the opening in the tonic key. It is this repetition – either exactly the same or slightly varied – that identifies the form as rounded binary. Here, Bach suggests a different harmony in m. 14 and he varies both voices in mm. 15–16. These last two measures remain in the tonic key and the piece concludes with an authentic cadence and a repeat sign. Ending the melody on the tonic and approaching it from a step below ($\hat{7}$ - $\hat{1}$), is very effective. Melodies that end $\hat{7}$ - $\hat{1}$ or $\hat{2}$ - $\hat{1}$ are extremely strong because they support a perfect authentic cadence and reinforce the tonality.

Figure 11.18

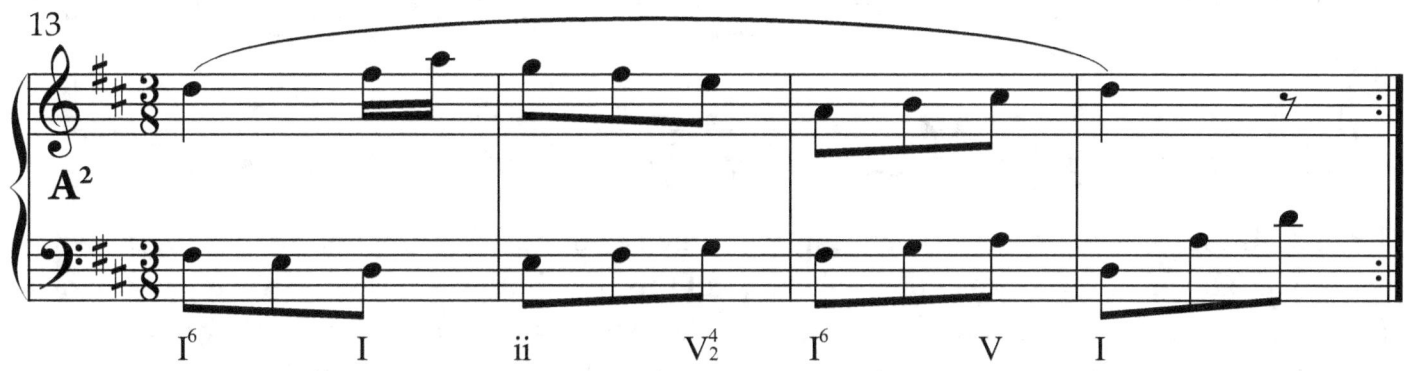

Imitation

Imitation can be an important element in two-part counterpoint. Play through the following example of a gigue, and listen for the exchange of motives between the two voices. The soprano enters alone, but the bass imitates the opening motive at the octave.

The first phrase ends with a half cadence in the tonic key in m. 4. The second phrase begins with a repeat of the opening measures in the tonic key, but this time both voices are active. If you decide to use a similar pattern of imitation, it is important to keep both voices moving once they have entered, rather than having one voice drop out in mid-section. If section A begins with imitation, usually the B section will also begin this way.

J.S. Bach wrote two part inventions to teach performance and composition to his son Wilhelm Friedman. These works do not have a specific formal structure. Although they vary greatly, one commonality is Bach's use of imitation in the opening measures.

The excerpt in Figure 11.19 illustrates this use of imitation. This invention is based on a three measure subject stated at the beginning in the treble clef. This subject is immediately imitated in m. 2 in the lower voice at the octave. Bach most often uses imitation at the octave, but occasionally he employs imitation at the 5th. These are the opening 12 measures of the invention and do not reflect a complete composition. Indicate the implied harmony for this excerpt using functional chord symbols.

Figure 11.19

Johann Sebastian Bach
Invention no. 8
BWV 779

1. Analyze the following piece. Name the form and label each section with capital letters on the score. Name the key, add functional chord symbols to indicate the harmony, and identify the cadences at the end of each phrase.

Anonymous
Bourree

2. Analyze the following piece. Name the form and label each section with capital letters on the score. Name the key, add functional chord symbols to indicate the harmony, and identify the cadences at the end of each phrase.

George Frideric Handel
Impertinence HWV 494

3. For the following menuet:

   a. Name the key.
   b. Give an appropriate tempo marking.
   c. Indicate the implied harmony using both functional and root/quality chord symbols.
   d. Name the cadence at the end of each phrase.
   e. Complete the piece in rounded binary form by writing eight more measures.
   f. Label the sections of the form with capital letters on the score.

George Frideric Handel
Menuet in B minor

4. Continue the following melodies to create two-part contrapuntal compositions in 18th century style in rounded binary form. Name the Baroque dances represented here. Mark the structural phrasing, indicate the implied harmony, and verify the form with capital letters placed directly on the score.

Dance: _____

Allegro

key: ___

Chapter 11: Counterpoint

Dance type:_____

Andante Grazioso

key:___

Dance type:_____

key:___

Chapter 11: Counterpoint

Writing a Two-Part Composition in Simple Binary Form

Simple binary form consists of two contrasting sections of equal length. Often, but not always, both sections are repeated.

$$\|: \underset{\text{8 measures}}{A} :\|: \underset{\text{8 measures}}{B} :\|$$

A typical assignment might require you to: Continue the following opening fragment to create a two-part contrapuntal composition in 18th century style.

As with rounded binary form, there are many options for completing such an assignment, but the next few pages will guide you through the steps involved in writing a 16 measure contrapuntal piece in simple binary form. The example we will use has been attributed to Henry Purcell (1659–1695), but it is now considered to be of doubtful authenticity (*Borry (Saraband), Zimmerman D 219/2*).

As with the exercise on rounded binary form, you should begin by planning the work, setting out the measures, and analyzing the implied harmony of the given fragment. Since the finished composition is to be 16 measures long, each section should consist of eight measures. This example does not contain repeat signs. However, repeat signs are a common element in this form and should be used in your composition.

Step 1: The A Section

The A section will consist of two four-measure phrases. The first phrase will be given to you. In this example, the composer ends the first phrase with an authentic cadence in the tonic key of D major. Another option would be to end with an imperfect cadence in the tonic key.

Figure 11.20

Chapter 11: Counterpoint

Now you can add a second phrase, following the style of the first phrase. This phrase might modulate to the dominant key or, for minor keys, to the relative major. In the second phrase of this piece, mm. 5–6 are in the tonic key and are related rhythmically and tonally to the opening phrase. In mm. 7–8, there is a modulation to the dominant, and the A section ends with an authentic cadence in A major. Note that there are no repeat signs in this example.

Figure 11.21

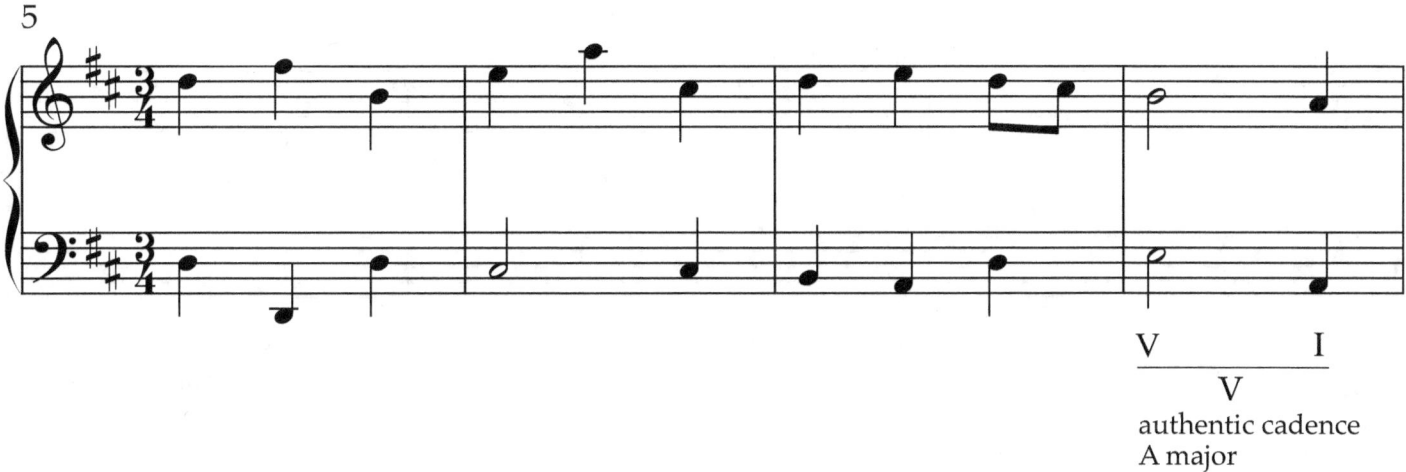

Step 2: The B Section

The first phrase of the B section opens in the new key – here, the dominant – but is musically related to the opening phrase. In this piece, m. 9 is an exact transposition of m. 1, and m. 10 is a variation of m. 2. The composer's choice to end the phrase with a tonicization of vi (B minor) lends harmonic variety to this section

Figure 11.22

In measures 13–14, the composer introduces a new sixteenth-note idea in the brief sequence featuring the secondary dominant (V^6/V). He concludes the piece with an authentic cadence in the tonic key, which is highlighted by the dotted rhythm on the last beat of m. 15. Again, there are no repeat signs, but repeat signs are a common element in this form and should be used in your composition.

Figure 11.23

Play through the piece in Figure 11.24 and pay special attention to the way Handel structures the four phrases. This minuet is in simple binary form. Note also the placement of the key and time signatures and the repeat signs. Handel modulates to the relative major (F major) at the end of the A section. Section B begins in the relative major but modulates back to D Minor in the final phrase.

George Frideric Handel
Minuet in D minor
HWV 462

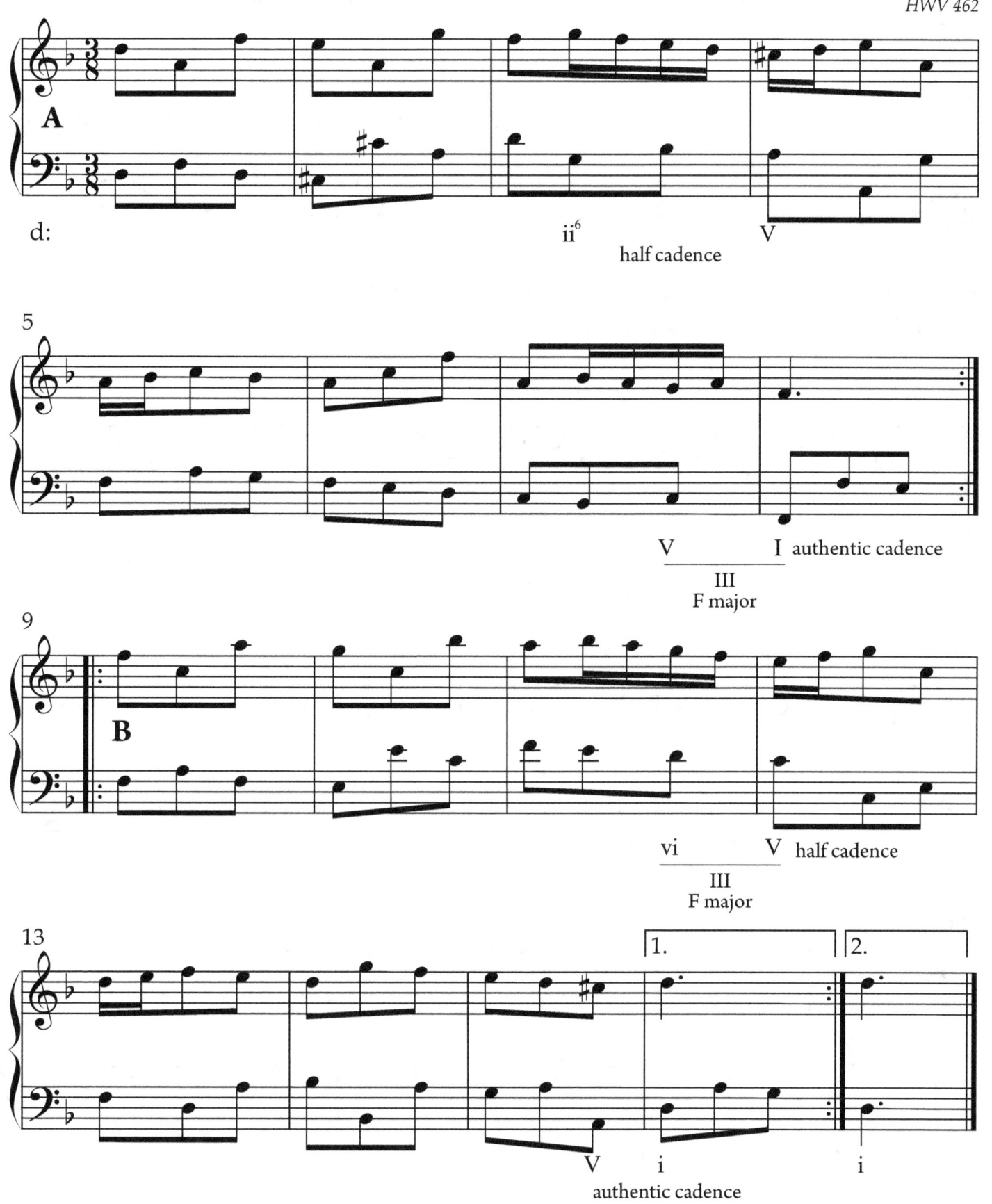

Chapter 11: Counterpoint

4. Analyze the following piece. Name the form and label each section with capital letters on the score. Name the key, add functional chord symbols to indicate the harmony, and identify the cadences at the end of each phrase.

attrib. Johann Gorrfried Heinrich Bach
Aria: Enlightening Thoughts of a Tobaco Smoker*
BWV 515

* original title: *Erbauliche Gedanken eines Tobackauchers*
Source: *Notebook for Anna Magdalena Bach* (1725)

5. Analyze the following chorale. Name the form and label each section with capital letters on the score. Name the key, add functional chord symbols to indicate the harmony, and identify the cadences at the end of each phrase.

Chorale text by Benjamin Schmolk (1672-1737)
Source: *Notebook for Anna Magdalena Bach* (1725)

6. Analyze the following piece. Name the form and label each section with capital letters on the score. Name the key, add functional chord symbols to indicate the harmony, and identify the cadences at the end of each phrase.

Georg Philipp Telemann
Fantasia in C minor
TWV 33:35 (Moderato)

7. Analyze the following piece. Name the form and label each section with capital letters on the score. Name the key, add functional chord symbols to indicate the harmony, and identify the cadences at the end of each phrase.

Georg Frideric Handel
Bourree in G major

8. For the following menuet:

    a. Name the key.
    b. Give an appropriate tempo marking.
    c. Indicate the implied harmony using both functional and root quality/chord symbols.
    d. Name the cadence at the end of each phrase.
    e. Complete the piece in rounded binary form by writing eight measures in the space provided.
    f. Label each section of the form with capital letters on the score.

Johann Sebastian Bach
Menuet BWV anh. 132

9. Continue the following openings to create two-part contrapuntal compositions in 18th-century style in binary form. Name the Baroque dances represented here and give an appropriate tempo marking. Indicate the implied harmony and verify the form with capital letters placed directly on the music.

Dance type:_____

Form:_____

Dance type:_____

Form:_____

Chapter 11: Counterpoint

Dance type:_____
Form:_____

199 Chapter 11: Counterpoint

Dance type:_____

Form:_____

200 Chapter 11: Counterpoint

Dance type:_____

Form:_____

Chapter 11: Counterpoint

Dance type:_____

Form:_____

202 Chapter 11: Counterpoint

www.ingramcontent.com/pod-product-compliance
Lightning Source LLC
Chambersburg PA
CBHW051405070526
44584CB00023B/3298